THE MANY FACES OF
ASPERGER'S SYNDROME

Tavistock Clinic Series

Margot Waddell (Series Editor)
Published and distributed by Karnac Books

Other titles in the Tavistock Clinic Series

Acquainted with the Night: Psychoanalysis and the Poetic Imagination
Hamish Canham and Carole Satyamurti (editors)

Assessment in Child Psychotherapy
Margaret Rustin and Emanuela Quagliata (editors)

Facing It Out: Clinical Perspectives on Adolescent Disturbance
Robin Anderson and Anna Dartington (editors)

Inside Lives: Psychoanalysis and the Growth of the Personality
Margot Waddell

Internal Landscapes and Foreign Bodies:
Eating Disorders and Other Pathologies
Gianna Williams

Mirror to Nature: Drama, Psychoanalysis, and Society
Margaret Rustin and Michael Rustin

Multiple Voices: Narrative in Systemic Family Psychotherapy
Renos K. Papadopoulos and John Byng-Hall (editors)

Psychoanalysis and Culture: A Kleinian Perspective
David Bell (editor)

Psychotic States in Children
Margaret Rustin, Maria Rhode, Alex Dubinsky, Hélène Dubinsky (editors)

Reason and Passion: A Celebration of the Work of Hanna Segal
David Bell (editor)

Sent Before My Time: A Child Psychotherapist's View of
Life on a Neonatal Intensive Care Unit
Margaret Cohen

Surviving Space: Papers on Infant Observation.
Essays on the Centenary of Esther Bick
Andrew Briggs (editor)

Therapeutic Care for Refugees: No Place Like Home
Renos K. Papadopoulos (editor)

Understanding Trauma: A Psychoanalytic Approach
Caroline Garland (editor)

Unexpected Gains: Psychotherapy with People with Learning Disabilities
David Simpson and Lynda Miller (editors)

Orders
Tel: +44 (0)20 8969 4454; Fax: +44 (0)20 8969 5585
Email: shop@karnacbooks.com
www.karnacbooks.com

THE MANY FACES OF ASPERGER'S SYNDROME

edited by

Maria Rhode and Trudy Klauber

KARNAC

LONDON   NEW YORK

For our families

First published in 2004 by
H. Karnac (Books) Ltd.
6 Pembroke Buildings, London NW10 6RE

British Library Cataloguing in Publication Data

A C.I.P. for this book is available from the British Library

ISBN 1-85575-9306

10 9 8 7 6 5 4 3 2 1

Edited, designed, and produced by Communication Crafts

Printed in Great Britain

www.karnacbooks.com

CONTENTS

ACKNOWLEDGEMENTS

Our thanks, first of all, to our patients and their carers for what they have taught us.

We are grateful to the Series Editor, Margot Waddell, for her comments, encouragement, and unstinting generosity. Thanks also to Leena Hakkinen and Oliver Rathbone of Karnac and to Klara King for meticulous copyediting. We are grateful to Professor Lionel Hersov and Elizabeth Bradley for helpful criticisms; and to Judy Shuttleworth for introducing us to the category of "multiple complex developmental disorder". Sally Hodges wishes to thank Dr Tony Lee for his comments on an early draft of chapter 2. We thank Biddy Youell for editorial suggestions and Marie Pearlman, Shirley Houghton, and Caroline Weaver for their generous secretarial and administrative support.

SERIES EDITOR'S PREFACE

A diagnosis of Asperger's syndrome can be a very mixed blessing: it is burdensome to some, providing little solace. For others it is a relief. Yet others remain puzzled and confused: What difference will a diagnosis make? What does it mean? What kind of help will be available?

What everyone will want to have access to is precisely the kind of information, insight, and wisdom that this book offers. Drawing on many years of experience in the Tavistock's pioneering tradition of psychodynamic work with autistic spectrum disorders, both editors believe in an open-minded approach to the many different factors contributing to both diagnosis and choice of treatment. They also believe in the value of multi-disciplinary work with so complex a disorder and in the unique history and presentation of each and every child, a presentation that vigorously defies tidy conceptualization or certainty.

The expertise of the professionals involved and the puzzling nature of such opaque states of mind are expressed in these pages with enormous clarity and sensitivity. For the first time a comprehensive account is given of the relationship between biological, environmental, and psychological approaches and as the various case studies unfold, the specificity and diversity of so broad a diagnostic spectrum is brought to life. Between them, the contributions provide a bench-mark in the current literature on the subject.

Margot Waddell
Series Editor

ABOUT THE EDITORS AND CONTRIBUTORS

Anne Alvarez trained as a Clinical Psychologist in Canada and the United States before training further in the United Kingdom. She is a lecturer at the Tavistock Clinic in London, where she recently retired as Consultant Child and Adolescent Psychotherapist and co-convener of the Autism Service. She is the author of *Live Company: Psychotherapy with Autistic, Borderline, Deprived and Abused Children* (Routledge, 1992) and co-editor of *Autism and Personality: Findings from the Tavistock Autism Workshop* (Alvarez & Reid: Routledge, 1999). She has published many papers on psychoanalytic psychotherapy with autistic, borderline, and traumatized patients. A book of her seminars at the Brazilian Psychoanalytic Society, *Anne Alvarez in Sao Paulo*, was published in 1999, and a festschrift, *Being Alive: Building on the Work of Anne Alvarez* (ed. Judith Edwards, Routledge) in 2002.

Jane Cassidy is a Child and Adolescent Psychotherapist who now works mainly in private practice. She is Chair of the Child and Adolescent Division of the Tavistock Society of Psychotherapists and Allied Professionals. She has a particular interest in the impact of trauma on families and future generations.

Lynne Cudmore originally qualified as a social worker and then worked for seven years in an inner-city social services department.

Since 1978 she has worked for the Tavistock Marital Studies Institute, where she is a senior couple therapist and Organizing Tutor of the professional doctorate and clinical training in couple psychoanalytic psychotherapy. Her research interests include the impact of infertility on the couple relationship, as well as the impact of a child's death on the parental partnership. She trained as a child psychotherapist at the Tavistock Clinic, qualifying in 2002, and now works part-time in the Infant Mental Health Team there. She has a particular interest in working with parents and infants in the perinatal period.

Sally Hodges is a Consultant Clinical Psychologist in the Tavistock Clinic's Child and Family Department. She has worked in the field of developmental disabilities for fourteen years, in Plymouth, in Redbridge in Essex, and, for the last eight of these years, at the Tavistock Clinic in both the Autism Team and what is now called the Learning and Complex Disabilities service. She was the organising tutor of the Tavistock course "Psychodynamic Approaches to Working with People with Learning Disabilities" and has published in the areas of learning disabilities, eating difficulties, and child protection. She is the main author of the book *Counselling Adults with Learning Disabilities* (with contributions by Nancy Shepherd: Palgrave McMillan, 2003).

Trudy Klauber is a Consultant Child and Adolescent Psychotherapist in the Child and Family Department of the Tavistock Clinic, where she is also Acting Head of Child Psychotherapy. She is the Organising Tutor for the Tavistock–UEL Postgraduate Diploma/MA in Psychoanalytic Observational Studies and also teaches on the clinical training in child and adolescent psychotherapy. Her clinical interests include work with parents, particularly those with severely disturbed children and with children on the autistic spectrum, and direct work with disturbed children and adolescents and those with autism and Asperger's syndrome. She has published papers and contributory chapters on her clinical work and on teaching and has given papers in the United Kingdom, Europe, and the United States. She hopes to write more about the Tavistock model of teaching and its impact.

Samantha Morgan trained as a Child Psychotherapist at the Tavistock Clinic. She currently works at Newham Child and Family Consultation Service.

Tanja Nesic-Vuckovic trained as a Clinical Psychologist before training and now working as Consultant Child and Adolescent Psychotherapist for the South Essex Partnership NHS Trust, and in private practice. She has a particular interest in working with severely disturbed children and adolescents and with those on the autistic spectrum. She is currently working on a project concerned with perceptual difficulties in children with Asperger's syndrome.

Caroline Polmear is a Training Analyst of the British Psychoanalytical Society. She works in private practice with adolescents and adults and is joint author of *A Short Introduction to Psychoanalysis* (Milton, Polmear & Fabricius: Sage, 2004).

Maria Rhode is Professor of Child Psychotherapy at the Tavistock Clinic and the University of East London. She has a particular interest in autistic spectrum disorders, language development, and infant observation and has contributed papers and book chapters on these subjects. She is co-editor of *Psychotic States in Children* (Rustin, Rhode, Dubinsky, & Dubinsky: Tavistock/Duckworth, 1997) and is currently working on an early intervention project for toddlers with communication difficulties.

Margaret Rustin is a Consultant Child Psychotherapist in the Child and Family department of the Tavistock Clinic and head of child psychotherapy training. She has a long-term interest in work with young people with complex needs and communication difficulties. She co-edited *Psychotic States in Children* (Rustin, Rhode, Dubinsky & Dubinsky: Tavistock/Duckworth, 1997) and has published widely on other topics in child psychotherapy. She is currently Chair of the Tavistock Clinic Professional Committee.

Graham Shulman is a Consultant Child and Adolescent Psychotherapist who trained at the Tavistock Clinic. He has a special interest in autism and is a former member of the Tavistock Clinic Autism Team and Workshop, where he was involved in setting up a multidisciplinary work-discussion group for professionals in the field of autism. He was a member of the autism sub-group of the Tavistock/University of East London infant observation research group and has been a Guest Editor of the *Journal of Infant Observation* on the subject of autism. He is Senior Tutor on the child psychotherapy training at the

Scottish Institute of Human Relations, where he is also co-leader of the autism workshop.

David Simpson is Joint Head of the Tavistock Clinic Learning and Complex Disabilities Service. He trained in psychiatry at the Maudsley Hospital and is a Consultant Child & Adolescent Psychiatrist and Programme Director of the Specialist Training in Child & Adolescent Psychiatry at the Tavistock Clinic. He is also Honorary Senior Lecturer at the Royal Free & University College London Hospital Medical School. He is a member of the British Psychoanalytic Society and works in private practice as a psychoanalyst.

Michèle Stern is a Consultant Child & Adolescent Psychotherapist who is currently working in a Child and Adolescent Mental Health Services team in Hereford. Her interests range from running adolescent girls' groups to more intensive work with complex disorders, including psychotherapy with blind children with autism.

Brian Truckle is Consultant Child Psychotherapist at the Birmingham Children's Hospital, and tutor on the clinical training for child psychotherapists at the Birmingham Trust for Psychoanalytic Psychotherapy.

PREFACE

Asperger's syndrome has recently become a frequent diagnosis, and it embraces a wide variety of children who in many ways are different from each other. This can be bewildering for parents, for teachers, and, as they grow up, for the children themselves. Parents look for answers to pressing questions. What does a diagnosis of Asperger's syndrome mean? What should be done to help their child as much as possible? What is the right educational placement—a question that often becomes pressing when the child is 10 years old and planning for secondary school becomes a reality? What kinds of relationships can their child look forward to as an adult? Can psychotherapy help?

As with autism, professionals hold widely differing views on the causes of Asperger's syndrome and the kinds of intervention that are appropriate. Children who are referred for psychotherapy in one locality would never be referred in others. Some psychiatrists, paediatricians, and psychologists feel it is an important component of a coordinated programme of intervention; others feel it is useless or even harmful. Such polarizations are unhelpful to parents, who may find it hard to access accurate information, and ultimately to the children themselves.

Our aim in this book has been to present a multi-disciplinary account of a psychodynamic approach to Asperger's syndrome. This includes a review of psychiatric and cognitivist theories, as well as of those psychoanalytically based ideas that inform the work of contemporary psychotherapists working broadly within the British Object Relations school. The present trend towards integrating these ideas with the findings of developmental child psychologists such as Colwyn Trevarthen, experimentalists like Peter Hobson, and numerous other researchers derives its original impetus from the writings of Anne Alvarez and Daniel Stern. It is our hope that multi-disciplinary contributions may help to reduce polarizations, which in our opinion are unwarranted and unhelpful. Conditions such as Asperger's syndrome, which have a biological as well as a psychological component, must eventually be understood through the bringing together of many professional perspectives.

The detailed clinical case histories in this volume are offered with two main aims in view. First, the reader will be able to form an opinion about the subjective emotional experience of these children, as well as about the process of therapy and the degree to which it was helpful. Second, these histories illustrate the wide range of individual differences encompassed by a diagnosis of Asperger's syndrome and underline the need for detailed consideration of each individual person. The clinical accounts are largely unencumbered by theoretical discussion; a brief overview of relevant psychoanalytic theories is provided in the Introduction for reference purposes.

This book is meant for child psychotherapists who treat Asperger's children, but also for teachers and other professionals who support them, for their parents, and for interested members of the public.

Maria Rhode and Trudy Klauber

Introduction

Maria Rhode

A sperger's syndrome has become a popular diagnosis. It is currently so widely used that it can be easy to forget how recently the English-speaking world was introduced to the work of Hans Asperger. The original paper by the Viennese paediatrician and educator was published in 1944, just a year after Leo Kanner delineated the syndrome of "early infantile autism". Lorna Wing first discussed the relationship between autism and Asperger's syndrome in 1981, but the English translation of Asperger's paper by Uta Frith was not published until ten years after that.

Since then, there have been many books and countless articles on Asperger's syndrome. As well as descriptive and theoretical work by psychiatrists, psychologists, and researchers, these include first-person accounts by people with Asperger's syndrome and by their families. Enough of a consensus has been established for Asperger's syndrome to be defined descriptively as a diagnostic entity in DSM–IV (the Diagnostic Statistical Manual of the American Psychiatric Association). However, a wide variety of opinion exists as to the relationship between Asperger's syndrome and other diagnostic categories such as autism, schizophrenia, and what Sula Wolff has called "schizoid personality disorder" in the young people she described as "loners". General awareness of the condition is sufficiently widespread for mildly eccentric academics to be popularly described as "Aspergers".

There is, in fact, a truth expressed in this inexact use of language. Quite apart from its controversial place in relation to autism and the autistic spectrum (Frith, 1991b; Klin, Volkmar, & Sparrow, 2000), Asperger's syndrome could be thought of as a spectrum in itself. The characteristics of the condition—social isolation and "oddness", special "interests" verging on obsessions, the eccentric and often pedantic use of language, physical clumsiness, and unusual sensory experiences are some of the most important—can occur to widely differing degrees. This variation interacts with the fact that every person with Asperger's syndrome (like every person with autism—Alvarez & Reid, 1999a, 1999b, and Alvarez, chapter 6 this volume) has his or her own unique personality. The outcome is a diagnostic category that embraces an enormously wide range. A single-minded stamp collector who spends all his time on his hobby, has no friends, is bewildered by social cues, and feels overwhelmed by bright lights and loud noises could attract a diagnosis of Asperger's syndrome. So could a child whose difficulties interfere with his life to a much more obvious degree, whose body image and sense of self might not be securely established, and who might feel the world to be an alien and threatening place and react by lashing out. Before the diagnosis of Asperger's syndrome became current, such children would have been described as borderline or "atypical" (Lubbe, 2000).

Though research in the field has been very active over the last decade, we are still only beginning to understand Asperger's syndrome. Klin, Volkmar, and Sparrow (2000) for instance, point out the extent to which the attempt to differentiate clearly between Asperger's syndrome and high-functioning autism is complicated by the lack of consistent diagnostic criteria, of reliable and appropriate measures, and of consistent methodology across investigations. It may be that increasing knowledge will lead to a narrower application of the term "Asperger's syndrome". In our opinion, however, the broad range it encompasses in present-day usage is not only a matter of our incomplete understanding. It also reflects the recognition by professionals that children diagnosed with Asperger's syndrome do not just tick the necessary descriptive boxes: they also share a "something" that people recognize, even if they present as differently as the borderline child and the socially bewildered philatelist. Indeed, this "something" is shared by some children who do not tick all the descriptive boxes necessary to justify a diagnosis of Asperger's syndrome according to DSM–IV. Thus, Gillberg (1991b) delineates the syndrome he calls

DAMP (Deficits in Attention, Motor Control and Perception), which, in its most severe form, overlaps substantially with autistic spectrum disorders. Similarly, Ad-Dab'bagh & Greenfield (2001) argue for a diagnostic category of Multiple Complex Developmental Disorder.

· This is one of the areas in which we feel that a psychodynamic approach has much to contribute. Psychodynamic psychotherapy is based on the belief that being responded to and understood by another person leads to a better understanding of oneself, and hence to a greater capacity to manage life's conflicts and demands. Psychotherapists work in a regular predictable setting, within a disciplined technique based on a highly developed capacity for attention and detailed observation. These are applied particularly to the transference (the evolution of feelings towards the therapist that derive from the child's internal emotional constellations) and the countertransference (the emotional response elicited in the therapist). This means that the psychotherapeutic relationship is a source of highly detailed knowledge of the patient's unique personality, including their characteristic anxieties and the self-protective devices they have recourse to. It follows that classifications of emotional conditions that are derived from psychodynamic considerations can diverge from descriptive psychiatric diagnoses. The clinical case histories in this volume are not just accounts of psychotherapy: they also permit the comparison across individual patients of characteristic anxieties and self-protective devices. Such comparisons should lead to a psychodynamic rationale for refining definitions of Asperger's syndrome, as well as to a deepened understanding of individual children.

This book provides the first collection of case histories of patients with Asperger's syndrome who were treated psychotherapeutically within the general theoretical framework of the British Object Relations school of psychoanalysis (see the discussion below of theoretical concepts). At present, in Great Britain, the offer of psychodynamic psychotherapy to children with Asperger's syndrome or autism remains highly controversial. There are several reasons for this. First, there exists a widespread misunderstanding that psychoanalysts and psychotherapists blame the parents for their child's condition. Two facts have contributed to this misunderstanding: Leo Kanner, who in 1943 first delineated the syndrome of infantile autism, wrote that the parents he met tended to be highly intellectual and emotionally cold (hence the notion of "refrigerator mother"), although, as David Simpson points out in this volume, Kanner stressed his belief that autism was intrinsic to the child's endowment. Neither the superior intelligence nor the emotional coldness have been confirmed by subsequent research, though they may have been accurate descriptions of Kanner's small sample. The second fact is that the psychoanalyst Bruno Bettelheim described the parents of the autistic children whom he had treated as having had a highly damaging effect on them. Bettelheim was the Head of the famous Orthogenic School in Chicago and was greatly respected in the United States. Again, his statements applied to a very restricted sample of parents: it would be surprising if no parents of children with autism ever had a damaging effect on their children, just as some parents do whose children are not on the autistic spectrum. It was a great misfortune that, like Kanner's, Bettelheim's statement was wrongly generalized by himself and others to all parents of children with autism, and in this way did an incalculable amount of harm. Having a child on the autistic spectrum can be a source of major trauma and grief for parents (Klauber, 1998, 1999a), who may for a long time be cut off from ordinary life. Parents whose children have any kind of serious problem are only too ready to blame themselves for it: the last thing they need is to feel—or to be—blamed by professionals.

Interestingly enough, statements of the contrary position by psychotherapists do not seem to have registered with those professionals who feel that psychotherapy is contra-indicated for children on the autistic spectrum. Frances Tustin, whose pioneering first book, *Autism and Childhood Psychosis,* appeared in 1972, wrote that the parents of the children she worked with were dedicated and sensitive, and that they inspired compassion and therapeutic ambition. Later psychoanalytic workers often conveyed a similar viewpoint: the psychoanalyst Salo Tischler (1979), for instance, described feelingly what it was like to live with an autistic or psychotic child. In spite of this, it is not uncommon to hear some professionals assert that Frances Tustin held parents to blame for their children's autism. Psychotherapists can sometimes feel that they will be seen as blamers of parents, no matter what they believe, say, or write.

This does not mean that parents do not have important work to do in helping their child with autism or Asperger's syndrome. The school of one Asperger child put it particularly well: "If your child were blind, you wouldn't blame yourselves, but you would know that how you responded to him would make all the difference." Parents of children with Asperger's syndrome, in common with parents of children whose difficulties are not related to the autistic spectrum, can find that they sometimes view their child's behaviour in terms of past experiences of their own, and that when this occurs it makes it difficult for them to respond as helpfully as they wish to. Clearing up misunderstandings of this kind is the aim of the work with parents that is an indispensable adjunct to child psychotherapy with any client group.

The second reason why psychotherapy for children on the autistic spectrum remains controversial concerns the widely held belief that autism and Asperger's syndrome are caused by a specific organic brain defect. In the opinion of many professionals, it follows that an approach that is concerned with emotional experience cannot be relevant or useful, and indeed will do harm by arousing false hope in the parents. It is not uncommon to find it categorically stated that psychodynamic psychotherapy has no place in the treatment of children on the autistic spectrum (Aarons & Gittens, 1992; Frith, 2002).

While a brain defect may well be implicated in autism and Asperger's syndrome, we do not agree with the conclusion that an approach to the emotions is out of place. We believe that such a conclusion confuses the issue of helpful treatment approaches with the issue of aetiology. Although overwhelming trauma has been associated with some kinds of autistic syndrome by psychiatric researchers (Rutter et al., 1999) as well as by psychotherapists (Cecchi, 1990; Reid, 1999c; Tustin, 1994b), it is clear that many children who have suffered a trauma are not autistic, and, conversely, that many children on the autistic spectrum have not experienced what other people might think of as a trauma. Like many other workers, we feel that a multifactorial aetiology is the most convincing.

Whatever the aetiology may be, even a purely organic defect would not be an argument against a psychological approach.[1] Someone whose way of being is different from other people's will benefit from help in understanding how this impinges on them. Understanding and managing the emotional ramifications can allow them to make the fullest possible use of their capacities. For example, Valerie Sinason has illustrated the impact of therapy on people with learning disabilities, which are frequently organically determined. However, this irreducible "primary handicap" (Sinason, 1986) is often greatly augmented by an emotionally based "secondary handicap", which can be significantly influenced by psychotherapy (see also Miller & Simpson, 2004). Similarly, Grotstein (1997) has proposed that the effect of psychotherapy may come about through helping someone with an autistic spectrum disorder to manage their condition, while Shuttleworth (1999) has argued eloquently for the need to recognize the reality of the experience of impairment that her adolescent patient communicated to her. Caroline Polmear (chapter 5) similarly felt that this acknowledgement marked a turning point with her patients.

Quite apart from such issues, recent research increasingly suggests that the long-standing dichotomy between organicist and psychodynamic views may turn out to be a false one. Tustin herself did not hold that no brain defect was present in the children she treated successfully: merely that no brain damage could be detected by the diagnostic methods that were available. The development of new techniques of brain imaging is making it possible to correlate emotional experiences with brain chemistry, physiology, and anatomy (Damasio, 2000; Kaplan-Solms & Solms, 2000; Perry, Pollard, Blakely, Baker, & Vigilante, 1995; Schore, 1994, 2001a, 2001b; Solms & Turnbull, 2002). Schore (1994, 2001a, 2001b), for example, has reviewed a great body of neurophysiological work investigating brain activity in mother–infant pairs. His conclusion is that the regulation of babies' emotions that takes place within their relationship with a responsive caregiver can be understood in terms of the immediate resonance between neurophysiological activity in the right brain hemispheres of the two members of the dyad. With neurophysiological patterns in the right hemisphere of each member reflecting those in the right hemisphere of the other, the caregiver resonates to the baby's emotions, modulates them, and the baby in turn resonates to the caregiver's modulated levels of arousal. Important brain circuits are often not adequately established in children who have suffered serious deprivation with regard to satisfying social interactions. Early traumatic experience, on the other hand, can lead to the over-use of neural pathways concerned with overwhelming fear responses. One consequence of this is that relatively mild unpleasant stimuli can travel down these "super-highway" paths and trigger responses that are much more extreme than the stimulus would normally provoke. (For a helpful review, see Balbernie, 2001.) None of this is an argument against the idea that a brain defect may be present from birth in children later diagnosed with Asperger's syndrome. It is, however, a strong argument against regarding the consequences of such a brain defect as being unmodifiable.

Like the interaction between baby and caregiver, the interaction between patient and therapist involves emotional resonance and modulation and therefore the possibility of the modification of brain structure and function. This is not to suggest that long-established neurological pathways can be made redundant, or that inbuilt or long-standing neurological deficits can be made good. What can happen, however, is that higher-order pathways can be laid down which make it possible to manage experiences that would previously have been overwhelming (Schore, 2002).

The importance of this line of thought can hardly be overstated in relation to psychotherapy for conditions involving a neurological element. As Caroline Polmear writes (chapter 5), her patients' "Asperger's-y" side remained, even though they had grown to be able to look after it better and their experience of other people and of themselves had been transformed. This, incidentally, is also true of people who are not on the autistic spectrum and who have psychotherapy for other kinds of difficulties. Probably every patient—and every therapist—at length comes to realize that aspects of their endowment and experience are there to stay. What can be changed, often dramatically, is the way these aspects are noticed, managed, and integrated and, by this means, the way they impact upon a person's life.

This raises two interrelated issues. The first concerns the question of how far psychological approaches that derive from psychotherapeutic work with people who are not on the autistic spectrum are relevant to people who are. The second concerns ways in which some aspects of psychoanalytic theory have evolved, partly in response to experiences with patients who were on the autistic spectrum or subject to psychotic states, and whose experience of the world, including the physical world, can be very different from the habitual experience of other people.

The first-hand testimony of some people with autism or Asperger's syndrome conveys their bewilderment at the behaviour of so-called "normal" people—a bewilderment and sense of alien existence captured in the title *An Anthropologist on Mars,* which Oliver Sacks (1995) chose for his articles on Temple Grandin, a university professor with high-functioning autism. Donna Williams, a woman diagnosed with high-functioning autism, has written that the reason she echoed people's words when she was a child was to convey the message, "Look, I can relate, I can make that noise too" (Williams, 1992). Not surprisingly, she did not understand why some people thought that she was making fun of them and got cross with her. Williams, in a book called *Autism and Sensing: The Unlost Instinct* (1998), suggests that the "system of sensing" constitutes an early way of apprehending the reality of other people and of objects that is qualitatively different from the "system of interpretation". It is concerned with the "is-ness" of people and things, as distinct from the reasons for their behaviour. She suggests that people with autism may learn the system of interpretation much later than is usual and may continue to rely on sensing in a way that others do not share and feel bewildered by. Gunilla Gerland, in a book (1996a) discussed in chapter 4, wrote about her experience of psychotherapy that it taught her a great deal about the motivation of other people but seemed to have no connection with how she herself experienced life. It was difficult for her to understand other people's motivation—cognitive theorists would say she did not have a "theory of mind" (see chapter 2)—but she was exquisitely sensitive to people's emotions, which she experienced in terms of a personal "language" of associated colours. In view of such testimony, it is perhaps not surprising that some people with Asperger's syndrome, like Gerland, can feel that "normal" people's attempt to construct psychological explanations for their condition is the imposition of an alien system.

To some extent this is no more than an extreme version of the problem that is bound to arise when one person tries to understand another. However much we exercise our sympathetic imagination in respect of someone else, our efforts are bound to involve the assumption of a certain degree of resemblance based on the fact that we belong to the same species. Are people with autism and Asperger's syndrome really telling us that we are a different species, and that our attempts to understand them are at best misguided and at worst imperialistic?

Gunilla Gerland herself (1996b) stresses the importance of the attitude with which a therapist approaches the experience of someone with Asperger's syndrome. By implication, an open mind, receptivity, and the absence of dogmatism are essential. (We would go further and say that this is true of psychotherapy with any client group.) Like Donna Williams, Gerland felt that psychodynamic interpretations concerning her family relationships somehow missed the point. Paula Jacobsen, the American author of a book entitled *Asperger's Syndrome and Child Psychotherapy* (2003), came to the same conclusion. She discovered in the course of her practice that the theoretical framework of classical psychoanalysis, in which she had been trained and which served her well in her work with her other patients, did not seem relevant to the issues confronting her patients with Asperger's syndrome.

Jacobsen responded by adapting her technique with such children. Instead of working on their emotional relationships and interpreting the children's friendly and hostile feelings towards her as a function of these (what psychoanalytic psychotherapists call working in the positive and negative transference), she concentrated instead on conceptualizing the children's difficulties in terms of two cognitivist theories ("theory of mind" and "central-coherence" theory—see chapter 2). Her own role was to offer supportive explanation.

We agree that it is important for psychoanalytic psychotherapists to understand cognitivist theorizations of autism and Asperger's syndrome, not just because it is essential to be aware of alternative approaches that can enrich one's own work, but also because these theories shed light on these children's perceptual experiences and social cognitions. Perhaps even more than other client groups, this kind of child benefits by professional input of many kinds. The child psychotherapy represented in this book is part of a cooperative network including parents, teachers, GPs, educational psychologists, Social Services, paediatricians, child psychiatrists, music therapists, and occupational therapists. Social skills groups and support groups can be enormously useful, as can perceptual training. All these professionals provide input for the child within the framework of an emotional relationship. In child psychotherapy, this emotional relationship is the focus of the work. The aim is not to teach strategies for specific tasks— that is a vital contribution by other people. Instead, the child psychotherapist addresses children's total sense of themselves. Improvements tend to generalize across a variety of specific situations.

The child psychotherapists who have contributed to this volume were all trained at the Tavistock Clinic in London; some were for a time members of the Autism Workshop there. Like the psychoanalyst Caroline Polmear, the psychoanalyst and child psychiatrist David Simpson, and the psychologist Sally Hodges, they work in the tradition of the British Object Relations school of psychoanalysis. The last sixty years or so have seen a flowering of work on psychotic and borderline states of mind and on experiences of existential anxiety, unintegration, and identity diffusion, both in patients who have been diagnosed as psychotic and borderline and in patients who experience similar anxieties but the whole of whose personality is not predominantly shaped by them. Work on these levels has led to the development of a variety of theoretical concepts that supplement those of classical psychoanalytic theory and are useful to the child psychotherapist who sees children with autism or Asperger's syndrome.

Before we proceed to give a brief account of some of the main contributions to psychoanalytic work with autistic children, we wish to emphasize two important technical developments that are highly relevant to this work and of which not all of its critics are aware.

First, present-day emphasis is much more on the here-and-now relationship between patient and therapist than it used to be and much less on an investigation of past experience. References to the past may serve to make the present more meaningful, but piecing it together is no longer seen as an end in itself. Peter Fonagy (1999), for instance, has proposed that the main means by which psychoanalysis leads to change is by providing the opportunity of learning new ways of "being with the other".[2]

A second development of capital importance has been the increasing emphasis on working through in the countertransference (Brenman Pick, 1985). Paula Heimann (1950), in a seminal paper, proposed that the therapist's feelings about the patient were vital information, not just something that interfered with therapeutic "detachment". The debate continues about many aspects of this topic, though all are agreed that it is essential for therapists to monitor their feelings closely in order to be aware of those aspects that derive from their own lives. The use of the countertransference requires disciplined cross-checking with evidence provided by the child's observable behaviour, supplemented where necessary by consultation with colleagues. However, it is increasingly recognized as a prime tool in the understanding of non-verbal communication and of emotional experiences that are difficult to put into words.

The well-known theory of containment developed by the psychoanalyst Wilfred Bion (1962) has provided a way of conceptualizing countertransference phenomena. These are seen as corresponding to unbearable experiences that the infant communicates to the mother by non-verbal means. Bion argued that the mother's capacity to receive the communication of an experience that the baby could not tolerate, while still retaining a balanced state of mind, made it possible for her to respond appropriately. This enabled the infant to take these experiences back, transformed now into something that had been tolerated and could be named and therefore thought about and owned. The baby internalizes more than the transformed experience: it also internalizes the capacities of a mother who was able to receive, process, and think about it.

Bion's theory of containment does not only permit the conceptualization of non-verbal processes of communication—it also underpins his revolutionary theory of thinking, according to which cognitive processes develop out of emotional relationships. This is in contrast to the traditional view that distinguishes sharply between emotion and cognition. The theory was not derived from work with children with autism, and it has a much more general application; but it will be obvious how relevant it is to the ongoing debate about which of the deficits characteristic of autistic spectrum disorders is primary—the social or the cognitive.

It will be clear to the reader how much there is in common between Bion's model of containment and Schore's formulations concerning the neurophysiological resonance between the right-brain hemispheres of baby and caregiver. Other developments in psychoanalytic theory link with the formulations by developmental psychologists and cognitivists in ways that we return to later.

The psychoanalyst Donald Winnicott worked extensively on basic existential anxieties, which he encountered in children as well as in psychotic adults and in the dreams of non-psychotic patients. These included the basic fear of not "going-on-being" as well as the fear of falling forever and of losing body parts (Winnicott, 1949). In his opinion, such severe disorders were largely the consequence of a deficit in the environment, primarily in the function he called "maternal holding". The psychoanalyst Esther Bick similarly emphasized the prime importance of the baby's interaction with a caregiver who could provide the infant with the sense of having a psychic skin capable of holding together all the parts of its personality. Without this, the child might attempt to hold itself together by its own efforts. Bick described a number of such "second-skin" functions, such as excessive reliance on the child's own athleticism or "verbal muscularity". Patients who did not feel held together sometimes felt that they were literally spilling out of their skins or were lost in space without anything to anchor them. One way of coping was by mimicking other people's surface characteristics, as though literally attaching oneself to a place of safety. This avoided the terrors of spilling out, but at the cost of the patient's individual identity (Bick, 1968, 1986).

None of these ideas was derived from work with people with autism or Asperger's syndrome, though they have proved fundamental to developments in that area. This very fact contains within it the controversial implication that some measure of autistic experience, whatever may have caused it, is a part of the human condition.[3] Indeed, this is implied by the fact that any psychoanalytic formulation relies on the countertransference experience of the therapist in conjunction with close observation. We shall return to this point after summarizing briefly some of the central contributions to a psychoanalytic understanding of autistic spectrum disorders. This summary is not exhaustive; it is intended to provide a background for references in later chapters to psychoanalytic work on autism, and in this way to avoid repetition and duplication. Very few psychoanalytic contributions so far specifically refer to Asperger's syndrome (Grotstein, 1997; Pozzi, 2003a, 2003b; Shuttleworth, 1999; Tustin, 1994a), though some undiagnosed cases are clearly recognizable as such (e.g. Rustin, 1997b).

Melanie Klein in 1930, before the publication of Kanner's or Asperger's papers, reported successfully treating a boy who would today be recognized as having autism. She considered that his extreme fear of the consequences of aggressive impulses had led him to withdraw from emotional contact, so that his symbolic capacities and interests did not evolve and his development had stalled. She felt that this stemmed from his own particular endowment, which had not been modified by interaction with his surroundings. Rodrigué, in 1955, put forward a similar conceptualization according to which his 3-year-old patient wanted nothing to do with an outside world that was felt to be overwhelmingly bad, in contrast to supremely good self-generated experience.

We have already mentioned the destructive outcome of Bruno Bettelheim's opinions on the role of parents. This was not only a tragedy for parents of children on the autistic spectrum: it has also led to the neglect of Bettelheim's acute observations of the children. He mentioned the salience of their experience of holes and of the mouth, though it was only through Frances Tustin's work that these facts came to be understood. He also emphasized that the central issue was the child's sense of identity and lack of proper personhood, and he was in touch with the life-and-death nature of the anxieties that led to the use of rituals and stereotypies. It must be stressed, however, that he provided what today might be called psychoanalytically informed milieu therapy, rather than the outpatient treatment provided by all the other workers under consideration. We would have serious reservations about some of his recommendations, which appear to be excessively indulgent and to stem from an over-identification with the children's point of view.

Margaret Mahler, also working in the United States, devoted many decades to the study of autistic and psychotic children. She posited various types of obstacles to successful separation–individuation from the mother. In accordance with the position of some schools of psychoanalysis, though not with Klein's position, Margaret Mahler believed that children started out in a state of fusion with their mother: one of her central publications is called *The Psychological Birth of the Human Infant* (Mahler, Pine, & Bergman, 1975). (This assumption also underlay Tustin's proposed early developmental stage of "normal primary autism", which she later came to feel did not exist). More recent research suggests, on the contrary, that infants come into the world ready to relate to another human being (Stern, 1985; Trevarthen, 1979, 2001; Trevarthen & Aitken, 2001). Mahler contributed many insights of lasting importance, including the description, quoted by Tustin, of the profound grief that she observed in many children who were to become autistic. She used the term "autistic armour" to describe the self-protective impenetrability of the children she worked with. The title of Bettelheim's book, *The Empty Fortress* (1967), refers to the same phenomenon and foreshadows Tustin's use of the word "shell".

Frances Tustin's first book was published in 1972; she wrote three further books on autism (1981b, 1986, 1990) as well as numerous papers. It was her small patient John who showed her his amazement at realizing, through the experience of watching a baby being nursed, that the nipple was part of the breast. Until then, he had thought that it was part of his mouth; in its absence, he felt that part of his mouth had been torn away, that it now contained "a black hole with a nasty prick". This alerted Tustin both to John's catastrophic experience of bodily separateness and to the overriding importance of bodily sensation. Her patients resorted to the use of what she called autistic objects and autistic shapes in order to feel safe: "Lacking an intra-psychic regulatory control system that has been generated by sensuous co-operation with the suckling mother, autistic children have generated an auto-sensuous barrier" (Tustin, 1994a, p. 114). This barrier, she thought, included both hard "autistic objects" that gave the child a sensation of strength and soft "autistic sensation shapes" such as their own breath or bubbles of spit, which were used for self-soothing. This allowed the children to feel safe from frightening outside impingements as well as from their own impulses and protected them against such terrifying physical experiences as spilling out, melting and dissolving, burning or freezing, or losing parts of their body. When children began to trust the therapist, they were able to communicate the experiences that frightened them, which had not previously been shared, understood, and regulated and because of this had remained extreme.[4] Tustin emphasized that this process was essential for good as well as bad experiences if the child was to be capable of a full range of modulated feeling.

The reader may well find such fears too outlandish to be believable: adults and children who are developing well do not live in this kind of world, though we are all familiar from dreams with the fear of falling.

Children in extreme states, on the other hand, inhabit this kind of world when they are awake. Autistic-spectrum children frequently have a highly unusual body image, such as the self as a system of pipes (Rosenfeld, 1984; Tustin, 1986; see also the case history of Kane—chapter 11), or the experience of losing body parts. For instance, a little girl with Asperger's syndrome dragged one leg behind her on the way back to the waiting-room where she would leave the therapist. It was as though she had lost the use of her leg. When asked what was the matter with it, she answered matter-of-factly, "It's come off."

Tustin thought that these extreme experiences, including the "black hole", occurred in other conditions besides autism: the thing that characterized autism, in her opinion, was the use of self-generated sensuous insulating devices. She distinguished between "entangled" children, who draw people into their world, and autistic, "encapsulated" children, who shut others out. Although she wrote this before the publication of Lorna Wing's (1981) paper on Asperger's syndrome, these sub-groups may be seen to correspond broadly to Asperger's syndrome and Kanner's autism, respectively. However, she also described a group of children who appeared to use what she called the "straitjacket" of autistic self-protective devices to keep themselves safe from schizoid dangers of fragmentation (Tustin, 1990, 1994a). (Sometimes a child who changes during treatment from an autistic presentation to the "borderline" type of Asperger's syndrome can be seen as belonging in this grouping.) Asperger children, in Tustin's opinion, had had a catastrophic experience of separateness at a later stage than children with Kanner's syndrome, and because of this their development of language had not been affected.

Donald Meltzer and his co-workers published in 1975 the account of their study group who had worked with a variety of children with autism (Meltzer, Bremner, Hoxter, Weddell, & Wittenberg, 1975). These ranged from a completely mute and severely delayed child to others who were less severely affected or whose behaviour had become psychotic rather than autistic. Some of the group's main findings concerned the children's need to protect themselves from a "bombardment of sensa". Meltzer understood this as resulting from a deficit in the internalized processing function described by Bion; it is also consistent with the way in which Schore formulates the neuro-psychological regulation that takes place in the mother–infant pair and with the well-known sensory hypersensitivity of children with autism. Meltzer's group also noted the children's difficulty with establishing a stable experience of space: their behaviour while looking through a window might oscillate rapidly, as though at one moment they were inside looking out and at the next moment they were outside looking in. They appeared to relate to surface characteristics by means of mimicry, as described by Bick, rather than to the insides of people or objects. Their capacity for maintaining a sense of three-dimensionality and perspective, both physical and emotional, improved during treatment. Meltzer thought that these children had become prematurely aware of depression in their mothers at a time when they could not cope with an unrealistic sense of responsibility for it. He suggested that they "dismantled" their sensory apparatus, which normally provides information about the world through more than one sense at a time, in such a way as to lose themselves in the input from one sensory modality and to protect themselves and other people.

The French psychiatrist and psychoanalyst Geneviève Haag (1991) has integrated findings from her clinical work with autistic children and from infant observation (a discipline that Esther Bick introduced into the training of child psychotherapists and psychoanalysts). This has led her to formulate a developmental theory of the role that the baby's emotional relationship with its caregiver plays in its ability to assume psychological ownership of its own body. The link between the mother and nursing baby is both emotional (mediated by eye contact) and physical (the nipple or teat in the mouth). All being well, these two means of contact together lead to a condition of proper "embodiment" in which the developing child feels in harmony with his body. Haag proposed that this dual link is progressively "incarnated" in the major joints of the body, in a developmental sequence that begins with the baby feeling that its head is properly joined to its shoulders. At about three months, the baby can support its own head; some two or three months later it sit up by itself; finally, somewhere between 10 and 15 months, the legs and feet have been emotionally linked to the trunk, and the baby has become a toddler who can stand and walk. This theory ties in with Alvarez's description (1980) of how children with autism "become vertebrate", which is itself related to Bion's more general distinction (e.g. Bion, 1991) between internal and external sources of strength—what he called the endoskeleton and exoskeleton. It is interesting that Pozzi (2003b) achieved a good therapeutic outcome with a previously hostile 12-year-old child with Asperger's syndrome through describing in detail what each part of his body was doing.

Finally, Anne Alvarez (1992b) has emphasized the active, "reclaiming" function of the therapist, whose lively qualities fulfil the same function as the mother's in providing the child with the sense of interesting and rewarding possibilities. Alvarez has integrated psychoanalytic theories with those of developmental psychologists: she stresses that the therapist needs to be aware of issues of deficit as well as defence (Alvarez, 1999a, 1999b) and to gear any intervention to the developmental level on which the child is functioning at that given moment, so that treatment becomes developmentally as well as psychoanalytically informed. One consequence is Alvarez's detailed attention to technical issues, to verbal and non-verbal adjustments that the therapist must make to be able to get a message across.

Like psychoanalytic workers in the tradition of Bion and like experimentalists such as Colwyn Trevarthen (1979, 2001) and Peter Hobson (1993, 2002), Alvarez sees problems in social interaction as being the primary deficit in autism that leads, in turn, to intellectual deficits and stereotypical behaviour. Intellectual deficits are not just the consequence of the child's native endowment, as a "one-person psychology" might suggest: according to a "two-person psychology", they can also follow from the child's identification with someone she does not experience as intellectually lively, or with the view of her own capacities she imagines this person to hold. Alvarez invokes Trevarthen's stage of "primary intersubjectivity", in which immediate emotional communication between mother and baby precedes the later joint attention to objects that characterizes "secondary intersubjectivity". Similarly, Hobson's book *The Cradle of Thought* (2002) traces the development of intellectual capacities from the baby's early emotional relationships.

Although the integration of different viewpoints has been attempted by some authors (Alvarez, 1992b; Alvarez & Reid, 1999a; Burhouse, 1999; Hobson, 2002; Tustin, 1994a, 1994b; Urwin, 1987), on the whole the theories—emotional, social, neurological, chemical—remain as varied as the people who are diagnosed with Asperger's syndrome. As Tustin (1994b) wrote, autism is situated on the boundary between biology, chemistry, and psychology: this, she thought, led her to recognize the appositeness of concepts derived from psychoanalytic schools and disciplines in which she had not been trained. Much further study will be required by neurologists, biochemists, and developmental psychologists, as well as by psychiatrists and psychotherapists. Our aim in providing case histories of Asperger's syndrome—like that of Alvarez and Reid (1999a) in their book on autism—is to document in detail the subjective experience of unique, individual people who all share a diagnosis.

This volume falls into three parts: (1) "This is Asperger's syndrome"; (2) "Is this Asperger's syndrome?"; and (3) the collection of clinical case histories. The first part begins with David Simpson's overview of psychiatric discussions of autism and Asperger's syndrome. He discusses their similarities and differences, as well as controversial issues such as the relationship of Asperger's syndrome to schizophrenia and the question of violence, and he proposes a way of understanding the lack of curiosity that can characterize the collector's approach to knowledge that is often seen in Asperger's syndrome. In the second chapter Sally Hodges contributes a critical review of the cognitivist theories that have been advanced in the attempt to understand Asperger's syndrome. She discusses the features of the condition that each of the theories accounts for or fails to account for and argues for the importance of considering the emotional as well as the cognitive dimension.

The following three chapters aim to enlarge the reader's understanding of what it is like to be someone with Asperger's syndrome, or to know them intimately. Trudy Klauber (chapter 3) offers a commentary on Asperger's original descriptive paper from the point of view of a present-day child psychotherapist and discusses the relevance of psychoanalytic concepts to Asperger's formulations. Maria Rhode (chapter 4) considers two first-person accounts by women with Asperger's syndrome in terms of similarities and differences, and also in terms of how far they link with or diverge from psychoanalytic formulations. Caroline Polmear (chapter 5) provides a meticulous account of processes in the treatment of adults with Asperger's syndrome—to our knowledge, the first published account of such work with adults. The articulacy of these highly intelligent women patients and Polmear's vivid rendering of her countertransference experience allows direct access to the world of Asperger's syndrome, even to the reader without previous knowledge or first-hand experience.

The second part, "Is this Asperger's syndrome?" begins with Anne Alvarez's assessment in chapter 6 of a teenage girl with a particular kind of Asperger's syndrome. As well as looking for indications in the transference relationship of whether psychotherapy might be useful, Alvarez discusses possible reasons for the chilling effect this girl sometimes had on other people and highlights a number of the elements of Asperger's syndrome that could eventually lead to a refined classification in terms of the horizontal and vertical axes of a "periodic table". Graham Shulman (chapter 7) provides an instructive contrast: his patient was originally diagnosed as having Asperger's syndrome, but other professionals disagreed with this opinion. Shulman considers the reasoning on either side and highlights the life-and-death anxieties that his patient shared with Asperger children. This chapter illuminates the well-known overlap between Asperger's syndrome and conditions characterized by poor impulse control (Ad-Dab'bagh & Greenfield, 2001; Gillberg, 1991b).

The third part consists of case histories by Samantha Morgan, Tanja Nesic-Vuckovic, Lynne Cudmore, Michèle Stern, Jane Cassidy, and Brian Truckle. These were chosen so as to illustrate the wide range encompassed by the diagnosis of Asperger's syndrome. For each of the three age ranges—under 5, 5–11, and adolescent—we have selected two accounts of psychotherapy, one with a child whose presentation was sufficiently florid so that they would previously have been diagnosed as borderline psychotic and another with a child who was more withdrawn and who might rely on obsessional coping devices.[5] All of these children, it should be stressed, had had a diagnosis of Asperger's syndrome from a child psychiatrist. Juxtaposing the two cases in each age range allows the reader to see the anxieties these children had in common and the differing means by which they attempted to deal with them. The part ends with an account by Margaret Rustin of the contribution a child psychotherapist can make to the ongoing management in the community of a young person with Asperger's syndrome who is no longer receiving treatment.

Many controversies about Asperger's syndrome remain unresolved. The contributors to this book would disagree on various points of theory, technique, or emphasis: this includes the two editors. At this very early stage in our understanding, we hope that this book will extend the debate, mitigate unhelpful polarizations, and help the reader to draw his own conclusions.

Notes

1. It is important to note that not all children with autism or Asperger's syndrome respond well to psychotherapy, and that a long and thorough assessment (Reid, 1999a, 1999b; Rhode, 2000a) is essential.

2. Learning these new ways can allow the child to express capacities which may previously have lain dormant. For instance, the development of a capacity to love is a recurring theme in the case histories in this volume; this capacity derives from the child's experiences with its parents, but for a variety of reasons may have been masked.

3. For psychoanalytically based examples, see, among others, S. Klein (1980), Tustin (1986, chap. 11), and Ogden (1989).

4. This line of thought links readily with the emphasis on regulation by American workers such as Greenspan (1997).

5. There is a higher proportion of girls among these cases than is true of children with Asperger's syndrome in general: this does not reflect a difference in those who receive treatment, but follows from the wish to select cases to illustrate our point concerning the contrasts between children with a shared diagnosis.

PART I

THIS IS ASPERGER'S SYNDROME

The chapters in this first part offer a number of different view points on the condition that is Asperger's syndrome. Hans Asperger himself wrote that the children whose condition was named after him formed an "immediately recognizable" group, but investigators since then have increasingly debated the differing ways of conceptualizing the relationship between the various features of the syndrome. Writing in 1991, Lorna Wing pointed to the confusion created by the absence of a comprehensive list of the features of Asperger's syndrome. This is no longer the case since the publication of ICD–10 (WHO, 1993) and of DSM–IV (APA, 1994). However, debate continues about the relationship of Asperger's syndrome to autism, to schizophrenia, and to various other syndromes such as Wolff's "schizoid personality in childhood" and Gillberg's DAMP (Deficits in Attention, Motor Control and Perception) (Gillberg, 1991b). Uta Frith's groundbreaking book *Autism and Asperger's Syndrome*, published in 1991, contains contributions by a number of authors who disagree on these and other fundamental issues. As Sally Hodges points out in chapter 2, it can be difficult to get a clear picture from research on basic issues such as the difference between Asperger's syndrome and high-functioning autism because of the lack of uniformity of methods and definitions employed in various studies, with the resulting consequences for comparability.

David Simpson, in chapter 1, provides a review of psychiatric perspectives on Asperger's syndrome and a discussion of its relation to autism, as well as to schizophrenia and to antisocial behaviour, including violence. Simpson is less convinced than some other authors of the continuity on an "autistic spectrum" of autism and Asperger's syndrome: instead, he sees the former as a psychotic condition of childhood and the latter as a lifelong personality disorder, as did Asperger himself. He reviews the conflicting evidence on the incidence of violent behaviour in people with Asperger's syndrome, an issue that has generated much heated disagreement. Finally, he outlines the contribution that psychoanalytic theories of cognitive functioning, which distinguish rote learning from a creative relationship to a field of knowledge, can make in bringing together a number of otherwise apparently unrelated features of Asperger's syndrome.

In chapter 2 Sally Hodges similarly discusses the relationship between autism and Asperger's syndrome, before going on to review a number of the most widely held and enduring psychological theories that have been put forward to account for observed behaviour. All of these theories were originally developed in relation to people with autism, but they have been widely invoked as explanations for Asperger's syndrome functioning as well. Hodges provides a comprehensive account of those features that are explained by each theory, as well as of those that are left unaccounted for. She stresses the essentially cognitive nature of all of these theories, which do not address the emotional experience of people with autism or Asperger's syndrome; as she illustrates by means of a clinical vignette, the relational stance that characterizes these two conditions is very different, even when the level of intellectual functioning is comparable. She concludes with a discussion of Peter Hobson's theory of autism, in which the developing child's interpersonal relatedness is accorded a position of primacy and which explains features that are not accounted for by purely cognitive theories.

Trudy Klauber, in chapter 3, provides a discussion of Asperger's original paper from the point of view of a present-day child psychotherapist. She shows how some of the seemingly disparate features of Asperger children may be subsumed under a unifying psychodynamic theoretical framework. Asperger emphasized the spitefulness of these children—a characteristic that has tended to be overlooked in subsequent writing. The exception to this is the different interpretation offered by such authors as Frith (1991a), according to whom spiteful acts are not expressions of a wish to inflict suffering, but derive from a failure to understand the experience of another person, together with the wish to elicit a reaction. In fact, these explanations are not mutually exclusive: a concern with pain, whether suffered or inflicted, is compatible with a failure to understand how to deal with it and with a failure to imagine how another person could do so. Some of the children described in the case histories in this volume needed help in managing their aggressive impulses—as, indeed, do many children without a diagnosis of Asperger's syndrome. Klauber argues that one of the motives underlying some of their aggressive behaviour was the need for it to be communicated and dealt with.

Maria Rhode, in chapter 4, discusses the first-person accounts by two very different women with diagnoses of Asperger's syndrome. Both of them received their diagnosis in adulthood, after they had battled to achieve a way of managing their condition. While each of them made use of various kinds of support, it is clear that their own courage and tenacity were decisive. These first-person accounts raise interesting questions in terms of "theory of mind" (see chapter 2), since both women report substantial problems with reading other people's motives, while at the same time their books are beautifully written and take full account of the likely state of mind of the reader. While some of the case histories in this volume illustrate the evolution of "theory of mind" in the course of therapy, the natural history of Asperger's syndrome remains an essential area for future research. Maria Rhode discusses these accounts in terms of developments in psychoanalytic theory. The importance of fears of falling, of sensory and perceptual impingement, and of failures of bodily integration emerges as paramount.

Finally, in chapter 5 Caroline Polmear describes two adults with Asperger's syndrome in psychoanalysis and psychotherapy. Here, too, sensory, perceptual, and bodily issues are of central importance, along with the gradual process of learning to manage emotions, particularly aggressive impulses. The image of dead or deformed babies occurs repeatedly in connection with the vulnerability of these women's infant self; this is an important feature of other clinical histories in this volume, and one to which we return in Part III and in the Endpiece. Another central issue in this chapter concerns the analyst's use of the countertransference as a means of understanding the patients' emotional communications when they are still incompletely verbalized; again, this is a salient feature of the other case histories. This use of the countertransference means that something that looks like an attack can be understood as a communication (Joseph, 1987) and used as a means whereby the therapeutic relationship can develop. In this way, the patients' fear of their aggressive impulses could be modified, and emotional contact, which had previously been terrifying, could be experienced as helpful. Polmear discusses the extent to which her patients felt impinged on by their own emotions as well as by the external world—what she calls a state of mind–body overfulness. This links with the issue of emotional regulation, which is a feature of many of the later case histories, and also with the degree to which these patients were frightened of contact.

Before the diagnosis of Asperger's syndrome became current, patients such as these would probably have been described as borderline with autistic features. This is an issue that it is useful to keep in mind while reading chapters 6 and 7, by Anne Alvarez and Graham Shulman, in part II, as well as the clinical histories by Tanja Nesic-Vuckovic, Michèle Stern, and Brian Truckle, in chapters 9, 11, and 13, respectively, of part III. We return to this question in the Endpiece.

It will be obvious that the authors of these five chapters hold differing opinions on various points of fact or emphasis. It is our hope that this will assist the reader in refining his or her own viewpoint.

CHAPTER ONE

Asperger's syndrome and Autism: distinct syndromes with important similarities

David Simpson

In 1944, Hans Asperger published his thesis *Die "Autistischen Psychopathen" im Kindesalter* [Autistic Psychopathy in Childhood] in which he described "a particularly interesting and highly recognizable type of child":

> The children I will present all have a common and fundamental disturbance which manifests itself in their physical appearance, expressive functions and, indeed, their whole behaviour. The disturbance results in severe and characteristic difficulties in social integration. In many cases the social problems are so profound that they overshadow everything else. In some cases, however, the problems are compensated for by a high level of original thought and experience. [Asperger, 1944, in Frith, 1991, p. 37]

In 1943, unknown to Asperger, Leo Kanner had published his seminal paper on "Autistic Disturbances of Affective Contact" (Kanner, 1943), in which he introduced the clinical entity of "early infantile Autism".

Asperger's syndrome and Kanner's autism* are, in my opinion, distinct clinical syndromes, although they show important common features. In this chapter, I consider Asperger's syndrome in the context

---

*In this chapter, I follow Frith's (1989, "Notes on Style") use of "Autism" for the clinical syndrome, distinguishing it from "autism" the phenomenon.

of Kanner's description of children with autism and highlight some important areas of difference as well as correspondence. I then discuss the relationship of Asperger's syndrome, first, to schizophrenia and, second, to violent behaviour and criminality. Finally I consider the difficulties that those with Autism or with Asperger's syndrome have with being curious. This is a feature that is important clinically but has received little attention and could be fruitful in furthering our understanding of both conditions.

Asperger's syndrome and Kanner's Autism

Early infantile Autism

Leo Kanner, like Hans Asperger, was born in Austria and trained in Vienna. After emigrating to the United States in 1924, he eventually became head of the Department of Child Psychiatry at the Johns Hopkins University Hospital in Baltimore. In his 1943 paper he gave a lucid description of 11 child patients. This description showed remarkable clinical acumen and laid the foundation for the definitions of the Autistic syndrome that are in use today.

With regard to the following three main features of Kanner's description there is virtually no disagreement with present-day views:

1. The children showed a profound lack of social engagement from or shortly after birth.
2. They showed a range of characteristic communication and speech difficulties. Three of his group were mute, but the language of those with speech was remarkable for features including, echolalia, literalness, and pronomial reversal.
3. They showed an anxious obsessive desire for sameness, exhibiting monotonously repetitive behaviours and utterances. This included an unusual relationship to the inanimate environment. They might, for example, not be particularly responsive to parents but be exquisitely sensitive to some sounds, or they might have major difficulties with transitions or changes in routines. They showed a limitation in the variety of their spontaneous activities but could be particularly fond of inanimate objects and might enjoy for example, continuingly spinning objects.

Kanner described these children as physically normal and attractive in appearance, with no associated medical conditions and with good cognitive potentialities, including excellent rote memories. He also mentioned that, in many incidences, their parents, and particularly their fathers, were remarkably intelligent and successful, but that their interactions with their child seemed strange: he noted obsessiveness and coldness in the parents' attitudes and in their marriages (Kanner, 1973, p. 42). However, since the children's Autism began virtually from birth, he stressed that the type of early parental relationship could make at most a limited contribution to the clinical picture.

With regard to these latter features, current views diverge from Kanner's formulations. Although isolated good cognitive abilities are recognized in Autism, it is now believed that about 75% of children with Autism also suffer from mental retardation (Rutter, 1979). A substantial proportion (25–40%) develop epilepsy, particularly in adolescence (Deykin & MacMahon, 1979; Olsson, Steffenburg, & Gillberg, 1988; Rutter, 1970; Volkmar & Nelson, 1990). With regard to the influence of parenting, Kanner is out of tune with those who consider Autism to be wholly the result of neurological and inherited factors; however, his opinion is surprisingly balanced. Kanner believed the fundamental problem to be an *"inborn autistic disturbance of affective contact"*, but he explicitly acknowledged possible environmental influences on this.

Kanner considered the syndrome to have two cardinal features (Kanner, 1973, p. 33): The first is *"extreme autistic aloneness"*, leading to an *"inability to relate themselves in an ordinary way to people and situations"*. He did not believe this to be a "withdrawal" from existing established relationships but thought that it was there from the beginning. From the start, he wrote, these children show "self-sufficiency"; they act "as if people are not there", "as if hypnotized". Any attempts to disrupt their aloneness is treated "as if it weren't there" or resisted powerfully as a distressing interference. Kanner quoted Gesell, who showed that in normal development infants as young as four months make anticipatory motor adjustments by face and body posture to their mothers lifting them. All the mothers of Kanner's cases expressed astonishment that their child did not do this.

The second cardinal feature is an "anxiously obsessive desire for the maintenance of *sameness*". The autistic child's world seems to be made up of elements that, once they have been experienced in a certain setting or sequence, cannot be tolerated in other settings or sequences or in any other spatial or chronological order. Kanner believed that the obsessive repetitiveness characteristic of children with Autism, their phenomenal memory and even their tendency to reverse pronouns might follow from this.

Kanner named the syndrome *"early infantile Autism"* (Kanner, 1973, p. 45), borrowing the term "autism" from Bleuler (1911), who originally used it to describe the self-centred thinking seen in schizophrenia. Kanner believed that early infantile Autism was related to schizophrenia, on the basis of the features of extreme autism: obsessiveness, stereotypy, and echolalia (Kanner, 1973, p. 40). He carefully noted how early infantile Autism differed from the usual description of schizophrenia in a number of important features—namely, the absence of any period of normal development; the child's undisturbed relationship to physical objects; and the general tendency of the children he observed to move out of their aloneness in the direction of increased contact with others, which contrasts with the usual tendency in schizophrenia towards greater withdrawal. However, he originally placed Autism within the group of the schizophrenias and described it as "the earliest possible manifestation of childhood schizophrenia" (Kanner, 1973, p. 55). This again contrasts with the current view, as discussed below in the section on "Asperger's syndrome, schizophrenia, and violent behaviour".

Asperger's syndrome

Hans Asperger was a paediatrician and an advocate of "remedial pedagogy"—a therapeutic educational approach for children with disabilities. He became Director of the children's hospital at the University of Vienna. In his 1944 post-graduate thesis, he gave a detailed clinical description of four boys aged between 6 years and 11 years who showed marked problems of social expression and interaction but who appeared to possess good linguistic and cognitive skills. (See also chapter 3, this volume.) Asperger's deep interest in these children is obvious from his paper. He favoured a holistic, observational, and intuitive approach to them, and he strove to gain insight into their way of being by describing their means of expressing themselves, consciously refusing to impose a system of explanation. He, like Kanner, believed that the disorder was determined by genetic factors (Maria Asperger Felder, in Klin, Volkmar, & Sparrow, 2000).

Asperger used the term "autism" to define the basic disorder that generated an abnormal personality structure in the child. Like Kanner, he adopted the word "autism" from Bleuler's original use of the concept in the context of schizophrenia. Autism in this sense refers to a "fundamental disturbance of contact that is manifest in an extreme form in schizophrenic patients".

In Asperger's view, it was the children's autism that disturbed and limited their interaction with their environment, shutting off a relation between themselves and the outside world. He considered autism to be the paramount feature that disturbed affect, intellect, will, and action in the children he described, as it does in schizophrenia. Unlike Kanner, however, he did not consider these children to be schizophrenic. In contrast to the picture in schizophrenia, the loss of contact in Asperger children was not progressive, but was present from the start, and they did not show a disintegration of the personality. In his opinion, they showed no more than a hint of thought disorder; in fact, he knew of only one child with this syndrome who went on to develop schizophrenia. He did not consider these children to be psychotic but considered their problem to be a fundamental disorder of personality. This disorder explained their difficulties and deficits as well as their special achievements.

Asperger noted many other common features in the children he described, although he stressed their individuality. Each child was distinguished not only by their degree of disturbance but by the originality of their personality and mode of interaction with the world. In all the children, their characteristic difficulties persisted over time. Asperger stressed the importance of the disharmony between their affect and their intellect and the way in which this caused a disturbance to both.

Affective disturbance was shown by the children's poor empathy and tendency to intellectualize, with problems in understanding social cues. Despite this, Asperger interestingly notes their extreme homesickness when admitted to hospital, describing "an exceptional degree of bonding to objects and habits of the home, bordering on the obsessional and causing these children to suffer much at separation". He believed that they were capable of very strong feelings.

Their linguistic and communicative capacities were, in his view, affected by a disturbance of the "contact-creating expressive function". He noted the impoverishment in their use of facial expression, gaze, and gesture and abnormalities in their use of volume, tone, and flow in speech. These features, which have more recently been described as the pragmatic aspects of communication (Volkmar & Klin, 2000, p. 31), underlie Asperger's observation that these children do not show appropriate modulation and reciprocity with their speaking partners. He believed that it was precisely the non-verbal and pragmatic aspects of communication that enabled the listener to tell "what is lie and truth, what are empty words and what is genuinely meant". He held that the route to this was not through intellectual understanding but through emotional intuition and that it was precisely this that was absent in children with this syndrome. Despite their difficulties, Asperger did not find their language to be delayed. Rather, they demonstrated a capacity to speak at great length on topics that interested them, although they showed an unusual use and choice of words and expressions.

Intellectually he also did not consider these children to be impaired. He reported their capacity for original ideas and advanced appreciation in science and arts, although he was aware of how this could be disturbed by their ego-centric approach and their tendency to perseverate with circumscribed interests. He described, for example, how individual children might be very interested in science, but their interests might be limited to types of smell, varieties of poison, or types of spacecraft, and their theories were often highly idiosyncratic. Mathematical ability might be very advanced, but basic number skills, like knowing tables, might be deficient. Asperger concluded that, in view of their non-compliance and tendency to pursue their own aims, it was not surprising that they showed severe learning difficulties, although they could perform well on IQ tests.

He observed difficulties and conflict in social groups, particularly their families, from an early age, which he viewed as following from their fundamental problems in socialization. Being unable to comprehend or communicate feelings, they could not relate and were easily misunderstood. He noted sadistic behaviour and frequent acts of malice, about which they showed delight. Asperger believed that these and other negativistic and aggressive acts were the result of their feelings of failure and frustration. They tended towards isolated and "alien" behaviour in relation to siblings. He described them as ego-centric and alone, tending to follow their own wishes, interests, and impulses and to ignore the wishes of others.

With regard to objects, Asperger considered their behaviour to be abnormal in that they either ignored objects or were obsessively fascinated with "collecting", which he described as "soul-less possession". He noted their clumsiness and postural difficulties, with poor mastery of their bodies and sense of rhythm. There were problems of cleanliness in all the children, and he described them as messy eaters.

Asperger believed the problem to be present almost exclusively in boys; he reported that out of 200 cases he did not see one fully formed presentation in a girl. He was convinced that the syndrome had an inherited cause, and he cited incipient traits in relatives in each of his cases. When fathers showed traits, they usually followed "intelligent professions". Although he went as far as to say that "the autistic personality is an extreme variant of male intelligence" (Frith, 1991, p. 84; see also "extreme male brain theory"—chapter 2, this volume) and quoted the view that boys tended to be better at abstract logical thinking while girls were better at the practical and concrete, he did report finding traits in mothers. He also noted an increased incidence in only children, which he explained in terms of autistic traits in their parents reducing their desire for reproduction. He noted how very few affected individuals married, but if they did, they had marital difficulties, which he believed to be a result of the disharmony between their affect and intellect that disturbed their desire for sex and reproduction.

At the same time, Asperger thought that these children were exceptional and were capable of unusual achievement. Although later he became more pessimistic about outcome, he stressed that the children's advantages outweighed their disadvantages and he believed they required special treatment.

Asperger's syndrome and autism:
similarities and differences

Asperger's and Kanner's descriptions are clearly similar, with a close correspondence in some areas, but they are not identical. During the past twenty years there has been considerable debate as to whether the syndrome described by Asperger is a variant of Autism. This debate is clearly very important scientifically and clinically. However, it is also powerfully influenced by the beliefs about individuals with particular disorders and problems held by society at large, which of course includes professionals. Avoidance of undue stigmatization, criticism, and misperception are important: so is the need for appropriate recognition and resource allocation. This is illustrated by Asperger's desire to avoid a label of social deviance and mental handicap. It is pertinent that his paper was published in the Nazi era, when the mentally handicapped and socially deviant were exterminated.

Asperger's paper was virtually unknown in the English-speaking world until Wing's review in 1981. She noted continuities with the syndrome described by Kanner and modified Asperger's concept to include the possibility of an early onset in the first two years of life, which might include the language delay and mild mental retardation that had by then been identified as more usual in autism than the high intellectual capacities described by Kanner. Wing coined the term "Asperger's syndrome" to avoid the term "autistic psychopathy", since in English—although not in the original German—"psychopathy" carries the connotation of antisocial, violent behaviour. She considered Asperger's syndrome to be part of the Autistic spectrum. Tantam (1988), although noting the distinction between Asperger's syndrome and Kanner's Autism, agreed that Asperger's syndrome should be placed on the Autistic spectrum. However, he believed that the term "Asperger's syndrome" should be retained as a strict definition for those showing autistic behaviour in the absence of language difficulty.

Volkmar and Klin (2000) equally do not favour broad definitions. They express the need for stringent diagnostic criteria for Asperger's syndrome and for validated research evidence to support any distinctions made between this disorder and related ones. They make a plea for an open-minded approach as to the extent to which Asperger's syndrome and Autism are the same or different, while noting a clinical distinction between Asperger's syndrome and Autism in respect of a number of features.

1. In terms of onset of disorder, Asperger emphasized normal development, including in language, which is not seen in Autism.

2. As regards circumscribed interests, these tend in Autism to involve object manipulation, visual–spatial tasks, music or savant skills, while people with Asperger's syndrome are usually preoccupied with amassing information.

3. Volkmar and Klin note that Asperger reported clumsiness and delayed motor skills not seen in Autism (although Kanner in fact did report this).

4. In terms of social functioning, Autistic individuals are not only

withdrawn but uninterested in others, while those with Asperger's syndrome are believed to be more active and to wish to engage, although their capacity to do so is impaired.

5. In terms of communication, people with Asperger's syndrome show less pronounced problems with intonation or quality of voice than do those with Autism. Unlike the picture in Autism, those with Asperger's syndrome tend to engage in talking to others, and although they may show considerable difficulty with reciprocity and the rules of discourse, they are frequently described as verbose.

Volkmar and Klin report on psychological profiles showing that people with Asperger's syndrome exhibit higher verbal than performance IQ, while the reverse is true for people with high-functioning Autism (Klin & Volkmar, 1995; Lincoln, Courchesne, Allen, Hanson, & Ene, 1998; Volkmar et al., 1994). Overall IQ is preserved in Asperger's syndrome compared with Autism; indeed, the diagnostic criteria for Asperger's syndrome mandate normal intellectual functioning. Klin and Volkmar (1995) also report a pattern of deficit in Asperger's syndrome in an area of performance consistent with "non-verbal learning disabilities" (Rourke, 1989); in fine and gross motor skills; in visual motor integration; in visual–spatial perception; in non-verbal concept formation; and in visual memory, which is not seen in high-functioning Autism.

Volkmar and Klin cite a family study (Volkmar, Klin, & Cohen, 1997) in which 46% of cases show a positive family history of Asperger's syndrome in first-degree relatives, particularly males. They suggest a much stronger familial component to Asperger's syndrome than Autism. Interestingly, this study also showed that 3.5% of siblings of probands with Asperger's syndrome had diagnoses of Autism, which suggests a genetic link between the two. Volkmar and Klin speculate that Asperger's syndrome might be the end result of several genes affecting socialization, and that Autism requires the activity of additional genes connected with language.

This suggestion lends support to the view that Asperger's syndrome and Autism are distinct conditions, but with an area of commonality as disorders of socialization. This is in keeping with the striking correspondence between Kanner and Asperger in identifying autism as the central feature in their separate descriptions of these syndromes; a common feature and mechanism in different clinical pictures. Kanner described a psychosis, while Asperger emphasized a disorder of personality.

Asperger's syndrome, schizophrenia, and violent behaviour

The relationship of Asperger's syndrome with schizophrenia and with violent behaviour are both controversial areas, and the preconceptions that people hold about these diagnoses and their implications impact on this.

To begin with schizophrenia: as I have outlined, both Kanner and Asperger considered the fundamental disturbance in their patients to be "autism", a trait that had been described by Bleuler as a fundamental characteristic of schizophrenia.

Kanner originally believed that his cases exhibited a form of childhood schizophrenia, although he distinguished this from the usual picture in important respects. Since 1970, following the work of Kolvin (1971) and Rutter (1970, 1972), the prevailing view has been that schizophrenia (and for that matter psychosis, with a few exceptions) does not occur in early childhood, and that the condition of early childhood Autism is distinguished from schizophrenia based upon various considerations, including family history and clinical features. It is usually stated that the symptoms and signs of psychosis, particularly delusions and hallucinations, are not present in Autism. This observation is, however, not in keeping with the clinical experience of many people who work intimately with such children, particularly with a psychoanalytic perspective, who not uncommonly report psychotic phenomena, particularly hallucinations both positive and negative (e.g. Rodrigué, 1955).

Asperger, however, was clear that his patients did not have schizophrenia, were not psychotic, but suffered from a personality disorder. Interest in the relationship between Asperger's syndrome and schizophrenia has persisted, and the possibility that people with Asperger's syndrome might be at increased risk of psychosis and schizophrenia has been suggested by some studies (Clarke, Littlejohns, Corbett, & Joseph, 1989; Nagy & Szatmari, 1986; Taiminen, 1994). Tantam (1991) has even suggested the possibility that Asperger's syndrome could be a link between Autism and schizophrenia. A clearer link with increased risk of schizophrenia has been made for children with schizoid personality (Werry, 1992). These children, described by Wolff and Barlow (1979), show features in common with Asperger's syndrome, although their level of social disability is less marked. Some researchers have questioned the strength of this link with schizophrenia (Ghaziuddin, Leininger, & Tsai, 1995) and have cautioned against confusing the style of elliptical thinking seen in people with Asperger's syndrome with the thought disorder characteristic of schizophrenia (Volkmar & Klin, 2000).

Despite the uncertainty, the possibility of a link between Asperger's syndrome and schizophrenia remains an important question, which, I believe, needs to be viewed in the context of the relationship between disorders of personality structure and psychosis. The relationship between Asperger's syndrome and schizophrenia parallels—and may have many features in common with—the relationship in adult psychiatry between borderline personality disorder and psychosis (Rey, 1994c).

Since the 1980s there has been interest, particularly in forensic psychiatry in the United Kingdom, in the association of Asperger's syndrome with an increased risk of violent and criminal behaviour. Asperger himself made a particular note of acts of malice and sadism seen in his children and the delight they take in these. He vividly described a 7-year-old who remarked coldly, "Mummy, I shall take a knife one day and put it into your heart, then the blood will spurt out and this will cause a great stir."

There are several studies and case reports that document violent criminal behaviour including several offences in people with Asperger's syndrome (Howlin & Goode, 1998) In her review, Wing (1981) concluded that a small minority of people with Asperger's syndrome had a history of bizarre antisocial acts (4 out of a series of 34 children, including one child who injured another by means of chemical experimentation). Mawson, Grounds, and Tantam (1985) described a 44-year-old man who was admitted to Broadmoor special hospital after a series of violent attacks on women and children dating from his teens, culminating in an attack on a baby. He had an obsession with finding a girlfriend and a fascination with chemistry and poison. Everall and LeCouteur (1990) and Tantam (1991) both described firesetting in Asperger's syndrome, Tantam mentioning five cases.

In discussing their case history, Mawson, Grounds, and Tantam (1985) suggested that the association between Asperger's syndrome and violent behaviour was more common than had been previously thought, and that many more people with Asperger's syndrome were to be found in long-term care institutions. This view is supported by the results of a study by Scragg and Shah (1994) of the entire male population of Broadmoor special hospital, in which they found that, out of a total of 392 patients, there were 3 cases of Autism and 6 of Asperger's syndrome. The combined prevalence of Autism and Asperger's syndrome in their population was just over 2%, which is considerably higher than estimates of the prevalence in the general population.

Despite this, as with schizophrenia, many people believe that there is little evidence to support the association of Asperger's syndrome with violent behaviour and criminality, and that the case histories exaggerate the problem. Tantam (1991) considered that violent behaviour, either in rage or sexual excitement, was rare in Asperger's syndrome, as were sexual offences, with the exception of indecent exposure. He also found that property offences were rare unless committed in the pursuit of the person's special interest. Ghaziuddin, Tsai, and Ghaziuddin (1991) reviewed accounts of 132 cases of Asperger's syndrome and found only 3 who showed a true history of violent behaviour. This compares with a rate of 7% for violent crimes in the under-24-year-old age group in the United States (U.S. Bureau of Justice Statistics, 1987).

Those who are unconvinced about the association of Asperger's syndrome with violence and criminality explain the reports of this behaviour in terms of the difficulty that people with Asperger's syndrome have in understanding social rules and as a consequence of their obsessional interests. Clearly, concerns about the validity of these suggested links and the distress of stigmatization are very appropriate. However uncertain and controversial these accounts, clinicians who work closely with young people with Asperger's syndrome, like Asperger himself, not infrequently encounter violent and sadistic phantasies, made all the more difficult to interpret by an attitude of emotional detachment. Most of these patients are luckily too inhibited to enact their phantasies, but this does not lessen the difficult task of risk assessment.

Difficulties with the development of curiosity: a psychoanalytic perspective

Finally, it is of particular interest to consider, from a psychoanalytic perspective, the difficulties that those with Asperger's syndrome have with being curious and with learning.

Melanie Klein pioneered one of the earliest psychoanalytic approaches to learning and the inhibitions it can undergo, which she attributed to the connection between a child's healthy curiosity and its aggression. She illustrated this link with material from the treatment of a 4-year-old "Dick", whom she described as suffering from schizo-phrenia but whom we would now recognize as a child with Autism (Klein, 1930). As did Kanner in relation to childhood Autism, Klein considered that Dick's difficulties resulted from an inhibition in devel-opment rather than a regression.

Klein (1928), like Freud (1909d), considered curiosity to be a mani-festation of the "epistemophilic instinct", or desire for knowledge, which she believed was part of the libido or instinct of love. In Klein's view, a child's curiosity, which involves a penetrative relationship between the child and the world around it, can become inhibited by anxiety engendered as a consequence of the passionate feelings that are associated with this. The causes of this anxiety are complex. Klein includes frustration at "not knowing" and the fear of punishment for entering and wishing to possess what are felt to be forbidden adult areas. The association of curiosity with aggression, which Klein felt to be part of normal development, was particularly important in her view, as she believed that if aggression was excessive, then this would inhibit the child, as a consequence of its fear for the damage that it might cause to the people and things that it loves. In this situation it follows that the expression of both curiosity and emotion would be inhibited simultaneously, as was the case with "Dick".

Bion (1962) extended Klein's ideas in this area but also differed from her in that he considered curiosity ("K" in his terminology) to be independent of love and hate (called "L" and "H", respectively). In his model, Bion adds a further crucial component, which, he believes, is necessary for the normal development of curiosity and learning—namely, the receptivity of parents to their child and his or her interests. Some children can be extremely sensitive to their parents' responses to their interests and perceptions. If the response is felt by a child, whether rightly or wrongly, to be unfavourable, then this can inhibit the development of its curiosity and learning.

Difficulties with curiosity are particularly relevant to Asperger's syndrome and Autism. In both these conditions children seem to for-sake their curiosity, withdrawing from mental penetration of the world around them and the route to understanding it through the minds of others. In children with Autism this is more complete. Those with Asperger's syndrome show more curiosity, but this tends to be cut off from feeling and expressed indirectly. Children with Asperger's syn-drome acquire knowledge tangentially, accumulating facts without really going into things and making contact with others, getting to know them and being known by them in a way that will promote the growth of their being. These children tend to "know" in the sense of accumulating knowledge, not of learning creatively. The psychoanalytic approach outlined here makes it possible to make some sense of the clinical phenomena.

Conclusions

In this chapter, alongside their similarities, I have stressed the differences between Asperger's syndrome and Autism—differences that, I think, cast doubt on the increasingly commonly held assumption that "Autistic spectrum disorder" is a valid entity. Indeed, I agree with the original views of Kanner and Asperger, respectively, that Autism is a form of psychosis while Asperger's syndrome is a disorder of personality development. The distinction between Autism and Asperger's syndrome could be compared to that between schizophrenia and schizoid personality disorder. Like Autism and Asperger's syndrome, these conditions share similar features and genetic loading; however, from a clinical point of view, their distinction is crucial. With regard to the common features of Autism and Asperger's syndrome, in addition to a withdrawal from affective contact and a constant desire for sameness, the difficulties that these children have in being curious is, in my opinion, fundamental.

CHAPTER TWO

A psychological perspective on theories of Asperger's syndrome

Sally Hodges

This chapter focuses on different ways of understanding Asperger's syndrome at a psychological level, which includes cognitive, emotional, and social processes. Psychological processes in autism have generated great interest in the literature. There continue to be disagreements and debate as to the process that may account for the cluster of symptoms that characterize Asperger's syndrome. Biological, genetic, and environmental factors in the origins of autism are beyond the scope of this chapter, though the importance of explanations at these levels should not be minimized. Present-day therapists working at the psychological level do not dispute the existence of biological or genetic factors, though they focus their therapeutic efforts on the more mutable aspects of the processes that occur as a result of any original or core "damage".

In order to consider relevant psychological processes—and at the risk of overlapping with other contributions to this volume—it will be important to define Asperger's syndrome as distinct from autism syndrome, particularly "high-functioning autism".

Autism

Autism—as David Simpson notes in chapter 1 in this volume—was first described in 1943 by Leo Kanner. His work generated much interest, but "autism" as a diagnostic category was not fully utilized until several decades later.

The concept of autism as a valid diagnostic entity comprising a consistent grouping of symptoms was strengthened in the 1970s by a large-scale epidemiological study (Wing & Gould, 1979). This showed that the core characteristics of autism consistently clustered into three areas: deficits in socialization, in communication, and in imagination. These three areas have since become known as the "triad of impairments" (Wing, 1988) and form the basis of the diagnostic criteria in the currently used schedules—for example, DSM–IV, the *Diagnostic and Statistical Manual of Mental Disorders* published by the American Psychiatric Association (APA, 1994), or ICD–10, the *International Classification of Diseases* published by the World Health Organization (WHO, 1993). The work of Wing (1988) and Frith (1989) in the 1980s identified three clear "subgroups" of autistic presentation: "aloof", "passive", and "odd". The recognition of subgroups led to the recommendation that the diagnosis of autism should be widened to that of "autistic spectrum disorder". Around this time, Wing (1980) also noted that there seemed to be another distinct group of able autistic children. She called their condition Asperger's syndrome because of similarities with children described in a paper by Hans Asperger (Asperger, 1944). Recognition has grown that the "diagnosis" of autism does not adequately cover the full range of presentations of "autistic symptomatology".

Asperger's syndrome

Asperger's syndrome is the name given to a certain cluster of autistic symptoms originally documented by Asperger (1944), and occurring in people with normal or nearly normal intelligence. As mentioned, the term "Asperger's syndrome" was not widely used until the 1980s, when the concept of autism was studied in greater depth. Lorna Wing (1981) initiated the use of the term "Asperger's syndrome" to describe the group of able autistic people who do not fit the "Kanner" prototype (see chapter 1, this volume). Currently the most used diagnostic classifications (DSM–IV and ICD–10), both suggest that a diagnosis of Asperger's syndrome should not be made when a person could be seen to fulfil the criteria for a diagnosis of autism. In other words, *autism and Asperger's syndrome are seen as different though related disorders.* According to the diagnostic schedules, in order for a person to receive a diagnosis of Asperger's syndrome rather than autism, they should display a later onset of symptoms and an absence of notable language delay. The notes in the text of both DSM–IV and ICD–10 suggest that motor awkwardness and "specific intense interests" are also more commonly associated with Asperger's syndrome, but these are not included in the diagnostic criteria.

There is ongoing debate in the literature as to whether Asperger's syndrome exists as an "entity" separate from autism and, if so, what are the dimensions or features on which it differs significantly from autistic disorder. These debates have yet to be conclusively settled and are further complicated by the growing number of related conditions that have been identified and defined in the literature. These include schizoid personality (Wolff, 1991), non-verbal learning disability (Johnson & Myklebust, 1971), right-hemisphere learning disability (Weintraub & Mesulam, 1983), and semantic–pragmatic disorder (Bishop, 1998).

Volkmar and Klin (2000) have reviewed a range of studies and diagnostic schedules, and from these have identified the clinical features relevant to the differential diagnosis of autism and Asperger's syndrome. These include:

1. age of onset;
2. circumscribed interests;
3. motor functioning;
4. social functioning;
5. communication.

They note that it is very difficult to compare the findings of studies exploring differences in the two conditions, since different workers use different diagnostic criteria, and since even within one research group these did not appear to remain stable over time (Volkmar & Klin, 2000). Many studies that have attempted to establish the validity of Asperger's syndrome in relation to a diagnosis of high-functioning autism have not yielded conclusive results or recommendations owing to these design flaws, and Volkmar and Klin recommend that further carefully designed research should be undertaken in order to achieve a more meaningful comparison. (Some of these areas of difference and similarity are discussed in chapter 1, this volume.) Recently, Frith (2004) has reviewed the literature regarding the diagnosis and nature of Asperger's syndrome. She concludes that autism and Asperger's syndrome are likely to be at least related conditions, though more research is still needed. She does, however, suggest that the category of Asperger's syndrome is necessary and important in clinical practice.

Although there are difficulties in drawing conclusions regarding the validity of the concept of Asperger's syndrome, we would agree with Frith (2004) that it continues to be a useful and meaningful clinical label defining a characteristic group of children. The actual experience for a therapist who works within the transference of "being with" a person diagnosed as having Asperger's syndrome can be quite different from being with a comparable person with autism. Take, for example, the following children:

"Peter"

Peter is 14 years old. In the therapy-room he is clearly nervous and agitated. He hops from one foot to another, asking the therapist what car she drives. His eye contact is fleeting, but he seems drawn to the therapist, asking about which cars she might be interested in, her journey to work, and her opinion of certain cars. He tells her in an urgent, agitated way about the relative merits of two different kinds of car: one can do 32 miles to the gallon but can carry lots of people; the other can do 48 to the gallon but only has room comfortably for one person or maybe two. Being with Peter is confusing and frustrating, and it is hard to shift him from his preoccupations. However, the therapist does get a sense that Peter is trying to make a connection with her, using the only strategies he knows.

"James"

James is also 14. In the therapy-room he does not seem interested in the therapist, and rather than having fleeting eye contact, he seems to look right through her, as though she were not there. He too concentrates on cars, but on the toy cars in the room. He lines them up, seemingly according to colour and size. When the therapist tries to engage with him, by holding up a car to look at or by talking about what James is doing, he calmly and without eye contact removes the car from her hand and restores it to its rightful place on the table. He shows no recognition that she has spoken at all, and the therapist is left with the sense that James has not registered her presence as another person, let alone someone who might be interesting.

Both Peter and James have IQs of about 80. Peter has a diagnosis of Asperger's syndrome, whereas James has a diagnosis of high-functioning autism. Both have good language skills, but they use language very differently. Equally, there is a different quality to the experience of being with these two boys. Peter is obsessively interested in cars, but he seems to want to make a connection with the therapist by means of this interest. His question and comments seem to be about how they can relate in terms of speed and space. In an agitated way, he seems to be trying to find any common ground for communication. James, on the other hand, does not use his language skills, and the therapist finds it hard to have a sense of how or what he might be feeling.

Although one could argue that these two children represent extremes of the autistic spectrum, with James perhaps falling into Frith's "aloof" subgroup and Peter into the "odd" one, the fact remains that *qualitatively* the experience of being with these two children is very different. The way one might approach treating these children would also be different—an issue that relates to the focus of this book, which is on ways of engaging with and drawing out people with Asperger's syndrome. While it may be an imperfectly defined category for diagnosis or research, the "label" of Asperger's syndrome can be helpful to clinicians and professionals, including those who focus on the qualitative aspects of being with another person.

What causes Asperger's syndrome?

Since the condition was initially recognized, there has been much interest and speculation as to what causes or contributes to Asperger's syndrome. Much research has been hampered by the lack of clarity about which features are specific to Asperger's syndrome and which are core or universal features of autistic spectrum disorders. Many features of autism—for example, learning difficulties or clumsiness—are not necessarily specific to that condition. As these features can be found in other conditions, they cannot be considered to be a direct consequence of autism.

As already mentioned, there are many indications that physical, genetic, and biological factors are important in the development of Asperger's syndrome. Convincing evidence exists of a genetic link between autism and Asperger's syndrome (and also of a genetic basis for both conditions). For example, there is an increased incidence of cognitive difficulties and autism in the siblings of children with Asperger's syndrome (Bowman, 1988; Burgoine & Wing, 1983). Luke Jackson, the teenager with Asperger's syndrome who has written two popular self-help books (Jackson, 2002a, 2002b), has a younger brother diagnosed with "Kanner type" autism. DeLong and Dwyer (1988) looked at 929 first- and second-degree relatives of children with autism and found a high incidence of Asperger's syndrome in the families of children with higher IQs. Gillberg (1991b), who studied the families of six people with Asperger's syndrome, found "Asperger" symptoms in at least one first- or second-degree relative of each of the six. It would be unwise not to recognize that a genetic predisposition must be present in at least a proportion of cases. If one agrees with the suggestion that Asperger's syndrome is associated with motor difficulties, this alone is evidence of a biological basis or of nervous system involvement.[1] However, taking into account all the evidence for biological and genetic involvement does not explain how Asperger's syndrome comes to be expressed at the behavioural, social, and emotional levels. This chapter is concerned with the processes by which these difficulties are mediated—that is, with Asperger's syndrome at the level of psychological functioning.

Theories of psychological functioning in Asperger's syndrome

There exist a number of accepted psychological theories at different levels that aim to account for the range of features seen in autism and Asperger's syndrome. They were developed in relation to children with autism and are assumed to apply also to other children on the autistic spectrum, including those with Asperger's syndrome. These theories can explain different features to varying degrees, but no one theory can as yet fully predict and explain the entire range. We look in greater detail at some of the most widely held and convincing theories, starting with the "theory of mind".

The "theory of mind"

One of the most influential theories is known as the "theory of mind". This theory has proved to be highly testable and has therefore appealed to researchers concerned with replicability. Uta Frith, Alan Leslie, and Simon Baron-Cohen have proposed that the range of symptoms seen in autism is due to a difficulty in being able to understand or think about other people's mental states or thoughts—in other words, to "mind-read". Baron-Cohen, Leslie, and Frith (1985) describe non-autistic persons' capacity to attribute independent mental states to themselves and others in order to predict and explain behaviour. An impairment of this process, it has been argued, leads to a range of social, communicative, and imaginative deficits. Theory-of-mind skills may be present to varying degrees. A "first-order" theory of mind requires a person to predict another's mental state ("I think that Claire thinks"). "Second-order" theory of mind, on the other hand, allows the processing of one person's understanding of another person's mental state ("Jane thinks that Claire thinks"). These two concepts have been used extensively in testing for theory of mind.

In order to ascertain whether a person is able to consider other people's mental states or has "meta-cognitive" functioning, it is necessary to devise experiments that demonstrate whether a person is able to predict behaviour based on a *false* belief (otherwise reality or the child's own beliefs would provide sufficient information—Dennett, 1978). A range of increasingly sophisticated false-belief experiments designed to explore a person's recognition or understanding of mental states in others (Baron-Cohen, Leslie & Frith, 1985; Happé & Frith, 1995; Mitchell & Lacohee, 1991; Perner, Frith, Leslie, & Leekam, 1989; Seigal & Beattie, 1991) suggests that autistic individuals do have a specific difficulty with theory-of-mind tasks when compared with children of a similar age and matched for IQ. However, it has been found that "normal" children have difficulty with this task until they reach the age of about 4 years. First-order theory-of-mind tasks are easier to pass, so second-order tasks have proved to be a more sensitive measure. It has now been demonstrated that children aged 3 may fail false-belief tasks though they are able to recognize a false belief

(Roth & Leslie, 1991). It is suggested that the "normal" theory of mind develops in the second year of life and accounts for the evolution of the capacity for symbolic or pretend play (Baron-Cohen, Leslie, & Frith, 1985).

Although this theory has been invoked to explain many of the features of autism, including the characteristic impairments in social behaviour and communication, there are some features it cannot account for. Examples include unusual skills such as jigsaw completion by shape (Frith & Hermelin, 1969), memory for unrelated items (Tager-Flusberg, 1991), or the ability to recognize faces upside down (Langdell, 1978). Nor can theory of mind account for some characteristic difficulties of people with autism, such as memory for sentences, memory for related items, or jigsaw completion by picture.

Trevarthen, Aitken, Papoudi, and Robarts (1996) point out that the theory of mind is essentially a cognitive theory and does not take into account the bodily expression of internal states (such as gestures, tone of voice, facial expression, and body movements). While it is an appealing theory on a cognitive level, its failure to account for such a wide range of autistic features suggests that deficits in theory of mind are not the core feature of autism, or indeed the only process taking place.

Another difficulty with theory of mind is that many people diagnosed with high-functioning autism or Asperger's syndrome have considerable success at theory-of-mind tasks (Bowler, 1992). Tantam (2000) suggests that this may indicate that performance on theory-of-mind tasks may be impeded by the language difficulties of people with lower IQ, rather than that people with Asperger's syndrome necessarily have an impaired ability to mind-read. He does, however, stress that people with Asperger's syndrome do see the world differently from other people. For example, they are less likely to use mental state terms, which reflects the importance of emotional or inter-relational components of their difficulties.

Happé (1994) suggests that Asperger's syndrome may be distinguished from autism by the development (or preservation) of some theory of mind.[2] She argues that if some capacity for theory of mind has been spared or has developed late, the ability to pass some theory-of-mind tasks could co-exist with difficulties in making and understanding relationships. She proposes that the late or unusual development of theory of mind may be associated with subsequent problems, which could account for the elevated incidence of positive symptoms of schizophrenia seen in people with Asperger's syndrome. She suggests, for example, that an "over-functioning" theory of mind could lead to hearing voices or to distortions of experience.

Peter Hobson takes issue with the use of Baron-Cohen's term, "mind-blindness", to refer to the essentially cognitive theory of mind. He points out that this term conflates cognitive and perceptual–relational functioning, which, he argues, need to be distinguished and given appropriate respective places in accounts of developmental processes. He does, however, consider the term to be very apt in relation to autism, as it draws attention to the possible significance of impaired perceptual or perceptual–affective functioning. His own research (Hobson, 1990, 1991) has highlighted how congenital blindness can lead to autistic-like features. We will return to Hobson's theory of the core difficulties in autism and Asperger's syndrome.

"Executive-functioning" theory

Workers such as Ozonoff, Rogers, and Pennington (1991) and Tager-Flusberg and Sullivan (1994) have put forward the theory that people with autism have difficulties in "executive functioning". It has been proposed that the a deficit in executive function underlies deficits in performance on theory-of-mind tasks—that is, the theory-of-mind difficulties outlined above are secondary to impairments in executive functioning.

Executive functioning consists of processes that are managed by the frontal lobes of the brain and include planning, complex cognitive tasks, impulse control, and flexibility of thought and action. It is argued that a dysfunction in executive functioning would lead to the presentation of many of the symptoms of autism. Individuals with autism or Asperger's syndrome tend to perform badly on tasks designed specifically to test executive functioning (Ozonoff, Rogers, & Pennington, 1991; Rumsey, 1985; Russell, Mauthner, Sharpe, & Tidswell, 1991). There is also some supportive evidence from neuropsychological studies (Bailey et al. 1998; Bishop, 1993; Dawson & Fischer, 1994) indicating that abnormalities or damage in the prefrontal parts of the brain result in autistic symptomatology

A major difficulty with this theory is that problems with executive functioning can also be found in many other conditions, such as attention deficit disorder, obsessive–compulsive disorder, and schizophrenia (Ozonoff, 1997). Pennington and Ozonoff (1996) have attempted to demonstrate that the executive-functioning impairments in autism are of a different nature and have a different onset, in order to suggest that a specific form of executive-functioning difficulty may be occurring in autism. However, like theory of mind, executive-functioning theory fails to explain various features of autism, especially those that fall into the emotional domain, such as unusual eye contact and facial expressions and emotional disturbance. Recent studies suggest that abnormal brain structure can be *caused* by behaviour and emotional experience, as well as the other way round (Schore, 1996).

Weak central coherence

This theory was first put forward by Frith (1989) in an attempt to account for the unusual strengths as well as the deficits that can be present in autism. Autistic features are thought to result from a specific imbalance—rather than a deficit—in the ability to integrate information at different levels.

In normal information processing, information is gathered together at many different levels in order to generate meanings and understandings relevant to the immediate context. Frith called this process "central coherence". In understanding any given situation, it is unusual to study each and every aspect of the environment; instead, an overall impression—"the gist" of the circumstances—is formed. This capacity allows for the quick understanding of the context-appropriate nature of ambiguous words such as meet/meat, sew/so, pear/pair (Happé, 1994). Frith (1989) suggests that this ability is altered in people with autism, who have difficulty in taking relevant contextual information into account. This theory would explain not only deficits in people with autism, such as in communication and social abilities, but, according to Frith (1989) and Happé (1994), might also account for some of their unusual abilities. Examples of these abilities include remembering unrelated pieces of information, recognizing faces upside down (as only parts of the face would be taken into account), and assembling jigsaws on the basis of the shapes of the individual pieces rather than the overall picture—all areas in which people with a diagnosis of autism have been shown to excel. Happé argues that central coherence could be thought of as a cognitive style that functions along a continuum. This distinguishes central-coherence theory from one based on deficit or damage, such as theory of mind or executive functioning, though Happé points out that deficits and cognitive styles can co-exist.

Central-coherence theory is still in the process of being more thoroughly researched, with the focus on pinpointing the levels in autism at which coherence may be weak. This theory is more able than those previously discussed to account for the unusual social behaviour that can be seen in autism. However, like them it is primarily a cognitive theory, and as such separates cognitive and emotional functioning.

Emotion (as Trevarthen has stressed, see above) can be conveyed through words and thoughts, but equally through bodily and facial expressions, movements, and awareness of self and others. Again, it is autistic people's notably different functioning in these areas that presents problems for central-coherence theory. Splitting emotional and interpersonal functioning from cognitive functioning hampers our understanding of the person as a whole and seems to be based on the premise that cognitive capacities in some way precede emotional capacities, if indeed they can be separated out. Later in this chapter we consider a theory that makes sense of autism by taking emotional and interpersonal development as central to development.

Extreme male brain theory

This is a recent theory that also focuses on cognitive styles rather than deficits. Baron-Cohen (2002) suggests that autism may be seen as an extreme expression of male traits, particularly of the tendency to "systemize" rather than "empathize". He proposes that women are more likely than men to rely on empathy: they attempt to predict behaviour through thinking about how others might be feeling. In contrast, men might base their predictions on an analysis of the variables in a system and a search for the underlying rules that govern the way the system operates. "Systemizing" is the process of gathering information by generating rules from observations, amending the rules where necessary to take account of contradictory evidence. Baron-Cohen contrasts this process with "empathizing", which, he argues, includes the processes of "mentalizing". This means using a theory of mind—the capacity to think about others' thoughts, beliefs, and intentions—but also includes the processes of sympathy and empathy. The "extreme male brain" theory suggests that the reason why so many more males than females develop autism and Asperger's syndrome is that the cognitive style adopted by autistic people is located on a gender-based continuum.

Baron-Cohen's theory has much indirect and anecdotal evidence to support it, but this still needs to be empirically tested. Once again, it does not take into account individual experiences of emotion or the development of the self in relation to others, and, like many theories of autism, it tends to emphasize the cognitive aspects of autistic functioning.

Impairments in relatedness: accounting for emotional and interpersonal experience in autism

Kanner (1943) suggested that most autistic children "have come into the world with an innate inability to form the usual biologically provided affective contact with people". He therefore held that the essence of autism lay in the disturbance of "affective contact"—the emotional experience of relatedness, that is, relationships with *people*—which appears to be universally impaired in diagnosed individuals.

Peter Hobson, at the Tavistock Clinic, has proposed a theory of autism that places "affective interpersonal awareness and relatedness" at the core of autistic presentation. Working from a base of psychodynamic understanding, Hobson has studied the processes occurring in normal social development from infancy onwards and compared this with developmental processes in autism (Hobson, 1993, 2002). He suggests that, in normal development, infants need to follow a path comprising three stages. First, they need to develop a sense of self in relation to other people; this is initially achieved through the sharing of experiences. (Hobson sees experiences as being *shared* with another person, rather than located in one person and communicated to someone else.) Only then is it possible for infants to develop an understanding of their relatedness to others, through the observation and monitoring of bodily expressions of relatedness such as actions, eye contact, tone of voice, and other aspects of affective contact. Finally, they come to recognize the relationship between their own subjective experiences and the bodily appearance of other people. In order to do this, infants must be born with "prewired" capacities to perceive and recognize interpersonal contact as such, or the whole process of interpersonal relatedness could not begin. Hobson suggests that the absence of this prewiring for the precursors of interpersonal relatedness could then account for the interpersonal and cognitive difficulties seen in autism, such as the failure to understand the minds of others.

In a detailed and convincing essay, Hobson marshals the evidence for difficulties and differences in the way very young children with autism function on the level of social and interpersonal relatedness, before the processes described as "theory of mind" have fully developed. This would imply the primacy of problems with affective contact.

Hobson cites both clinical and experimental evidence for this proposal. Clinical evidence of unusual affective contact exists from Kanner's own observations onwards. Anyone who has had interactions with a person diagnosed as autistic will be able to recognize the experience of difficulty in establishing a mutual affective relationship.

From a research perspective, many studies illuminate the difficulties autistic people have in understanding and responding to emotions. For example, Weeks and Hobson (1987) found that autistic children were less attentive to facial expressions of emotion than were matched non-autistic children when they were asked to sort photographs according to characteristics. This implies that, in autism, the ability to recognize emotions in others—a core component of intersubjectivity—is underdeveloped. In another study Hobson, Ouston, and Lee (1988) asked autistic children to match photographs of facial emotions with vocalizations of the same emotions. This was controlled with photographs of non-emotive actions and sounds (such as types of walking). The autistic children managed to match up the non-emotional stimuli much better than the emotional stimuli, which again suggests a significant difficulty in recognizing and understanding expressions of affect. A number of other studies (e.g. Tantam, Monaghan, Nicholson, & Stirling, 1989; Ozonoff, Rogers, & Pennington, 1991) have reported similar supporting findings.

In yet another study, Hobson and Lee (1989) compared the responses of autistic and non-autistic adolescents and young adults on a psychological test that involved pointing to a word that was represented by one picture out of a set of four. The young people with autism scored significantly worse than did the control participants on pointing out words with an emotional basis such as surprise or horror.

Hobson stresses the significance of research on many aspects of interpersonal relatedness in autism, including the unusual or idiosyncratic nature of autistic children's emotional expressiveness (Kasari, Sigman, Mundy, & Yirmiya, 1990); the reduced level of indicating gestures such as pointing (Mundy & Sigman, 1989); and the unusual nature of social referencing processes (Yirmiya, Kasari, Sigman & Mundy, 1989). He concludes from the substantial body of research data and clinical evidence that in most, if not all, cases of autism, abnormalities in perceptual–relational, non-verbal communication, and interpersonal affective coordination are present from a very early age, even before cognitive deficits are recognizable. He suggests that the cognitive deficits should be viewed as developmental sequelae to the abnormalities in interpersonal relatedness, rather than the converse, as other workers have proposed. However, he argues that even this division is not clear-cut, and that in infancy it is not really possible or helpful to split affective–cognitive and conative processes of interpersonal relatedness, as they are all interrelated and interdependent.[3]

Hobson (2002) has recently put forward some implications for research that follow from his own experimental data and theorizing. He suggests that the appropriate "unit of study" needs careful consideration, and that the understanding of autistic processes may benefit from a study of what happens *between* people, on the interpersonal level of functioning, as opposed to a focus on the individual child's thoughts, feelings, and beliefs.

Hobson's theory centres around what occurs between people: the interpersonal relationship or what Trevarthen (1979) has called "intersubjectivity". He describes how difficulties in the processes of interpersonal relatedness could lead to an autistic presentation. This is very much a "two-person" theory. Alvarez (1999a) has suggested that primarily cognitive theories such as theory of mind could be viewed as "one-and-a-half-person psychology": they do focus on understanding others on the level of cognition or rational inference, but without addressing the affective aspects of relationships. In support of Hobson's theory, she notes the increasing range of professionals who, like psychoanalysts, are now placing feelings at the heart of cognition. For example, developmentalists such as Trevarthen (1980) and Murray (1991) see emotions as core components of functioning. Most interestingly, brain researchers are also writing about the centrality of feelings in normal development (Damasio, 2000; Perry, Cohen, & DeCarlo, 1995; Schore, 1996). Schore and Perry both stress that emotionally loaded events such as the experience of severe trauma can impact on neurological development, for example by increasing neural connections in parts of the brain (see Introduction). This adds weight to the clinical and research finding (Reid, 1999c; Rutter et al., 1999; Tustin, 1994b) that trauma or aversive events can contribute to autistic presentation.

Summary

In this chapter we have looked at some of the most enduring and widely held theories about psychological processes occurring in autism. The majority of these theories focus on cognitive processes. Their proponents consider that cognitive deficits occur prior to the social and emotional features of autism. Theories that see cognitive processes as being central to the development of autism or Asperger's syndrome assume that cognitive processes precede other aspects of functioning, but also that cognition can be understood independently of feelings or interpersonal relatedness.

From a converse perspective, Hobson's theory of interpersonal relatedness and autistic development takes into account the difficulty in isolating different aspects of functioning, particularly in infancy, where these processes are so inter-dependent. Hobson offers a model that can account for some of the more unusual social and affective difficulties to be seen in autism and that are difficult to explain using a purely cognitive framework. His theory also allows for the possibility of interventions that address difficulties in relatedness. Considering autism as having a basis in very early interpersonal processes makes it understandable that so many domains of functioning should be affected and suggests how therapists who work at the interpersonal level could affect the development of the children whom they see. The process of engaging with autistic children through the relationship that is created in psychotherapy can allow for damaged interpersonal relatedness to develop in a more helpful way.

Notes

1. A psychological understanding of physical impairment is provided by the work of Geneviève Haag (Introduction).

2. As does Grotstein (1997), writing from a psychoanalytic perspective.

3. This links with Bion's clinical work on the development of the capacity for thought out of emotional factors such as the tolerance of frustration (Bion, 1962). See also Britton (1989) on the connection between the incapacity to tolerate the parental relationship and some forms of thought disorder. Alvarez (1992a) has contrasted a "one-person psychology" of cognitive deficit and a "two-person psychology" that takes account of a child's internalized expectations of the way in which his capacities and actions will be viewed by significant others.

CHAPTER THREE

A child psychotherapist's commentary on Hans Asperger's 1944 paper, "'Autistic Psychopathy' in Childhood"

Trudy Klauber

In this chapter I reflect and comment on a number of aspects of Asperger's syndrome, as described by Hans Asperger in his original 1944 paper (Frith, 1991c). Asperger uses the term "autistic psychopathy" for what, since Lorna Wing's paper (1981), we now call Asperger's syndrome. I want to think about some of the difficult questions raised in the paper, of which one of the most important is whether or not there is meaning in the children's behaviour and what the meaning may be. Asperger himself faced this difficulty in looking at the behaviour, test results, and other communications of the boys about whom he wrote. There is a misleading quality in so much of what goes on, and it is easy to become muddled about what is meaningful and what is not. Other questions include the difficulties the children have in learning simple and practical things and the attraction towards complexity, and their "severe and characteristic difficulties of social integration". I also include some comments on aggression and the question of malice and some brief thoughts on imagination and phantasy.

Asperger borrows the term "autism" from Bleuler to define the pathology of the group of boys with "autistic psychopathy" who "have severely disturbed and considerably limited interaction and who are not psychotic. . . ." He also states that they have, "severe and characteristic difficulties of social integration . . . in many cases . . . so profound that they overshadow everything else" (trans. Frith, 1991c). He concludes that they seem to have a kind of personality disorder (see chapter 1, this volume). There are detailed case histories of Fritz V, aged 6½ years, Harro L, aged 8½ years, Ernst K, aged 7½ years, and, briefly, Hellmuth L (possibly around 7 years). From them and other children Asperger draws out the clinical picture of the children, their appearance, intelligence, social behaviour, drive and affect, and, finally, genetic and biological factors.

Asperger emphasizes the "social value" of the *autistic psychopath*, and throughout the paper he shows great feeling towards the boys he describes—and with whom he had a lot of contact in the University Paediatric Clinic in Vienna. The warmth and the ability to identify with the dilemmas and suffering of the boys—especially when they report that they have been teased or bullied—is present alongside clear-sighted descriptions of coldness and malevolence, in two boys in particular, and some fascinating descriptions of certain aspects of the sensitive and thorough testing process in the clinic.

Asperger lets each child's personality appear from behind the type. He writes that personalities and special interests are often outstandingly varied and original. While the problems presented vary over time, essential aspects are unchanged. The children in his sample "cannot learn simple practical skills or social adaptation. They present at school with learning and, or, conduct disorders, and they have job and performance problems at school." He does not mention the impact of puberty directly, but he does comment on sexuality and the fact that, from his limited observation at that time, these individuals often had social and marital conflicts in adulthood.

He observes that there is little eye contact, they hardly ever fix on someone or something, and it is difficult to see if the glance is to a place "far out" or turned inward. He wonders with what they are preoccupied, noting that look does not meet look and that they tend to gaze past him, touching visually only accidentally in passing. He notes that they "seem to perceive mainly with their peripheral vision . . . a surprisingly large amount of the world around them." He comments on eyes lighting up when some were ". . . intent on a malicious act". He sees tension and worry as well as slack and empty faces, lost and far-away-looking, with a limited number of facial expressions, and that they may be constantly moving in a stereotypical way.

Asperger mentions his own use of intuition—perhaps similar to the psychotherapist's use of countertransference (see below)—in attempting to understand the boys. He notices that, in these children, ". . . the language feels unnatural". He is extremely interested in their intelligence, neologisms, unique expressions, and points of view, and he forms the opinion that there is "surprising maturity" in their ability to see things from a new perspective.

He gives examples of an interest in natural sciences, and he comments on a "chemist" who stole to fund his experiments in a single-minded way that horrified his family, while another was obsessed with poison and stole cyanide. He refers to the complex arithmetic of one of the boys, Fritz V, and believes it to be a special skill (see chapter 5, this volume) while also noting that using such special skills as complicated ways of solving simple arithmetical questions failed from time to time, and the children often could not do simple things.

Asperger mentions "particular introspection" and comments that the children are constantly self-observing. He says that they are good judges of character. This discussion is an interesting one. He notes that the children recognize falseness and hypocrisy and are drawn towards those who genuinely feel for them. It is not possible, it seems, to put on an act as a good teacher or carer—this is easily exposed. (On the children's sensitivity to others' moods, see chapter 12 and Endpiece, this volume.)

He goes on to mention one boy who felt homesick in hospital (noting his surprise at how many of the boys he met did feel like that). The boy, with his head on a bolster, made a strange noise and needed to be very quiet for a long time—the description shows clinical observation of fascinating detail, which tells us much about Asperger's empathy with these troubled boys. The boy in question had a kind of fantasy or hallucination of his teacher with a tiny head and said that when he pressed his eyes, a picture got better, and then he put his head on a bolster and lay quiet until the strange noise in his ear went away. Homesickness—whether a result of extreme distress at minor change or an "exceptional degree of bonding with objects at home"—was something that Asperger linked with self-observation and interest in the functions of the body. I shall return to this and other questions in my commentary.

"Prodigious crackpot interests":
the attraction towards complexity

The first Asperger child I ever met was one of those with a special, narrow interest—in his case, upholstery on the upper deck of a particular make of double-decker bus. He found it riveting, as he did information about tickets, ticket rolls, and small differences between bus-ticket printing machines. He had the capacity to concentrate on such areas in immense detail, to remember them, and to collect data that others would have found boring. Eventually, with this boy, I found it possible, using close observation and monitoring the countertransference (known elsewhere as reflexive or self-reflective practice) in the setting of regular weekly sessions, to distinguish between different feeling states in relation to his extraordinary concentration on detail. I felt able to tell the difference between when it was driven by extreme anxiety or fear and when it had become habitual and unnecessary and was preventing him from developing other, essential aspects of his mental life.

Anne Alvarez (1999b) has suggested that rituals and the stereotypies of autism take the place of play in autistic children's lives. I suggest that the narrow range of interests in Asperger children is similar. These kinds of behaviours seem to develop as a means of self-calming high anxiety, reducing panic, and distracting the child, and they can easily become habitual. Alvarez recommends that the psychoanalytic psychotherapist needs to monitor closely the emotional atmosphere of the moment in order to understand whether panic, anxiety, or fear is still the unconscious driving force. The psychotherapist, using close observation of the child and the feelings in the consulting-room, is often able to distinguish accurately between redundant rituals and the use of similar behaviour in an attempt to dissipate extreme emotional states that are felt to threaten the child's existence or safety.

Regardless of whether the Asperger child or adolescent is neurologically different from others—and there is some evidence to suggest that they are—it is always important to note the *feel* of what is going on. My patient's interest in bus upholstery was conveyed in a monotonous tone, in lengthy sentences with few pauses for breath. The effect of his delivery on me was mostly to induce boredom and sleepiness. For a long time I thought that I must concentrate very hard and search for meaning, *against* all that I was feeling. On one occasion I recall pursuing a line of thought that had something to do with his interest in travel, his interest in arriving at a destination, and that he might even wonder whether or not I travelled around, perhaps by bus. I feel clear now that I was quite wrong. My emotional reaction to the material eventually led me to consider seriously that it was by then just part of his habits of mind, and that such habits were as unhelpful as his insistence, aged 11, that his mother should watch him take a bath (for an hour or more mainly totally submerged) or find his socks for him every morning. I dared to suggest that he was stuck somewhere lifeless and uninteresting in his mind, and that perhaps he was not sure that he wanted to go anywhere else; in any case, he did not know how to try. (That is to say, I felt that he was not using the interest as a regulator of extreme anxiety, although originally, long ago, he might have been, but that he had simply got washed up somewhere and mentally did not or could not move away.)

The atmosphere in that particular session changed and came to life, and so did he. He was irritable and cross and immediately told me that we were going to play at schools (he would be the teacher), and I was to go into detention. I was to stay for 90 minutes, and when I dared to speak again, I was given several more days of detention, where I was to be left by myself, doing nothing but boring tasks similar to the ones to which he seemed so attached. I suppose in his mind he had kept me fixed in that way—not able to move nor to make unwelcome comments. His mother, who was supported by a colleague in the clinic, began to resist the demands to search for the socks. He became very bossy with her, and she resisted. He also discovered that he knew where his socks were. He even seemed to be pleased with himself about that and about other ordinary achievements too.

Adult resistance to the pull into dead-end activity allowed something else to develop. It became clearer that he really was in a panic about apparently simple things like choosing between one sport and another on games afternoons. But he never showed it: he simply stood very still, thereby confusing his teachers, who thought he could choose if he wanted to. It became more possible to distinguish between what was felt to be too frightening or difficult, where he needed sensitive and thoughtful support, and developmental challenges which now could be faced—albeit later than by his peers—had he not spent so much of his life in such a paralysed state of mind. This lost developmental time had, of course, steadily widened the gap between his development and that of his peers, and that of his younger sister. I am suggesting that some of his insistence on focusing most of his mind on something very detailed had prevented him from knowing about *manageable* anxiety, suggestive that it had developed at an earlier time in his life, when he did feel a need to withdraw himself. The very fact of taking up so much of his life's time had, I think, slackened his grip on life and on the real assertiveness that is needed to tackle significant developmental tasks. In such a state of mind the mildest assertiveness from self or others can be experienced as disproportionately aggressive and dangerous.

It seems to be a feature of the condition that adults will often feel confused. What is habitual and could be given up can feel very similar to a deadening diffusion of feeling used as self-protection by a child who feels the external world is truly dangerous. Distraction can appear to be deliberate or naughty when it is in fact being used as a means of un-focusing the mind from extremely fearful states. The distractions can include certain kinds of behaviour, but also the very use of language itself. Large amounts of detailed information, a monotonous tone, or the refusal to allow a response from the other person may all be means of avoiding meaningful links or strong emotional reactions in the course of trying to control an unpredictable and frightening external world.

The special and narrow interest in Asperger children seen as self-protection against primitive fears can become a form of psychic retreat (Steiner, 1993) from which it is difficult to break out. Asperger himself comments on how his group of boys ". . . make life difficult for themselves" when it comes to learning, and one boy says, "I don't like little sums". This boy, Harro, had particular idiosyncratic ways of solving arithmetic problems and was frequently, but not always, correct. His convoluted, subjective system is both fascinating and tiring to follow and is not entirely logical. It feels as if he is highly intelligent, but why does he love the complexity of big numbers and idiosyncratic methods? It might, indeed, be a neurological problem, but surely not a function of his hard wiring alone? It might be that there is a sense of safety in burying himself in the detail, rather similar to the way some people with the syndrome talk at great length in a way that reassures them but is not always communicative (see Youell, 1999).

Simple procedures and shorter sentences would allow space for unbidden, spontaneous thought and feeling. Verbosity, cataloguing, complex routes to simple destinations fill up time and space and, perhaps, create an apparently safe haven for people who do not understand the world and dare not risk allowing the space and time in which to discover that they might.

There is also something dangerously addictive about all forms of psychic retreat, and the longer the time spent in them, the greater the fear of emergence. This form of self-protection is not unique to Asperger's syndrome or to autism, but it might be a factor in making treatment of both groups more difficult, especially when the children are in latency. Treatment in early childhood is more likely to be effective than in the latency period (when more developmental time has been used up and there has been more time for the symptoms to become established), but, equally, the physical and psychological upheaval of early adolescence provides a window of opportunity when putative order and control are challenged by the return of the upheaval of physical and emotional experiences from toddler life. In adolescence, there is a chance to re-work them. I certainly felt that it helped me to offer friendly challenges to my patient, which he felt able to take up and to move a bit away from his circumscribed life and interests. One day he gave me an interesting piece of work to do in detention. I had to draw a safety poster on which the slogan to be written was, "No children or pets are allowed out on *bornfire* [sic] night". Anything to do with birth, movement, moving on was not allowed out according to his diktat.

The attachment to time-consuming, mind-filling activity raises another point. Such activity is an extraordinary example of over-use of one particular part of the mind. That part, like an over-developed muscle, becomes super-fit through regular exercise and use. It is like exercising one arm only. Other parts of the mind are under-used and are less ready to move into action. The over-use of one part of the mind—the gathering of facts and mental cataloguing—might, I suggest, actually contribute to the difficulty in exercising more free-floating reflective capacity and the development of more imaginative (as well as anxiety-provoking) use of the mind.

Play, the medium through which children are in touch with thought and feeling and where they can represent and mentally work through their preoccupations and anxieties, is not easily available to children with Asperger's. There is an excess of self-consciousness, tension, and anxiety that inhibits play and the potential development it offers. The absence of play inevitably inhibits the development of the capacity to symbolize and leaves the children in a more concrete and literal world in which the difference between phantasy and reality, internal and external worlds, dream and reality is unclear. Perhaps difficulties in speaking spontaneously rather than laboriously, or the problems with physical coordination that Asperger mentions and that is much in evidence in many of the clinical chapters in this volume, can be linked to such inhibitions in play and playfulness. There is a kind of stiffness and poor coordination in mind and body.

Alvarez suggests that there is a "secondary autism", as she calls it, which comes into being to deal with the "early sensitivities and deficits" of primary autism (Alvarez, 1999b and see Meltzer, 1975a). If Asperger's syndrome is part of the autistic spectrum, which I think it probably is in some cases, then Alvarez has the idea that experience-driven, secondary autistic symptoms and behaviour are further inhibitors of more ordinary development. Secondary symptoms seem to maroon autistic and Asperger individuals in a place from which change becomes threatening in itself. Asperger described something he called a "distraction from within", which I take to be a kind of mental interference. External interference, according to Asperger, may also come inadvertently from (some) parents' overvaluation of their children's originality and inventiveness, which can be confused at times with maturity. While this might be the case, it is also surely born out of something else he mentions: the despair of teachers—and surely, by inference, of parents—at the tortuous efforts required of them and the children to get simple tasks done and understood. The children lack the ability to relax and to access also the autonomic and procedural systems for getting on with things. They can seem actively and consciously to interfere with the process—as if their internal world is dominated by interfering rather than friendly or supportive figures. Psychotherapy can, for some, provide a bit more mental freedom and space for clarification and for distinguishing real attempts to use the imagination from varieties of psychic retreat.

Emotional regulation

Asperger's description of the clinical picture and his detailed examples of the four boys include familiar descriptions of situations that suggest that emotional regulation and self-control are absent. This is particularly poignant in the descriptions of how the boys came to the Clinic—not managing ordinary classroom and school situations in particular. He says: ". . . in everything the children follow their own impulses and interests regardless of the outside world" and "Causes for open conflict are multiplied." Merriness can become immoderate and turn into jumping and rampaging. There is a hint, in the description of the boy suffering from homesickness lying on his bolster until the noise in his ears goes away, that he is trying to regulate his emotional state by physical means. There are other examples where apparent playfulness changes into something else, which suggest that it can feel impossible for the children to calm themselves once feelings start to escalate, and that things can soon get out of hand. This is a familiar picture to many of those who work with Asperger children.[1] Asperger's description of "internal impulses" hints at something that, from the psychoanalytic point of view, is central: that there *is* an internal world, with an influence on the external situation.

The emotional regulator is often described in psychoanalytic thinking as an internalized benign and helpful figure with whom we can identify. This figure, like a parent or a well-functioning parental couple, helps us to know when to stop something, that we are able to stop, that we can calm down or we can move on to something else. In the hypersensitive individual with Asperger's, the interference of unregulated anxiety, the pull towards distraction, and the difficulty of not resisting the pull into over-absorption is much less regulated. There is both excessive emotional reaction and a pull into retreats. Whether or not there is a neurological deficit, it is likely to be exacerbated by manoeuvres that inhibit internalization of a regulating function in infancy. Parents' and others' attempts to introduce it are, in turn, met with resistance or distraction, and they become discouraged. Psychoanalytically informed interventions can address the question and can begin to strengthen self-regulatory processes, which, in turn, allows more space for other aspects of the mind to develop.

Very frequently Asperger children need to regulate pleasure as well as other emotions such as sadness at separation or loss (cf. Tustin, 1981, 1986). In a recent example a boy was very excited coming into the clinic and greeted his therapist with a broad smile. However when she came to fetch him for his session, he was buried in a comic book and then held it ahead of him as he walked all the way to the therapy-room. The pleasure and anticipation were gone as if they had never been, and there was no opportunity to look forward to the session to come. He seemed to be obliged to turn away, as if the feelings might otherwise get too great and overwhelm him. He poured emotional cold water on them and seemed to have killed them off completely. This, of course, inhibited further exploration—for example, of whether his therapist had given him a warm smile or was pleased to see him and was herself looking forward to a potentially interesting and satisfying session for them both. It took him 20 minutes of the session before he would give up his withdrawal (reading the comic, drawing monsters he had drawn many times before, and setting up endless fights between them). After the therapist had endured the 20 minutes and had begun to feel that things were not about to change, while feeling aware that she also felt rather anxious and breathless, he suddenly looked up, as if it were now all right to do so. He said, " Did you know there is an interactive version of this game?" Interaction now seemed possible and regulated. Of course he had lost 20 minutes of his interactive time, but he had not lost it all. The waste of potential developmental time taken up with this form of regulation through cut-off and emotional withdrawal amounts to a loss of years of developmental time and consequent emotional developmental delay, before one even begins to look at possible deficit.

As I mentioned earlier, there is a link between specialist and narrow interests (often caricatured as train-spotting) and emotional regulation. The collecting of information often seems to be a kind of attempt to keep feeling down. It is as if the idea of making a good connection is either absent or felt to be anything but good. Real emotional connections with others also bring other risks—particularly of natural endings or breaks: something else that is frequently felt to be unbearable. Change and breaks in routine are extremely difficult for most people with Asperger's syndrome. Change can feel overwhelming or disastrous. The imperative of seizing control appears to offer the illusory hope that there will be no change, time will not pass, and there will be no partings or separations. Then children like the first patient I mentioned above cannot participate too deeply in reality. Not concentrating is not always enough to keep reality out, and active concentration on something else offers hope. Certain activities, like list-making or attention to minutiae, seem to offer something more active at diffusing the attention and the affect. Some young people demonstrate that they are able to concentrate on many such activities at once—watching television, listening to music, and perhaps playing a portable electronic game, for example—as if they have to work extra hard at keeping feeling out and the attention well spread. Some of these children collect prodigious amounts of factual information of many kinds. Of course the difficulty of putting together a realistic picture of the way the world really works then becomes extremely great. Common sense is not available in ordinary or in psychoanalytic terms. I comment further on why this should be later in the chapter, when I address problems with the imagination.

"Autistic acts of malice"

"Acts of malice", according to Asperger, occurred mainly within the families of the children he describes. With uncanny certainty, he writes, the children can sometimes do whatever is the most unpleasant or hurtful thing in a particular situation. However, he writes, since their emotionality is poorly developed, they cannot sense how much they hurt others, either physically, as in the case of attacks on younger siblings, or mentally, as in the case of parents (p. 77).

In the detailed descriptions of Fritz V, Asperger describes how "he committed mischievous acts, typical of this type of child". He goes on to say that the same boy who had been sitting listlessly would jump up with his eyes lit up, and, before one could intervene, he would have done something mischievous—for example, knocking everything off a table or bashing another child, usually younger and smaller, who was scared of him. He would turn on lights or water, suddenly run away, or throw himself into a puddle impulsively—always in the worst and most embarrassing circumstances, according to Asperger, who later uses the word "malicious" rather than "mischievous" when he suggests that it is no wonder their behaviour ". . . often appears altogether "calculated".

Asperger seems to feel, sympathetically, that there is some difficulty linked with poor physical coordination, or "sheer restlessness", in addition to an inability to gauge degrees of hurt. However, when he uses expressions such as "malicious", "calculated" (Fritz), "sadistic", and "primitive spitefulness" he is writing about something more than mischief. A number of child psychotherapists would concur with this view of some of the children (see for example, Alvarez, 1999b). Asperger mentions that the children often turned nasty when they were treated nicely, and he describes a boy who told his mother he wanted to plunge a knife into her heart and would relish the outflow of blood. The same boy wanted to be a wolf that could rip people and sheep apart, making the blood flow. This is shocking, "calculated" stuff and is different from the hot-blooded and unregulated self-defensive behaviour of Ernst and Harro when they are teased and bullied at school. It may be a primitive ruthlessness, as Polmear's patient suggests (chapter 5, this volume) or it could be a counterphobic reaction in an individual who becomes identified with something deeply and primitively feared.

The psychoanalytic point of view would include a number of other factors in discussing the apparently sadistic or sado-masochistic behaviour of some. These would include the kind of identification made by some of the children, some internal explanation of the need to withdraw from normal contact, and questions about aggression and excitement. All of this also needs to be set in the context of the perceptions and misperceptions that often develop between parents and their children who are difficult to read and to reach.

I begin with this latter point. Difficult-to-reach individuals like Asperger's Fritz will have had a lifetime of experience of confusing, worried, or angry responses from parents and carers. Fritz additionally seems to have been really extremely emotionally deprived. Such experiences are, for many individuals, misperceived as evidence of their own unacceptability or even that they deserve to be mistreated and hated. Asperger himself observes—and it seems highly relevant—that the children do take in a great deal of information at high speed, using peripheral vision and hearing. Their understanding of the information taken in so quickly is idiosyncratic, such as, for example, their reading of a frowning face or a loud or irritated remark.

Fritz, a "highly unusual boy", could not manage social integration: he could not play and was easily wound up by other children, who no doubt goaded him into lashing out. His attempts at seeking affection felt unpleasant—"as abrupt as a fit", according to Asperger—and he "did not care if people were sad or upset". He seemed to invite others' anger and he lacked appropriate distance, shyness, or respect. He was one of those children whose fleeting glances seemed to take in so much.[2] He had no sense of physical rhythm, was uncoordinated, and might have been dyspraxic (see Introduction and Endpiece). Asperger notes that he says to another child: "I am so horrible because you are cross so nicely."

Locating crossness in another child and identifying himself as the horrible one at least makes him an active bully rather than a passive victim. One might go one step further to suggest that in his bullying and with the "detectable malignant glimmer in his eye" he was identified with a superior adult bullying kind of internal figure, which might suggest that his subjective understanding of some of his experiences was not simply that he was neglected or deprived—which he undoubtedly was, in my view—but that he was not likeable or loveable, and that he found that idea exciting.

A further problem for many parents is that they *are* truly frustrated by what look like gratuitous nasty acts: attacks on them or on others or the apparently wilful destruction of property. It becomes almost impossible at home not to feel and actually to be retaliatory at times, as

many have honestly admitted (Klauber, 1998). Therapists can sympathize, as they are often provoked in similar ways and may need to
suffer and struggle to understand the meaning and to respond helpfully (see, e.g., chapter 12, this volume).

Occasional parental anger sometimes plays further into some children's distorted picture of relationships between parents and children.
Once the distortions have begun, many factors, including parents'
questioning of their children, can cause further withdrawal from what
is felt to be so persecuting. Such hypersensitive individuals can easily
begin to behave as if the whole world is cruel and as if they have no
choice but to identify with the cruelty (and sometimes the coldness)
that they believe is there. In some extreme cases, individuals are so
coldly withdrawn—or un-drawn, as Alvarez has noted (1999a)—that
they scarcely feel that they or others are human.

We must also take into account how many people with Asperger's
syndrome have actually *been* bullied and teased for being different.
Difference or oddness induces fear as well as insincere responses in
some children and adults. Falsely friendly adults who are themselves
anxious or afraid—Asperger mentions some whose behaviour is more
mechanical than truly empathic in the paper—are a further complica-
tion in an already powerful and confused set of messages. It is plausi-
ble to hypothesize that the fact that Asperger children are quick to pick
up on insincerity is more than likely to encourage them to withdraw
further from a confusing and frightening social world.

It has been well understood in child and adolescent psychotherapy,
since Valerie Sinason (1992) first published accounts of the extent of all
kinds of abuse among learning-disabled children, that children and
young people with any marked difference or disability are in danger of
abuse. It is also, by now, well documented that identification with the
abuser is an outcome for many who become abusive and sometimes
cynical to others in their turn. In respect of Fritz's attacks on younger
and smaller children, the classic picture of bullying, locating the discomfort, fear, and hatred in another, is not unusual. The identification
with bully rather than victim evokes the idea that there are only two
positions available, and Fritz chooses the former, probably unconsciously. All this adds to a heightened sense of persecution.

The glint in Fritz's eye, which Asperger associates with malig-
nancy, suggests excitement associated with inflicting hurt. I want to
link this with another comment from Asperger himself. He observed
that a lot of the boys were apparently addicted to masturbation, often
in public and without inhibition. Hellmuth L is one such boy. When

sexual arousal and excitement become associated with cruelty, then there is a psychologically dangerous situation: one that may become addictive as well. First, it is non-developmental because it is self-stimulation, and, second, it increases the tendency to turn away from social life and physical attraction in the belief that it is bad or dangerous. It can lead to aloofness and an addiction to further activity that induces mindlessness—always making the return to mindfulness feel more filled with persecution. When persecution and excitement are linked, sadism can become the route to arousal, and this may be a factor in the boy Asperger describes who seems so attracted to violence and blood-letting. At the onset of puberty and in adolescence such arousal combined with the lack of ordinary social contact can lead to excessive, "strange excitement" (Alvarez, 1999b).

When this kind of activity is present in young people with Asperger's, all sorts of habitual activity can take on distorting confusion in the mind. In one patient of mine, as a young adult, when I mentioned that he was doing something unpleasant in his mind and with his body—he was secretly masturbating during his session—his giggly and frightened response made it clear that he felt my remarks to be intrusive and attacking, and he found that arousing and liked to get me to talk about it if he could. That seemed to lead him far away from what seemed like a really frightening idea—that he would have to struggle extra hard to learn about how to make good social contact and to try to get to know himself and others (Klauber, 1999b).

Fantasy and imagination

Asperger describes some fascinating comments by some of the individual boys—notably when they are asked in tests to distinguish between two things. In two examples there are hints of powerful and frightening fantasies. Fritz is asked about similarities and differences between a cow and a calf. "Lammer, Lammer, Lammer", he responds rapidly, and when asked a further question—which of the two is bigger—he says, "The cow, I would like to have my pen now", which sounds like someone getting quickly away from the subject of cows and calves. Asperger suggests that Fritz was following his own internally generated impulses, and I think he was right. It would appear that Fritz is troubled by a picture that really upsets and disturbs him, and "Lammer" is intended to obliterate it. Perhaps he is communicating that the idea of a mother figure and her baby, even if they are animals, is intensely troubling and painful. We know from Asperger that Fritz's mother found motherhood difficult. Perhaps Fritz is demonstrating how persecuting and painful such an image would be if he took it in and thought about it—so he doesn't. I am suggesting that for Fritz, and perhaps for some other Asperger children, the measures used to obliterate difficult images or ideas are extreme and distorting to cognitive as well as emotional functioning. The exaggerated response to a relatively ordinary question might further tend to suggest that it is not an ordinary image for Fritz: the discomfort of it, or perhaps the pain, seems too much for him to manage.

If we turn to another of Asperger's boys, Harro, he describes an exaggerated and frightening fantasy. (Asperger says, "Again and again he went off at a tangent and had to be brought back. Very often he shut off completely. . . .") Asperger asks him about the differences between a fly and a butterfly, and he quickly becomes over-excited, talking about a fly mother laying many eggs in gaps in the floorboards. The eggs quickly become maggots, and Harro says the floor can talk to him and he could die laughing. Such a graphic fantasy could be interpreted. The fly-mother breeds many babies in the gaps in the floor (the gap is an evocative image in the play of many children with the syndrome). The maggots seem to be merged with the talking floor, which causes Harro to feel he could die—the laughter sounds fearful rather than amused at the idea. It seems possible that Harro has a highly disturbing picture of any space around mother becoming infested with numerous nasty babies, which upset his mental balance. Whether such an interpretation might seem credible or not, it is worth noting that Harro's response to the question he is asked produces a highly disturbed and unusual response.

I want to suggest that the responses of Fritz and Harro seem to be part of the suffering linked with something excessive and frightening in using the imagination. For some Asperger children, relinquishing the alleged safety of their narrow and detailed interests allows access to subjectively distorted and frightening contents of their mind. For example, the ordinary fantasies about rival children who might make many of us feel jealous becomes the horror story of Harro's fantasy: maggot creatures everywhere, in every tiny gap. It is clear how it interferes with Harro's capacity to stay on task.

These extremes, which in themselves encourage increased avoidance and retreat, also appear further to insulate the Asperger child from ordinary and manageable experience. The absence of ordinary play, especially imaginative social play in the toddler years, is a tragic and sometimes irretrievable loss. That particular period of life is so intensely involved with working out how to manage further stages in step-by-step separation from the family and entry into the social world. In little children's social world the possibilities of working collectively at ideas linked with parents' relationships, the making of new babies, the struggle with jealous exclusion, and so on, is managed so much through repeated and shared play and fantasy. The mental work of that stage of life sets the scene for a more realistic idea about allowing space between oneself and mother. Language and looking develop and permit communication across space, and the growth of an active life of the mind where scenes and stories are acted and re-enacted. The fascinating and difficult work of understanding how one fits into a world with others, with the freedom for oneself and others to move out and back, is a desperate struggle for the Asperger child, where rigid clinging to sameness so easily makes any movement feel frightening and where rigidity obstructs so many developments and confuses many who would like to assist.

Asperger's paper and his honest and detailed observations are highly evocative and full of feeling. His children are recognizably Asperger children as we would think of them today, whose lives are often so hard and whose reactions and behaviour are difficult to manage and to understand. Asperger wrote at length about his "autistic psychopaths", yet it is only in the last decade or so that Asperger's syndrome has been accepted as a diagnostic entity and that there has been such a proliferation of interest in the diagnosis and in searching for ways to help the isolation and deep feelings of difference that are so prevalent. My attempt to apply a psychoanalytic understanding to the pursuit of narrow interests, the difficulties of emotional regulation in making contact, using the imagination, and what meaning there might be in acts of malice, is a subjective response to Asperger's paper and his attempts in 1940s Austria to make sense of the children's behaviour and suffering.

CHAPTER FOUR

What does it feel like?
Two first-person accounts
by adults with Asperger's syndrome

Maria Rhode

In this chapter I discuss recent books by two women who were diagnosed with Asperger's syndrome when they were adults. Gunilla Gerland has called her book *A Real Person: Life on the Outside* (1996a); the title of Liane Holliday Willey's is *Pretending to be Normal* (1999). Both of these titles suggest something of the struggle that people with Asperger's syndrome can face in achieving a sense of identity in a world of people whose experience, in many important respects, is so different from their own.

I have chosen these two books from among many recent first-person accounts because they convey particularly vividly what it is like to live in an "Asperger's" world, with sufficient detail to allow comparison. This chapter may usefully be read in conjunction with the following one, in which Caroline Polmear describes the experience of adults with Asperger's syndrome in analysis and in psychoanalytic psychotherapy.

A real person

I shall begin by discussing some of the events and themes that particularly stand out in the mind after a reading of Gunilla Gerland's (1996a) book. I shall consider how her account is illuminated by what has been learned through psychoanalytic psychotherapy with people on the autistic spectrum, and also how it adds to this. I must emphasize that this is in no way an attempt to "psychoanalyse" the author of a book, although people who are not familiar with the fundamental importance of the psychotherapeutic setting could conceivably misconstrue it as such. Outside this very particular, disciplined setting, and in the absence of the transference relationship that evolves within it (see Introduction), no therapist has the information that is necessary for suggesting an interpretation of any particular utterance or piece of behaviour. This is true whether the behaviour is described in a book or occurs in the course of ordinary social relationships. However, all psychotherapists' understandings are ultimately derived from what their patients have told them or shown them, and some of these understandings will be relevant to the experiences described in first-person accounts. Equally, psychotherapeutic knowledge is extended by experiences that cannot be comfortably subsumed under existing theories, so I shall highlight some aspects of Gerland's narrative that surprised or puzzled me.

Gerland describes an achingly lonely childhood in which she felt cut off from everyone except for her elder sister, Kerstin. Kerstin, she felt, genuinely liked her as she was—she knew how to make up games that they both enjoyed, in spite of Gunilla's very limited understanding of cooperative pretend play. Her mother, however, seemed to want something of her—and it was not until long afterwards that she realized that this something was her love. It felt threatening: being asked for her love was indistinguishable from being asked for a piece of her body. (This confusion between feelings and body contents has been highlighted in much psychoanalytic work on autism and borderline states—see Grotstein, 2000; Rey, 1979; Tustin, 1981b). When in distress—and she had to endure a great deal of distress—it would never have occurred to her to turn to her parents for comfort: she had no idea that comfort came from other people, and she never felt that her mother understood the first thing about her. Instead, she found refuge behind an old brown armchair and allowed herself to become absorbed in contemplating the pattern of warp and weft in the material. At times when—as she writes—her soul felt scratched, this offered some sort of healing. Another source of comfort was feeling the curved surface at the bottom of bottles. Nobody understood her need for these curves, and she was unable to explain: curves, she writes, were by their nature comforting, just as self-evidently as "green was green". Perhaps, she speculates, these curves provided some sort of necessary corrective to her own nature, which was so "straight" (in the sense of direct and literal). In any case, her father used to tease her by holding bottles just out of her reach. Her need, she writes, was as urgent as a need for food or for the lavatory might have been, though she was completely unable to explain this in a way that others might have understood. We are shown the disturbing discrepancy between her father's viewpoint—he liked teasing his daughters and thought they should practise "learning how to take a joke"—and her own helpless panic when she was deprived of the particular kind of sensory input that she needed in order to keep on a more-or-less even keel. Indeed, she conveys very vividly the degree to which experiences that most people can learn to cope with remained for her a matter of life and death. Others did not understand the degree of her hypersensitivity and often made things worse by "teasing" or by taking advantage of her vulnerability. Her task became to find ways of managing as best she could.

Gerland's father seems often to have behaved with considerable cruelty, though she insists that this was merely his way and that he liked getting a reaction out of people. This went as far as locking Kerstin inside a mill-tower and pretending to leave her. Gerland describes increasing violence between her parents, along with her mother's slide into alcoholism and mental illness. Her father moved in with another woman, leaving his two daughters to take care of their mother. After the death of her grandparents, all the relatives met to discuss the inheritance. Gerland was sent to summon her mother, who was drunk in bed. After cursing at her and sending her away, her mother eventually came downstairs, stark naked and raving. As the shocked relatives melted away, one aunt said to Gunilla, "You're strong, you'll manage." She was then 13 years old.

Gerland stresses the difference between her sister Kerstin's reaction and her own to events of this kind. She sensed Kerstin's distress in terms of physical phenomena: the way Kerstin's head wobbled on her neck, or the dull red colour that she felt Kerstin emanated when she was in despair. She was fond of Kerstin and did not want her to be upset, but she could not understand the degree of her distress. How her parents went on, she thought, was nothing to do with her, though she realized that Kerstin wanted a companion in her anguish and she was sorry that her different way of experiencing events made her an inadequate ally for her sister. Instead, she sought the company of teenage outcasts from middle-class society, where she could come closer to a sense of being like other people. Like them, she turned to drugs and to casual sex as a means of being with someone without needing to communicate. As she puts it, there was one other girl in the gang—the pretty blonde one who would not sleep with the boys—and that left vacant for Gunilla the slot of the "unattractive" one who would.

She was always looking for someone to model herself on, to show her how to live. For a while she seemed to have found this in a boyfriend, but he began to complain that she had no thoughts of her own. Next she attached herself to Annie, a girl on the fringes of addiction and criminality, with whom she went to Spain. She lived with a heroin addict and supported herself by selling blood. Dicing with death provided a certain sense of reality (see also chapter 5, this volume), as though it fittingly embodied her long-familiar experience of the life-and-death quality of situations that other people might think quite ordinary. However, she realized that what she was risking was not a quick death but gradual, relentless deterioration, and it frightened her. Where someone else might have faltered in their determination to give up drugs, her single-minded tenacity meant that she set herself a goal and carried on "until it was done".

Back in Sweden, Gerland worked in a nursery. She had a gift for understanding the children—which is, indeed, remarkable in view of the widely held opinion that people with Asperger's syndrome have theory-of-mind impairments (chapter 2, this volume)—though the schedule exhausted her, and relationships with colleagues and with the children's parents remained problematic. She had wanted to go to university, but she could not pass mathematics at secondary level. As a mature student she found, as she had at school, that some kinds of abstract thought presented major problems, though she was excellent at recalling information.

In the meantime, she had obtained public funding for psychotherapy. She attended for four years, with mixed results. On the one hand, as she writes, it really was time that someone took an interest in her welfare; and, despite her many criticisms of the process, she seems to have sensed that her therapist genuinely did so. On the other hand, she could not engage emotionally: it felt like an intellectual exercise with her "real self" sitting outside yearning to be let in. As so often in her life, it was as though other people knew "how to do it", and she could not find the secret, even when she brought tissues along to her sessions in the hope that crying might make her feel more involved. Listening to her therapist's interpretations "taught" her about other people's motivation, she felt, but not about her own. Then, when her reading led her to think that she might be on the autistic spectrum, her therapist urged her to "have the courage" not to think of herself as autistic. Gerland interpreted this as a denial of her experience and a refusal to learn anything new. She consulted Christopher Gillberg, an expert on the psychiatric demarcations between various conditions on the autistic spectrum, who said that she had an autistic condition and might have been diagnosed as having Asperger's syndrome when she was a child. Although this confirmation at first depressed her greatly, she ultimately found that it helped her to find a perspective on her experience. Through further reading and reflection she has since "become [her] own expert" and considers the right diagnosis of her condition to be attention deficit disorder with autistic features.

Against the background of this overview, which inevitably does not do justice to the subtlety of Gerland's writing and leaves out many important incidents, I wish to discuss some of the features of her story that seem to me most significant. These include Gerland's proposed diagnosis; the relevance of her parents' behaviour; her descriptions of bodily aspects of her experience; some features of how she related or failed to relate to other people; and her views on psychotherapy. I shall pay particular attention to ways in which her testimony links with or contradicts psychoanalytically based views on Asperger's syndrome.

Diagnosis

The question of diagnosis is complicated to some extent by the heroic degree to which Gerland has fought her way towards an ability to manage in what remains an alien world. As she says at the end of the book: ". . . you have such complicated rules in your world! And all the time I have to think and think and think about them." It is obvious that her high intelligence has served her as a life-line. Still, from the time she was a child she sensed that there was something "wrong with her", and her parents' reassurances only made her feel misunderstood.

Professor Gillberg is an expert on the differential diagnosis of conditions on the autistic spectrum, and his reported opinion that she suffered from Asperger's syndrome as a child and retained features of autistic spectrum disorder must be convincing.[1] Gerland's self-described motor clumsiness (except in the swimming-pool) is characteristic of people with Asperger's syndrome; people with autism, in contrast, are often physically deft, though in therapy it is clear that both groups share the fear of falling. Gerland does not mention any delay in language development. This too is characteristic of Asperger's syndrome as distinct from autism. Her self-diagnosis of attention deficit disorder with autistic features seems to me less persuasive. Her difficulties in maintaining her attention in a classroom situation where she was not receiving individual attention were related, according to her account, to the degree to which she felt impinged upon by distracting stimuli, whether perceptual or social. She was lost when the teacher forbade her to doodle, as this had been her way of maintaining a foothold in the present and following the lesson. In contrast, children diagnosed with ADD (attention deficit disorder) can find it hard to sit still and to inhibit impulsive behaviour. They often cannot maintain their concentration for any length of time, even on their own choice of activity, whereas Gerland was capable of an outstanding degree of single-minded determination. However, the diagnoses of autistic spectrum disorder and ADD certainly overlap. Graham Shulman (chapter 7, this volume) describes an impulsive boy who was at one time treated with medication for these problems, and who showed many of the anxieties characteristic of autistic spectrum disorders.

Parental influences

The behaviour of Gerland's parents raises the whole embattled issue of psychotherapy for autistic spectrum disorders and of psychotherapists' supposed tendency to blame parents. A false polarity has grown up between the view that these disorders are biologically based, on the one hand, and that they have important psychological and emotional dimensions, on the other. The reader is referred to the discussion of these questions in the Introduction. At this point, I shall merely re-emphasize that the idea that parents "cause" their child's condition is a simplistic one that has done a great deal of harm in the past, and one with which no psychotherapist would agree nowadays. Though it is hard to imagine that any child could have escaped emotional damage if their parents behaved like Gunilla Gerland's, this is not to say that they caused her Asperger's syndrome: Kerstin did not develop this, though she did suffer greatly. Indeed, Gerland goes so far as to speculate that she herself might have been more autistic—more turned away from other people—if she had had less to contend with at home, and less need to anticipate potentially devastating pieces of behaviour. This speculation—which, incidentally, contradicts the idea that autistic behaviour is completely neurologically determined—seems questionable to me. It goes against the experience of many devoted parents who make tremendous efforts to understand their children with autistic spectrum disorder and who do actually succeed in helping them to manage better in the "ordinary" world (Alvarez & Reid, 1999b). What is certainly the case is that psychological disturbance makes it more difficult for people to see their children as they are and to avoid inflicting their own problems on them, whether or not the children have autistic spectrum disorders. Gerland did not feel that her parents were capable of understanding her experience, which was different from their own, or indeed that they were interested in doing so. Her father seems not to have realized that some of his behaviour would have been likely to terrify a small child. Her mother, once her husband had left, intruded on her daughters with her own sexual preoccupations and constantly prophesied that Gunilla would never find a man. It is understandable that Gerland's therapist should have seen her feeling of alienation as being a reasonable response to such behaviour, but it leaves out the essential dimension of unusual sensory and bodily experiences in Asperger's syndrome, to which I now turn.

Sensory and bodily issues

Such experiences constitute a foreign language for most people, as indeed do the reactions of the child with autistic spectrum disorder, however logical from the child's point of view. Even if Gerland had felt that her parents actively wished to understand her, this is not easy for anyone to do. (As one mother of a child with autism said, "He should have come with instructions.") To my mind, one of the most valuable aspects of this book is the clarity with which Gerland makes these experiences accessible.

Some of Gerland's earliest reported memories concern the impingement of sensory and social stimuli, the need for a refuge from them, the experience of a body that did not feel properly put together. On a map of her body, she writes, her feet would have been white—unknown territory. Her feeling of connection to any given part of her body was inversely proportional to its distance from her head. Her skin was unbearably sensitive to touch, and for years she experienced horrible feelings at the nape of her neck, which sound like a mixture of the skin crawling and the spinal cord liquefying. At the same time, she had the very high pain threshold that is often found in autistic spectrum disorders and can, in extreme cases, look like a dissociation between mind and body. She had a particular phobia of jewellery, which she could not bear to touch and which sent shivers down her spine. The more convoluted the design was, the worse she felt: the horror extended even to the sound of the word "convoluted". The noise of a mechanical saw, or of a motorbike revving up, made her feel completely disorientated and overwhelmed—in her words, "skinless"—so that everything threatened to fall out of her. Being locked in a dark room by a spiteful fellow pupil felt like losing her eyes, her sense of which way was up and which was down—in fact, her sense of self. Physical education was a torment because of her fear of falling; she was always out of step with the other children in music or dancing classes. She developed a sense of being "wrong", which was added to by each successive failure. She catalogues the effect of constant admonitions: "'Pick up your feet! Look what you're doing! Sit up! . . . Don't be so lazy. Don't be cheeky. Don't be . . .' My inner refrain went: 'No real person—no real person—no real person'" (pp. 134–135, italics added).

Many of Gerland's experiences make sense in terms of recent psychoanalytic findings. Her vertigo, her feeling of bodily clumsiness except in water, her experience of losing herself when she was part of a classroom group—all of these link readily with the formulations of Bick, Winnicott, Tustin, and Haag, which were discussed in the Introduction. More specifically, the way she felt the impingement of unpleasant stimuli as her spine liquefying and as a horrible feeling at the nape of her neck may seem unexpected in terms of most people's shared experience, but it makes sense in the light of Haag's hypothesized developmental schema according to which a child acquires physical mastery and psychological ownership of successive joints of the body, beginning with the neck and progressing downwards (Introduction). So does the fact that her feet—rather than her hands, for instance—felt like terra incognita and that, as she said, her sense of familiarity with any part of her body stood in inverse proportion to its distance from her head. Similarly, her difficulty in judging the speed and distance of moving vehicles may have been compounded by the ease with which hypersensitive people can experience approaching objects as a psychophysical impingement. For example, a boy with autism regularly covered his ears when men approached through a door: interpersonal impingement seemed to be mapped onto sensory hypersensitivity, so that it was experienced as auditory intrusion (Rhode, 1997b). It is interesting that Gerland's ability to judge distance is one of the things that improved: it may have had a neurological basis, but it got better with her greater experience and self-knowledge (as well as with practice). Equally, she explains her predilection for biting—human flesh, for preference—as a need to still the horrible sensations in her teeth. While this need may well have had a neurological component, it too disappeared as she developed; and it makes perfect sense in terms of Tustin's description of the sense of damage and incompleteness in their mouths that children with autism suffer.

Her horror of jewellery has the unreasoning, self-evident, shivers-down-the-spine quality of most phobias. While many relevant levels of meaning are likely to be involved, it sounds like the kind of horror that literally makes the skin crawl—in other words, that has an important component on the level of skin function.[2] It may be significant that Gerland's horror increased with the degree to which the surface of the piece of jewellery or button—a kind of "skin" of the object—was broken up into small constituents.

Rhythm is an element that many psychoanalytic workers have considered to be fundamentally important to the bodily sense of self and to basic levels of communication (Maiello, 2000; Meltzer, 1975b; Rey, 1994a; Tustin, 1986). As a small child, Gerland particularly loved singing along to the sound of the car engine on family outings: it was only in these circumstances that she was able to sing, and she was deeply upset when the adults forbade it. She seems to have needed the rhythm or "song" of the car on which to model her own, just as children in so many activities need a model whose example they can follow.

Relationships with other people

When Gerland was little, she writes, [my family] "were a kind of UNIT, a mother–father–big-sister unit, and I was another unit quite apart from them" (p. 14). This is a degree of exclusion well beyond what we all have to tolerate as part of growing up. Melanie Klein (1961) described an unrealistic fantasy constellation of a parental couple who seem to be mixed up together, a constellation that can lead to consider-able disturbance if it is too prominent in a child's emotional life. Children on the autistic spectrum can experience something even more extreme, in that mother and father can be imagined to form the kind of physical unit that Gerland describes, which seems to leave no space for the child to be seen and understood, though a sibling may be thought to participate in it (Rhode, 2003). This unit is often wrongly blamed for the child's feeling of alienation.

However, when Gerland was about eight, there was a turning-point: she discovered the notion of "inside". Before that, she had regarded all houses as though they were flat stage sets: only her house had an inside, because she had experienced being in it. Discovering that "insides" were a generally applicable concept helped her to generalize in other contexts. The link will be clear with the emphasis placed by Tustin and, particularly, by Meltzer on the "surface", adhesive mode in autistic spectrum disorder. Acquiring the notion of three-dimensionality is a turning-point in many of the case histories in this volume as well. The circumstances surrounding Gerland's momentous discovery seem to me important: she was lying near the border of the family garden, playing with the neighbours' cat who was on the other side of the boundary, in the garden next door. I believe it may have been very helpful that the "inside" of the neighbours' garden was inhabited by a living creature that responded to her—a very different situation from the one she usually encountered in relation to the "inside" of other people's minds.

Though Gerland says that she was not attached to her parents, she describes her complete panic when left at school, or with her grandparents over the holidays. She did not believe that people who left would ever come back—perhaps her grandparents were her new parents?—and when her parents did come back, she was not really sure that they were the same people. Everyday links, including cause and effect, were a mystery to her: perhaps her mother's return, which was preceded by all the children's assembling in a particular room, could be hastened by going into that room, whatever the time of day. This calls to mind Tustin's (1986) statement that children on the autistic spectrum typically construct idiosyncratic linkages between events and objects in terms of their own experience—most often, their own bodily experience. Gerland constructed many such systems of linkage to try to make some sense of a world that bewildered her. How could she find her way back to her own classroom, through a maze of unrecognizable corridors? How could she remember which of all the hundreds of "empty faces" (people outside her immediate circle) belonged to children in her own class? How did other people know all these things? Perhaps, when someone said "You'll enjoy going to school", this meant that they could actually read the future.

Gerland describes becoming so used to the difference between her own reality and other people's that eventually no experience felt authentic to her unless it stood out against what seemed to be the conventional order. She came to rely completely on her own opinion and judgement, without ever losing the feeling that there existed a "right" way of living that eluded her. The need constantly to work things out in her head, to maintain a mental running commentary on what she was doing, to formulate every sentence before uttering it, made spontaneity impossible. By the time she had worked out what she wanted to say, the conversation had moved on. Her description calls to mind a number of children with Asperger's syndrome who keep up a running commentary on their own actions as though they were telling a story about someone else. ("Linda" did this in the early stages of treatment—see chapter 9, this volume.) Sometimes this seems a way of keeping at a safe distance from their own experience when they do not trust an adult to help them through it; sometimes it is even more basic, a way of providing for themselves a sense of ongoing existence.

Gerland was hypersensitive to other people's emotions, which she apprehended in terms of an idiosyncratic colour system, much like the borderline adults treated by the psychoanalyst Henri Rey (1994b). However, putting herself in other people's position and understanding their viewpoint (capacities associated with developing a "theory of mind"—see chapter 2, this volume) was another matter. She explains her inability to read other children's malicious motives by what she says was her own lack of envy and spite, which meant that she did not expect to find these emotions in others. This suggests to me that she may have shared a difficulty that many children on the autistic spectrum show in a clinical setting: that of maintaining a sufficient grasp of their own identity so that they can think themselves temporarily into the mind of another person.

Interestingly, the literary skill with which Gerland writes—it comes as no surprise to read that she always got top marks in Swedish—implies an ability to gauge the reader's response, which at first seems at odds with her reported bewilderment at what motivates other people. Her writing (like Willey's, which is precise, evocative, and often poetic) displays none of the typically "Asperger's" obliviousness of the reader's likely reaction. In this they contrast with various personal statements by intelligent adults with Asperger's syndrome cited by

Happé (1991). Unlike them, Gerland writes with a flair that carries the reader with her. Probably many different elements enter into this capacity, including her own experience and her ability to reflect on it, her wide reading, and her therapy. In any case, her account of her early experience rings completely true, though it is seen through the lens of her later understanding. She makes clear what perils every hour of the day can hold for a person with Asperger's syndrome, and we are left in no doubt about their life-and-death quality. Although she maintains that her emotional detachment had nothing to do with protecting herself from painful emotions, her description of realizing that the object she was banging a door against—BANG, BANG, BANG—was the head of her mother who was lying on the floor in a drunken stupor calls to mind the way Caroline Polmear's patient used "cartooning" (the reporting of images of horrific violence devoid of emotional meaning—see chapter 5, this volume).

As with so many children on the autistic spectrum, Gerland's capacities were patchy. Her teachers could not understand that the same girl who excelled at Swedish composition handed in blank papers for her maths exams, and they put it down to laziness or dumb insolence. This patchiness can be a major source of confusion to the parents of children with autistic spectrum disorder, as well as to anyone who works with them and to the children themselves. For a long time, Gerland could not understand her failure to grasp things that other children seemed able to do naturally: was she "retarded", and people were keeping it from her? This is one of the reasons that a diagnosis can come as such a relief to people with Asperger's syndrome, as well as to their parents: as long as it is not used as a substitute identity, or seen as placing an automatic ceiling on development, it can make sense of an otherwise bewildering assortment of traits and validate the perception that one's experience and coping strategies may be significantly different from those of other people.

Novel contributions

I would now like to highlight two of Gerland's experiences that puzzled and intrigued me. As a child she would hold her mouth and vagina when standing up, and she was greatly annoyed by the adults' assumption that they "knew" she needed the lavatory. I confess I would myself have assumed that she was worried about something spilling out of the two places she was holding, though not necessarily that she needed to urinate. I might also have wondered whether moving through space when she got up had perhaps heightened her sense of vulnerability at these two bodily apertures. In fact, the reason for her behaviour was that she was "trying to press back the horrible thing creeping at the nape of my neck and down my spine . . . to press it back from both directions so that what was unpleasant couldn't grow and become bigger than me". As well as being associated with nasty sensations, the horrible thing was semi-personified and was felt to exist inside her. A therapist would not know this without being shown or told about it.

The second example concerns Gerland's need to move her head quite violently from side to side before going to sleep. She provides no explanation for this, and I can only speculate. Caroline Polmear's patient moved her head in this way to provide herself with the reassurance of sensory stimulation when she was attempting to look at her analyst. Though Gerland was not trying to look at anyone, falling asleep is something that many children can find difficult: unless they expect a safe place in which to take refuge, it can literally feel like falling. It may be that the violent movements gave her some sort of sense of mastery over the feeling of vertigo that arises when one moves one's head from side to side; it may be linked to the reassurance that children on the autistic spectrum derive from spinning in circles. I have no way of knowing, but reading Gerland's account will alert me to similar behaviour in the children I see.

Pretending to be normal

Liane Holliday Willey had a very different life story. Though her concerned parents consulted professionals over her failure to conform as a child, the usual diagnosis was "smart and spoiled". Her parents seem to have given her their total support whenever she fell out with authority. When they were summoned by a teacher whom she had driven to distraction by refusing to lie down on her mat like everyone else, they asked her whether this was so and why. She replied that it wasn't: she didn't have a mat, the thing she had been given was called a rug. Her parents advised the teacher to use the word "rug" in future.

Whatever the teacher may have thought of this, her parents' attitude seems to have given her confidence in the legitimacy of her own experience. This self-belief stood her in good stead in later life, though the separation from her parents and her accustomed surroundings laid her open to a major crisis of alienation and despair when she went to college. Even this was far from Gerland's conscious resolution that she must lay herself open to everything, including the worst experiences possible, so as not to be in a position in which anything could take her by surprise.

Like Gerland, Willey could not do maths, but she had excelled at other school subjects, had got on well with her classmates, and had anticipated a successful time at university. Leaving home for a big campus in a foreign city was a disaster. She suffered all the confusion, disorientation, and inability to find her way—both literally and meta-phorically—that Gerland went through on starting school. Once re-moved from her familiar setting, Willey found she could not read people's intentions, and she lived an isolated life with a houseful of pets. A particularly valuable part of her book is the checklist of points to consider when a person with Asperger's syndrome goes to univer-sity or starts a new job, in order to avoid being overwhelmed by sensory stimuli. The psychoanalyst Donald Meltzer (1975a) has written eloquently of the "bombardment of sensa" that can assail children with autism. Psychoanalytic findings that link sensory and emotional expe-riences (H. S. Klein, 1980; Meltzer, 1975c; Rhode, 2000b) provide a bridge between such seemingly diverse approaches as psychotherapy and sensory integration.

Willey did not, in fact, realize what Asperger's syndrome was until one of her daughters was diagnosed as having it, and she realized that she shared many of the same difficulties, particularly with regard to sensory overload. In retrospect, she thought that her father had some Asperger's features. She writes movingly of how her family have learned to help each other through the associated difficulties. She and her husband will reassure her daughter that they understand why she gets into the shopping trolley and covers herself with groceries to avoid sensory overstimulation in the supermarket. Her daughters, in turn, will warn their mother when she is talking too loudly or display-ing what she calls her "typical Aspie temper", or dressing in a way that seems eccentric to them, though not to her. Like Gerland, she panics at the idea of finding her way in an unfamiliar place. The profound importance of bodily foundations comes over even in her choice of metaphor: "There are days when I stand on a precipice, precariously ready to fall beyond who I am and into someone whom I cannot believe I ever was. . . . There are days when I stand on a terrace, ready and able to embrace new insight and a clean awareness." The reader is left with a sense of great respect for the courage, integrity, and persist-ence that have enabled her to build up a successful academic career and, even more significantly, to establish what is obviously a loving and mutually supportive family life. When things are bad, she writes, "I reach for my husband." Together they have found a way of manag-ing their family relationships which allows different modes of experi-ence to be acknowledged and valued.

The stories of these two women, different as they are, show the extent to which extreme bodily fears can co-exist with a high degree of achievement. Though one might question how far they sometimes see their past through the lens of their present understanding, their de-scriptions of their experience as children and young adults rings movingly true. There is abundant evidence of the courage and tenacity that Caroline Polmear highlights in her Asperger's patients (chapter 5, this volume).

How useful was therapy?

Willey felt that therapy—which seems to have been supportive coun-selling, possibly with a cognitive orientation—helped her to manage at college, and she recommends it for fellow "Aspies". Gerland, as already indicated, had major reservations, though she did feel her therapist cared about her. What happens between two people in a therapeutic relationship is something no outsider is in a position to judge. It is possible that the tendency of some people with Asperger's syndrome to use their intellect as a life-line may have contributed to bringing about the "intellectual exercise" that Gerland complains of. It is certainly true that less attention seems to have been paid to bodily experiences than therapists working in the tradition of Bick and Tustin might be inclined to do. Tustin (1994a) agreed with Donna Williams, a woman with high-functioning autism, that interpretations concerning family relationships have very limited relevance, particularly in the early stages of treatment. We are not in a position to know how much Gerland told her therapist about her sensory experiences. She did talk about her overwhelming loneliness, which was of quite a different order from the ordinary human loneliness that is the lot of everyone and that is eased through understanding and companionship. The therapist's recognition that the patient has Asperger's syndrome can be a crucial element of this understanding (Caroline Polmear, chapter

5, this volume; Shuttleworth, 1999). It is conceivable that the force of long habit persisted and that it remained difficult for Gerland to feel that her experience could be authentic if it was not in contradiction of someone else's viewpoint. What is important is that these two women fought their way through overwhelming difficulties in a way that must be inspiring to other people with Asperger's syndrome, as well as to those of us who do not have it. This fact, and the amelioration of such symptoms as Gerland's inability to judge speed and distance, her extreme sensitivity to touch, the feeling at the nape of her neck—all symptoms that might be thought of as having a neurological basis—indicate something of the improvement that can come about by one means or another. "Remembering", as Willey says, "can set me free". Of course, as she points out, it needs to be a balanced and disciplined kind of remembering.

Chapter 5 provides an account of the way some of these issues were addressed within the transference relationship, in the case of adults in psychoanalysis or psychotherapy.

Notes

1. Information is relatively patchy about the degree of improvement achieved in later life by people with autism and Asperger's syndrome. Some can improve significantly, even in the absence of specialist input, but many do not achieve independence. Many factors influence the outcome, including, obviously, intelligence levels. Recent follow-up studies tend to show better outcomes than earlier ones, although comparability is affected by differences in design (Howlin, 1998).

2. The central importance to the developing baby of feeling contained inside its own skin was first described by Bick (1968, 1986). Failures in this skin function play a particularly important part in autistic spectrum disorders (Meltzer, 1974, 1975a; Tustin, 1994a, 1994b).

Finding the bridge: psychoanalytic work with Asperger's syndrome adults

Caroline Polmear

Z ara came to her session, one Friday morning in July, exactly on time. She had been in analysis for nearly nine years.

Her barely audible double ring of the bell alerted me to the fact that she was feeling particularly raw. She had perfected a technique whereby she could make the bell vibrate just enough to let me know she was there without making it utter its harsh, shrill sound, which could completely annihilate her fragile sense of self. I tried to respond to her two short rings with a response played on my door buzzer that followed the allegro con vivo beat she had established. Her appearance confirmed my suspicions that today was a difficult day for her. She came into the consulting-room with her pillow clutched tightly to her front, her clear nail-varnish bottle in one clenched fist and her "see-through" key ring in the other. After taking up a position on the floor to the side of my desk, she began to gather herself. With her compelling wish to communicate, however difficult it might be, she told me that she wasn't normal today and that she had a list of items to talk about.

We worked together for half an hour or so, going through the degrees of hopelessness, helplessness, hope, and despair that characterize our work together, and eventually managed the contact we were striving for. Zara relaxed and began to speak directly, with an arresting purity. She said that now, just from this term, she had started to feel what it was like to be "normal": not all the time, but sometimes. For the first time in her life, she had a sense that she was like other people some of the time, not an alien species. She said she didn't know how this had come about, but she thought it was because I had found a bridge between our two worlds. She didn't know how I knew what she felt, because I was "normal", not like her. But when I found the bridge, she felt more "normal".

It has been my privilege to work with two adults with Asperger's syndrome. "Zara", a young woman lawyer, completed a 10-year psychoanalysis (five sessions a week) five years ago. "Catherine", a woman in her late forties, an archaeologist interested in the very earliest civilizations, completed a twice-weekly psychotherapy that lasted for four years.

My patients were able to convey to me their experience of a world constantly threatening to overwhelm and annihilate them with unmoderated sensory experience. It is a world where perceptions are as sharp as raw nerve endings; where broken-off body parts and violent explosions can erupt at any time; where rigidity and ritual offer only a partial protection, and psychic retreats (Steiner, 1993) afford the only peace and respite from unmitigated and exhausting terror. Small wonder that such retreats feel infinitely preferable to the painfully assaulting world of "reality".

Adults with Asperger's syndrome are seldom referred for intensive treatment. They may function well enough with a false self (Winnicott, 1960), relying on a meticulous attention to detail, a capacity for mimicking relationships, and an occupational setting that is syntonic with their particular capacities. In many cases they function extremely well. It is thought that some great thinkers over the centuries may have had the condition. Asperger commented on "the particular originality of thought and experience, which may well lead to exceptional achievements in later life". Perhaps regrettably, Catherine reported that her photographic memory and her capacity to compute arithmetic at great speed reduced as she improved and began to feel more normal. It seems that unintegrated functioning of some parts of the brain works better than when the ego is stronger and the various functions more integrated.

People with Asperger's may seek help when they change jobs and the people and activities holding projected aspects of themselves and providing a kind of exoskeleton (Bion, 1991) are lost. Alternatively they may feel troubled by their difficulty in relating, or a relative or friend may suggest that they need support. A sense of feeling different, alien, of not fitting, may lead to a search for help, although without a well-developed sense of self it can be difficult for the person in this situation to want or need anything for themselves. They may accept help if it is seen as helping others.

The experience of having Asperger's syndrome makes one feel different. It requires something subtly different from the analyst too. I hope that it will become clear that, while retaining a firmly analytic attitude,[1] the analyst has to go beyond what is usually required in understanding and responding to the experience of another.

From my limited experience I recommend psychoanalytic treatment if both parties feel they can manage it. Intensive treatment gives patient and analyst the opportunity to experience the encapsulated terror of traumatic contact and separation many times and, hopefully, to work towards understanding and containing this. The process is testing and demanding for both parties, and I have been impressed by, and grateful for, the courage and tenacity of both of my patients.

This chapter is in two sections: in the first, I give clinical examples to convey the patients' subjective experience, and in the second I discuss the treatment of adults through psychoanalysis and psychoanalytic psychotherapy.

The subjective experience

Contact and avoidance of contact

Ordinary human contact, which warms and gratifies and gives meaning to life, was experienced by my patients as a threat to their and my survival. They might yearn for a soft contact but then feel the need of hard contact to maintain the shell of self that saved them from annihilation, from non-existence, or from their insides spilling out (see Introduction). Besides, loving contact could feel ferocious and devouring and had to be avoided in order to protect the loved one.

Saying "Good morning" at the door or looking at me on entering the room felt to Zara like lasering me with such an intensely focused beam that I would be dispersed into fragments, vaporized, or burned up. Catherine described in vivid detail car crashes in which death was instant, violent, and gory and the bodies were splattered around the scene of the accident. I soon came to respect the fact that contact meant impact and violent death by explosion. The two of us were indistinguishable at the moment of impact, and neither survived. On other days I was warned that if I came too near at the door, I risked death from the fallout of the explosion of a nuclear bomb.

In the early days of treatment, the experience of feeling understood by me also felt like unbearable contact. It was immediately dispersed in a range of ingenious ways. Zara would typically whiz off into a flurry of cartoon images of me as a Monty Pythonesque person made up of human-like machinery bits, with no meaning or purpose. She laughed uproariously at the mental image of me on ritual tramlines, moving backwards and forwards day and night between my chair and the door, dehumanized and safe and yet, sadly, utterly useless to her, of course. Sometimes when something I said made real and helpful sense, she would instantly tell me of herself in the helping role doing for someone else a version of what I had just done for her. She could preserve something of the learning by removing from it any knowledge of me as a separate alive person, and thus removing the element of contact, which so terrified her.

Helpful contact could also be experienced as unbearably exciting and overwhelming. In this state, Zara found herself speaking in a robotic, computerized voice while trying to hold onto what I'd said. The words within the sentence were detached from each other, and the experience of being understood—longed-for but overwhelming—was stripped away from the intellectual content. That way the thought could be preserved while the emotional experience of it was neutralized. It would be tempting to see these defences as envious and destructive, yet it was clear to me that they were efforts at preserving rather than destroying. If Zara's experience of me could be split up like this, then at least some of me could be retained at this stage.

While emotional contact felt like dangerous physical contact, actual physical contact, for example in the moment of taking the bill from me, was almost impossible. Catherine would hold her breath in panic and turn her face away, flapping one hand and arm frantically to rid herself of overwhelming anxiety and a physical feeling of being invaded. All openings in the face—eyes, ears, and mouth—had to be shut tight. Even so, Catherine shuddered involuntarily as she grabbed the envelope and rushed for the door.

It became clear that contact could mean the coming together in an instant of primitive ferocious, biting love and ruthless, violent hatred, with very little ego to moderate the impact of the hatred with something more loving. As both patients gained in ego strength, new ways emerged of managing this seemingly impossible situation. One day, Zara, eager to take in what I was saying because we were well in contact that day and the session was feeling fruitful, listened intently to what I was saying while giving a complete simultaneous translation into German. This seemed to lessen what could have felt like the penetrating physical impact of my words, by discharging them through her mouth while she retained the understanding.

The fear of being touched or physically impinged upon was always present. On one occasion, Zara recalled the fear of being cuddled by her mother, which she said physically hurt her (see also Gunilla Gerland's experience—chapter 4, this volume) and made her feel violent and evil. When contact was not mutually destructive, it was feared as a dangerous merger (Stockdale-Wolfe, 1993). Zara accused me in patent terror of "locking on" to her so that I took over her mind, leaving her "brain-dead".

Identity, self, and self-experience

I think that before treatment, my patients had little sense of self as it is ordinarily understood. When I spoke about "doing something to yourself", Zara replied incredulously, "I don't have a self!" In fact, my suggestion put her in a panic, which I later understood to be related to the dangers of having a self. The unconscious fantasy that emerged in a hundred different ways was that as soon as one came into existence as a self, one would be destroyed. If I thought she had a self, then I must be about to annihilate her. Ringing the doorbell proved that she existed, and she expected its harsh, shrill sound to shatter her at the moment of existing if it rang fully.

Such experiences seem to me to link with a severe problem about being recognized. I imagine an infant whose basic primitive communication with its mother or carer fails for some reason. It cannot recognize itself in the other, or perhaps cannot bear the contact enough to feel contained. When this is repeated during treatment, the analyst experiences it as a failure of projective identification.[2] The patient, on the other hand, feels that she is communicating powerful emotions but getting back no feeling reaction. The analyst receives a communication from the patient of something either dead and empty or "otherwise engaged" and self-sufficient. This failure of fundamental recognition and of communication with the analyst at first feels irreparable and devastating to the patient, as I assume it must have been in her early experience. The whole enterprise feels doomed, and failure seems to stare both patient and analyst in the face.

While these patients feels "selfless", in fact they exist inside others. My patients located their whole selves in me, where I could begin to learn about them. They described me as dead, as "brain-dead" or "brain-damaged". They said that I was someone deeply split within myself, that my mind was out of touch with my emotions. I was someone from another species, an "alien form", unrecognizable as human, cut off, unfeeling, and mechanical in all my interactions with other people. I was psychopathic and had no conscience; I had an empty mind, was unable to think for myself, someone who mouthed psychoanalytic theory without understanding and without concern for my patient. Equally important was my quality of wrongness. I was the wrong shape, an uncomfortable angular shape. Catherine said that I made her feel sick in her stomach and that she wanted to sick me up. I was of the wrong culture and of the wrong theoretical persuasion. All this was pushed into me with a violence and primitive hatred that made it hard to bear.

My sense was that I was being made to experience how it felt to be Catherine and Zara; I was also learning about their expectation that a significant person wouldn't really take them in, couldn't bear them or stand them, perhaps even wanted to kill them. Zara in fact believed that when her mother was pregnant with her, she had starved herself in an attempt to deny the pregnancy. Catherine thought that her mother had nearly miscarried her (both women's mothers had in fact suffered more than one miscarriage). In-between bouts of violent attack on me, I felt I was sometimes being offered a lifeless "baby" to treat, perhaps in the mistaken belief that that was what I wanted. Perhaps my patients unconsciously wished to restore the dead babies to their mothers.

Gradually, a sense of a deep internal split emerged in both patients. It seemed like an experience of traumatic and unmetabolized rupture at the very heart of the self. I am struck by the similarity with those patients described by Balint in *The Basic Fault* (Balint, 1968) and assume that they were to varying degrees autistic or that during treatment they hit upon autistic "pockets" (H. S. Klein, 1980; Tustin, 1981b, 1986).[3] Zara described a chasm of unbridgeable proportions that could suddenly open up. The floor of the consulting-room became plates in the earth's surface, and she was convinced that I had only put a rug there to hide the fault line. It was as if the internal experience of rift was mirrored in the outside world. The space between us was frequently an infinitely deep hole, and she could not trust me to want to reach across the chasm and make contact with her. If she risked it herself, she might fall into the death gap[4] to annihilation. Better not to want contact.

> At a time when Zara's anxiety was at its height and she was beginning to experience a wish to make contact with me, she arrived for a session in a panic, flapping her arm to get rid of some of it and blowing out as she entered the consulting-room. "Big, enormous hole outside" she gasped, tapping the surface of my desk to hear the hard sound with hollow tones in it. "It wasn't there yesterday." (I realized she must have been talking about some road works she had passed.) "You pulled up that plant; there's an enormous gap in the garden; there's nothing there. Oh no! Where is that book, there's a gap in the bookshelf." Now quite frantic, she tried to look at me, and as she did so she threw her head from side to side, scanning me as a way of reducing the impact of taking me in through her eyes. She began repeating something over and over, getting more and more anxious as I failed to grasp what was terrifying her. Finally I got it: "Dead budgerigar; dead budgerigar, dead budgerigar. Why would anyone wear a dead budgerigar on their suit?" I realized that she saw my ellipse-shaped, plastic tortoiseshell brooch as a dead bird, perching on my jacket lapel. The gap between the sessions, the terror of not being able to trust that one or other of us could get safely across the gap to make contact with the other, the near-certainty that she would look to me for life and contact only to find a dead hole, and a belief that I'd uprooted our connection, miscarried her, and left a yawning chasm for her to disappear into, fell into place in my mind.

Though I am describing the lack of an integral sense of self, my patients did have various identities. At one level there was the professional person, renowned for their exceptional intelligence, diligence, wacky sense of humour, and absolute integrity. The capacity for detail and the degree of focus of people with Asperger's syndrome lends itself well to certain professions, particularly the more academic ones. At a deeper level, though, there is a more painful identity as "alien". (In Oliver Sacks's account of his meeting with Temple Grandin he captures this alien feeling in the title: *An Anthropologist on Mars*—Sacks, 1995.) I wonder whether part of this lies in the feeling of being unrecognized and in the lack of a feeling of physical fit with others. I certainly found in my patients a yearning for body moulding and fit with another. But as our work progressed, the identity as alien seemed to recede, until Zara could describe feeling "normal" when I found the bridge between our two worlds.

Another feature, which seems to contribute to the identity as alien, is a sense of living in a primitive part of the brain. Any sophisticated thinking feels like something learned, or grafted on: false and not to be trusted. Primitive experience of a sensation world is the "truth", while the world of people interacting with a mixture of self-interest and interest in others is the world of "lies". What is felt in the body is real. In my patients' material there were numerous images of damaged babies; babies born with the front part of their brain missing, their foreheads short and sloping backwards; and of early forms of mankind. Both Zara and Catherine felt more related to animals than to people (see also chapter 11); Catherine was sure that she was descended from a different evolutionary branch. In the early years, I often felt that Zara's analysis was dominated simply by fight/flight reactions. The first dream she brought concerned *a homunculus with its eyes wide open left on a shelf to die*. I think she felt at that point that she hadn't even reached conception. I have already mentioned that both patients' mothers had suffered several miscarriages. Perhaps unconsciously conception itself was felt as the first destructive contact (see also chapter 9, this volume).

This profound sense of alienation—in the early days, when she was in a dispersed state of "selflessness", Zara described herself as a hologram—suggests another perspective on the continuing attacks on me. Zara might have felt compelled to provoke and attack me in order to elicit a "real" reaction, and in that way feel real herself. If she failed to throw me off-track, she would go off on a manic flight of violent "cartooned" attacks on me, describing with glee how she was picking me up by the legs and banging me rhythmically against the wall—bang, bang, bang—then swinging me around her head before letting go and sending me off to outer space. My task was to find ways of containing the excitement of all this before she crashed into the alternative state, which she experienced as having "flopped". Both Catherine and Zara explained to me, and showed me, the problem of swinging between two extreme states: one over-reactive, over-active, too excited and "hyped up", too focused, "like someone with all the dials on the radio receiver turned up too high"; and the other a flopped, turned away, timeless sleep state.

Shells, wrappings, and retreats

Much has been written about the autistic shell, notably by Frances Tustin (1972, 1981b, 1986, 1990). What I became most aware of with my patients was the dual function of the "shells" they used. They served both to keep *in* the psychopathic, pre-ruth (Winnicott) violence and to keep *out* the annihilating penetrating other. Equally, the shell was both to avoid contact and, in its choice of medium, to communicate and make contact. It was to control the intrusion of external stimuli like light, noise, and smell, then playfully, taking that same stimulus, to turn it into a barrier to further intrusion.

For example, a troubling light shining into the consulting-room unusually brightly was at first hated, as was I for allowing it, then turned into a delightful ritual light show for the patient's benefit, created by moving her head around in a fast circular motion to play with and control the way the light fell on her face. The shell preserves a liveliness, a fast-moving flapping and tapping world full of humour and connections, yet paradoxically in its very use it creates deadness. At times it can feel imperative to the patient to keep the shell going when the alternative might be either the deathliness or the deadness of contact. In so doing the possibility of contact and real life is lost. Anything can be used as a barrier—autistic hard objects (Tustin, 1981a) such as nail-varnish bottles, jangling sets of keys, coloured glass bottles, shiny pens, rubbish bins; more or less anything that comes to hand, and the more glittery and shiny, the better. Something that catches the light and plays tunes at the same time—like a bunch of keys that jingle at different frequencies, on a see-through key ring that reflects then refracts the light and offers wonderful patterns in a kaleidoscope effect—is sheer joy! Herein lies an important aspect of the barrier. It is created as a defensive, protective shell but becomes a retreat of sheer pleasure. My ordinary world could scarcely compete with such a multi-media experience.

On the soft side, a pillow into which one can press one's shape and have it mould reflectively to one's face feels receptive and comforting, as do soft padded jackets and big soft toys.[4]

"Shells" based less on sensation do, of course, exist. Gomberoff and de Gomberoff (2000) describe a way of using language as an insulating wrapping. My patients used language in various ways, but usually with the dual aim of communicating and hiding. The pace of most sessions was hectic. Masses of detailed descriptions half finished, interrupted by two or three more descriptions, raced by. Sometimes it seemed as if I was being given a complete account of all the meetings and interactions, the papers read, the lectures given, of the few days since we'd last met. All this was delivered in about five minutes, in a tone that implied, "I'm just getting rid of all this, take no notice!" Yet taking notice always helped. There were always important communications in the content and level of anxiety, and if I could find a way to speak about them, the patient could be helped towards contact and out of the ritualistic recitation. Sometimes this happened several times in one session as we dipped in and out of being in touch. At other times it was necessary to bring my patient back from a very deeply turned-away and cut-off place where she felt utterly alone and helpless, "left for dead". It was an important moment in Zara's analysis when she conveyed to me just what this felt like.

> Shortly after we had re-visited the encapsulated trauma of rupture, she repeatedly berated me for my failure to empathize. She was absolutely sure now that there was something completely missing in me: the "missing link". Things had gone badly wrong here because of my utter failure to empathize, and now she was damaged. I'd made her ill, so much worse. Everything I said was simply defensive, just self-protection. Now she had to do it all on her own, had to try and keep her baby self[6] from dying. She then told me that she'd had a consultation and taken full recordings of some of our sessions to a senior analyst to discuss. He'd said it looked as if I were completely out of touch. She reiterated how greatly I'd harmed her. I went through a range of feelings, but most particularly felt a devastating hurt of an almost physical quality, as if she'd stuck a dagger into me. I felt something in me begin to disintegrate, as if all my professional foundations were crumbling. It was as though I were abandoned and defenceless against an ultimate catastrophe. I knew in my guts what Zara meant when she talked about her baby self dying. In the silence that followed, heavy with failure, I felt shocked and shaken. Zara began making agitated, rustling, and flapping noises under the blanket, which she now had over her head covering her face. My silence was clearly making her anxious. I said that I thought that if I spoke, my words and voice might feel unbearable, like a dagger going into her, and yet if I were silent that felt dangerous and bad also. She lay quiet and very alert. Emboldened, I continued that I thought her rustling sounds in the warm air around her head were the only protection she felt she had from me annihilating her altogether. After a silence she said, "Well

that's good, at least you're trying to understand. You've taken in what I've said and made an effort."

Rhythm and music formed another barrier/retreat/shell communication: contact could sometimes be made without some of the violence. In a turned-away state, Zara often tapped on my desk. If she were just "ticking over", staying alive, possibly imagining that she was providing for herself inside my space, there would be a gentle *andante* heartbeat rhythm. It felt calming, though sad, like keeping something going without coming dangerously to life. On other days the tapping would be less regular. After a missed session, Zara began with a list of the all holes she had circumnavigated in getting to me. There followed stories of people who had lost limbs, or died, or been irrevocably separated. She seemed to experience each story in her own body as she sped through them. She bought the terror of the gap into the room. Her drumming on the desk became recognizable: the heavy slow rhythm of the Death March. Dum, dum, de-dum, dum, de-dum, de-dum, de-dum. The "rag-and-bone" man went past in the street outside, ringing his bell. "Bring out your dead, bring out your dead!" she called.

Separation

As all this implies, the developmental step of separation has not been achieved. Instead, separation feels like a sudden shocking rift (Tustin, 1972). I think the example above in which the Death March was tapped out illustrates this to some extent.

Holidays and weekend breaks were always difficult. Early in treatment the defences of being one's own carer (Winnicott, 1960) could take over, but after a while this no longer worked. Both patients noticed that for a time they became ill, or injured themselves, during holidays. The difficulty lay in not being able to symbolize feelings when these are equated with body parts (Grotstein, 2000; Rey, 1979). An example might be helpful:

Zara's anxiety was palpable as she entered the consulting-room on a Friday shortly before a holiday break. In response to my "Good morning", she rejoined, "Bad morning; bad, bad, bad." She did not look at me, and she held a favourite little glass bottle pressed into the ear nearest to me. "A broken arm and crushed finger! Ugh!" she continued, shuddering. "I see the break, the fracture, broken bones everywhere, and he didn't look well, it's a shock for him. And I didn't know. I didn't see it in your face. You're all cool and calm. You don't realize a break is serious. And now I think of Gerry's arm broken" [a loved and loving member of her family]. "Broken bones . . . break, break, break. Gerry drives at night. How did your husband do it? A car accident, a crash? I can't bear to think about it; and you didn't tell me it had happened" [shuddei ing and flapping frantically]. "You're not distressed; you should be looking after him. He probably shouldn't be working, you know."

Zara had seen my husband leaving the house with his arm in a sling and a bandaged finger. I spoke of the shock of suddenly seeing something of my world that she didn't know about, of my reality; of her panic about not being able to control the breaks, and her experience of the break as a physical fracture that was not happening to her, but to people she and I loved. I addressed her fear that she should be able to control it but couldn't, and her lack of hope that I, or anyone, could protect her from breaking. I said that she felt afraid I was careless and unaware of the terrible danger that I put her in and that she put the world in. Earlier in the analysis it would have been impossible to speak about a "break", since all separation was denied, along with any attachment. But at this point, my talking calmed her, and she responded by saying that she thought it probably was "the break" that was distressing her, clearly meaning now the break in our continuity.

Discussing holiday dates was always difficult. My patients became watchful for any sign that I was about to mention them. It seemed vital for them at least to feel in control of what they expected to be a shocking experience. Catherine learned to sense exactly the day I would raise it and would come in with studied nonchalance saying "It would probably be a good time to give me the holiday dates." The underlying terror remained palpable. For Zara, the shape of the break was important. It had to be exactly a full week, ending on a Friday and beginning on a Monday. Another shape would unleash a torrent of abuse about my irresponsibility and carelessness, putting people's lives at risk. I can only think that it was my failure to ritualize the separation that was so unforgivable. In knowing that I really was separate and could leave at times she had not defined, she seemed to feel defenceless against the frightening experience of being unable to protect herself or those around her.

In the context of separation, it is interesting that both Catherine and Zara experienced difficulties in moving on from one activity to the next. It seemed that an awareness of time meant being aware of loss and separation too. They would "get stuck" in an activity and find it almost impossible to change to another. This made it hard to keep to times and arrangements. Catherine said that, in order to get to her evening appointment with me, she had to ask the secretary at work to tell her to leave the building: if she became engrossed in her work, she might be hours late.

The treatment process

Most of the examples in this section are drawn from Zara's analysis, since daily sessions offer the opportunity to work at greater depth. However, the phases I discuss were recognizable in Catherine's psychotherapy too.

Following the collapse of the "false self" (Winnicott, 1960), I think that there are two phases in treatment, not following exactly one upon the other but often contiguous and overlapping. Gradually one becomes aware that the first phase has more or less given way to the second. I think of these phases as the "contact containment" phase and the "developmental thrust" phase.

Contact containment phase

From my description of the patients' subjective experience, it will be clear that the first hurdle for patient and analyst is to establish a way of making and retaining contact that does not obliterate them both. Add to this the fact that the retreats are not only essential to the patient's survival but often feel so good, so amusing, and so far superior to anything the analyst has to offer, and you have a problem! Since contact can feel so painful, it can unleash violent primitive hatred. Catherine described her feelings as "primitive savagery" and reported images of herself as a lion holding me in her mouth as she growled and ripped me to bits with the blood dripping down her chops. The analyst has to be able to bear a seemingly never-ending amount of attack without being destroyed. When I could understand that the attacks felt to my patients to be coming from an uncontrolled, primitive part of the brain, ruled by fight/flight mechanisms and un-moderated by passage through the ego, then I could join with them in trying to understand and moderate the fear of annihilation and the need to destroy me in order to survive. Later on in her analysis Zara could warn me with a mixture of glee and dismay: "Oh no! They're at it again! Now I'm chopping you up into little bits and turning you into a meat loaf. That's horrible!"

I was helped, too, when I realized that all that I was being subjected to, day after day, was but a taster of my patients' experience of me, and their world, day after day and year after year. If I felt assaulted, what must they feel like? I could see the attacks as both a way of surviving and a way of communicating to me their overwhelming experience.

In the light of this, I find the traditional view of autism, as a failure to attach, a failure to feel, a condition of "autistic mindlessness" (Meltzer, 1975a)—all descriptions that stress the absence of ordinary human qualities—does not fit with my experience of Asperger's patients. Rather, the attachment is enormous: too overwhelmingly intense, too possessive to be bearable to the patient, too greedy and oral to be manageable, too ferocious to be survived. Equally the so-called failure to empathize or feel human feelings seems to me to be more like its opposite. The experience of others' feelings as if they were in one's own body is so strong, so overwhelming, that it must be evacuated or dissociated if the patient is not to be assaulted by feeling that cannot be moderated or contained. So for "mindlessness" I would say "mind over-fullness" or perhaps, more accurately, "mind body over-fullness".

This shift in thinking is important because it allows the analyst to be ready to catch the wish to make contact, or to recognize the need for the retreats for a recovery period at a particular moment in the session; to realize when language and action are being used not simply as a barrier, but as a communication too. Without this state of mind in the analyst, all communication could be experienced and misunderstood simply as destructive attacks. For example, for months Zara "cartooned" scenes in which she sprayed me with bullets. She described how my body jumped from the impact of the bullets and fell into lifelessness between shots. At last, one day, into my own thoughts came my three failed attempts to sit through the whole of the film *Apocalypse Now*. Each time I had had to give up and leave the room, sick and faint with the unremitting impact of the violence, the music, the spray of bullets, and the unmoderated brutality. Meanwhile, Zara seemed to feel engaged in an amusing, though worrying, activity. "Oh no!" she said. "I'm doing it again! Spraying you with bullets. There are bloody holes all over your jumper", and so on. The feelings were dissociated by turning the violence into a "cartoon". Over time we were able to understand many aspects of this activity. The spraying action of the bullets conveyed the danger of her looking at me and dispersing herself, in bits, violently into me. At the same time it expressed her wish to make contact with me—with the real inside of me—as well as the danger of doing so. Would I be able to stand it, to see it through? In conjuring up my own private memories and feelings, Zara did manage to get through to me by non-verbal communication, which was an enormous step forward. Usually I was left "cold" and puzzled by these attacks. There was communication too in the image of my lifeless body coming alive in "contact" with the bullet. Our contact brought us both to life but was bound up with instantaneous death. Between moments of contact she, or I in the cartoon, fell back into lifelessness.

There is another important "mind shift" for psychoanalysts working with these patients. Sandler wrote of the analysts' collection of theories and part theories, which he holds in his preconscious mind and around which he organizes the patient's material (Sandler, 1983). We call them up as required to help us make sense of our experience and observations. At the beginning of Zara's analysis, I lacked a theory, or even a description, in my preconscious collection that could help me make sense of the roller-coaster of intense physical and emotional experience that characterized the work with her. To think in terms of defences seemed to deny the raw undefended quality of our contact. I think we both longed for "defences" but could find them nowhere. Her turned-away, flapping, tapping retreats were the only place she appeared to be able to go for any relief and protection against overwhelming experience. The dissociation and concreteness seemed psychotic, yet here was a fine mind in some intellectual areas, in someone holding down a tough job.

When I read Oliver Sacks's essay, "An Anthropologist on Mars", I was able to recognize that my patient had Asperger's syndrome. With a neuro-psychology view added to my armoury of theories, I felt freer to "believe" my patients' communications as fact, not fantasy. When she talked of being "brain-damaged" or "brain-dead", I had assumed she was telling me about an unconscious fantasy of what she had done to her mind. Actually she was telling me that she experienced herself as brain-damaged, and, in fact, she was. I think that this shift in me must have helped her feel better understood and known by me. I can only guess at how often in the early part of the analysis my communications had felt subtly wrong and like foreign bodies being put into her.

Recognizing the non-verbal communication is essential. Flapping and tapping are never quite so ritualistic as they might seem. Each instance will express a different rhythm or a different quality of panic. At this point, skills derived from infant observation[7] are the most useful ones. It is not always possible to go on thinking while under attack, or while being rejected and ignored. Concentrating on observing and on thinking about one's observations, sometimes out loud if the atmosphere permits, sometimes quietly to oneself, keeps the process going and counters the patient's compulsion to turn the analytic process into one of their own rituals.

While retaining a separate mind in this way, one needs at the same time to join the patient's world. Cecchi (1990) describes beautifully how the analyst joins the alien world of Mariela, a little girl with autistic syndrome, as a step towards greater separateness. The examples I gave earlier of listening out for musical rhythms, or responding to the rhythm of the bell with the rhythm of my buzzer, were attempts to do this. Sometimes, however, there is a force that works against this empathy. A powerful countertransference can arise, matching and mirroring the patient's own hatred of being invaded or intruded upon. Catherine, for instance, shuddered and flapped away contact, saying, "Get out of me: come near me, and you're dead meat!" The countertransference equivalent is: "No! I'm separate; I'm not part of this mad world of yours!" I can only understand this as part of the traumatic rupture of separation and the failure of pre-verbal communication as a developmental stage in attachment and early containment. The pressure on the analyst is to get rid of—abort—the patient. Staying with my patients' experience moment by moment seemed to help them to feel more contained.

Developmental thrust phase

It seems to me that when there is good-enough containment, an internally driven developmental push comes into play. Perhaps it owes something to the tenacity and courage of these patients; perhaps it is common to all of us. Once we could establish a working relationship enough of the time, my patients set about trying to make up on the developmental steps that they had missed.

For Zara, this phase began after a holiday break. She entered without acknowledging me and looked anxiously around, flapping one arm and hand in a panicky, evacuating movement. Instead of going to the couch, she sat on the floor beside my desk. She was very still and mostly hidden from view. I thought of a child playing dead. Inevitably, she was afraid that I would object. In fact, it felt like an act of freedom, which suggested she now inhabited herself. I was allowed to witness her terror and to talk to her about it in a different way. Her courage and determination to pursue the truth were our allies. She set us on a path of trying to understand her feeling that she was of a different species, and of searching for developmental stages that she felt she had not achieved. Her terror of contact was palpable, and she had to gather herself together before each session. She often brought reading material, drawing paper, or puzzle books to hold her attention in case I failed her. She communicated conflicting messages to me: "go away" on the one hand, and on the other a desperation to be able to make contact, and a fear that if we failed she could die.

Though sometimes she continued to provoke me, she increasingly recognized how much this was meant to create an excitement that made her feel real. This was her dilemma: contact of that kind offered only momentary triumph and was followed by hopelessness. Getting in touch less violently was harder.

Drawing became helpful. When I first commented that in her drawings she was showing me how she thought in pictures, she was excited that I could know this, and suspicious that I might use the knowledge to intrude. But soon she used drawing as a way of expressing what she could not say in words.

The drawings showed her inside various sorts of steel casings, or in thick padded spacesuits and impermeable protective shells. She might be a dot inside a steel box, safe but still dying from lack of oxygen. The steel box could swiftly become a coffin.[8] Gradually she began to represent herself and me, usually separated by a brick wall or by something even safer and stronger. Then a drawbridge appeared in the wall, or grids, which could be opened or shut as necessary (see also Adam in his bunker, but with one antenna up—chapter 13, this volume).

It seemed that the need for a feed or for "oxygen" could be contemplated so long as she controlled the amount of opening time. We came to think of this as the need for a concrete regulator, or moderator of a blast from the outside world, in the absence of an adequate internal cushion or filter.

Sometimes Zara dispensed with drawing and experimented with objects to hand. She placed the rubbish bin and her legal briefcase in front of herself as a barrier against me and gingerly moved a little away from the desk, so that I could see her—and, on days when she felt able to look, she could see me. Sometimes a movement that looked like grasping and pulling the door-handle of a heavy safe let me know that she was trying to open a little crack for me, though she might immediately shut it again to make sure she could. When I understood that she wanted to let me in and needed to be able to control my invasiveness at the same time, she readily agreed.

She was sure that it was important to try to look at me, but this was really difficult. She felt that she had lost an important part of her development through her terror of looking into dead eyes, and summoned up her courage to try. Often she threw her head from side to side while flapping or tapping away her anxiety; this was the scanning I mentioned earlier. She could manage catching sight of me in passing if at the same time she provided herself with muscular stimulation and sensations to counteract the potentially annihilating effect of taking me in through the eyes. If she were really anxious when arriving in the consulting-room, she would say "dead eyes; dead eyes; dead eyes", as if this mantra could keep them at bay. Any changes in my appearance, or in the consulting-room or house, heralded the opening of a dead and empty chasm into which she might fall.

Zara's wish to look at me persisted. She explored various ways of "logging on", or "docking", or "plugging in". My desk was the medium, the control panel that she could link up with. From the beginning of the analysis my desk had fascinated her, with its numerous little drawers, which could hide everything away and keep things organized and separate. Well before she could have acknowledged any relationship with me, she joked that she was having "a long-term relationship" with my desk. It seemed odd to her at first when I spoke of the desk as a safer representation of me: solid and enduring. (I quote: "This desk is older than you and will be here when you are dead.") But this idea seemed to fit the facts over time and became acceptable as a way of thinking about her attachment to the desk. Sometimes, when she felt suicidal, she would move up very close to the desk and silently rest her head against it.

One way of trying to come in to land was to "dock" or "log on" to me by means of a visual image, which she enacted, of tuning in her radar, getting me on her screen, and attaching to me. What surface I seemed to offer her depended on her state of mind. As she imagined herself attached by a cord, gradually being pulled in to land, my surface might feel jagged and inhospitable, and landing seemed as dangerous as running a ship onto the rocks in a heavy sea. On easier days, when the fit seemed better, my surface might feel smooth to her, more malleable and receptive. When I appeared smooth, there was another danger: that I might turn glassy, and she might slip off.

As she became able to look at me and talk directly to me at the same time, she would check my clothes, then shudder as though she herself were wearing them. Rubbing her neck, she told me that my sweaters were too itchy on her skin, my collars too hard. She felt the discomfort of my clothes on her own skinless surface. Getting inside my clothes seemed to be a vital part of reconnecting. It did not feel intrusive, and I wondered if this was an attempt to get inside, as a baby does when it pushes its hand inside its mother's mouth to explore. I did not experience the old countertransference wish to evacuate her. Sometimes it felt quite playful.

Separations clearly disturbed Zara, but now it was possible to talk more about them. Although the repeated traumatic ruptures of the early part of the analysis were re-visited many times, these episodes were shorter, and contact was never completely and devastatingly severed. She often described an experience of being attached to the desk/me by a life-line, and she would make brave attempts to move a little out into the room, or look around it from a different perspective. She was terrified that the life-line might detach, leaving her to float off. Neither of us would be able to do anything about this catastrophe. It brought to mind Piontelli's work on the ultrasound observation of foetuses (Piontelli, 1992), and I wished we could see a video of Zara's life in the womb to see if there had been a dangerous rupture and near-miscarriage. Perhaps a partial detachment of the umbilical cord had led to a temporary shortage of blood supply to part of her brain.

As our work progressed, Zara began to experience existing. Perhaps a new feeling of having the right to exist came together with the emergence of a stronger ego. However, with each experience of existing came the conviction that she would be destroyed, almost immediately, either by her colleagues or by me. There were periods when she seemed to be exploring a split in her mind. She was ambidextrous, and if she were struggling to communicate something too frightening and found that her words were becoming disjointed and unavailable to her, she would occasionally change hands and see if she could draw or write it with the other hand. She explained to me that by using this side of her brain she could maintain a bit more distance from the overwhelming emotions that stopped her functioning. While she could move between sides like this, she still lacked the flexibility to use her whole self, to integrate thinking with action, or to look at me at the same time as feeling and relating. She had experienced me as unable to integrate my thoughts with my feelings in the earlier part of the analysis. Now she knew it in herself. She thought of this difficulty as lack of communication between the left and right hemispheres of her brain.

Both of us wondered whether we were seeing an ego and sense of self that had been traumatically obliterated or had never developed properly because the capacity for ego development had not been "wired in" in the first place (Alvarez, 1992b; Shuttleworth, 1999). My patient felt more drawn to the theory that the wiring was not right. I do not feel I know. I thought that the world-view that Zara showed me was one created by an intelligence and inventiveness without strong-enough ego—for whatever reason—and without a sense of self. Developmentally, in analysis she seemed to be trying to move from body ego (Freud, 1923b) and brain, to mind and psyche, with internal representations that promote the development of a containing, and moderating, ego.

Imperceptibly, Zara's sense of herself grew. Despite her despair at recognizing her autistic features, she felt the beginnings of a sense of identity through getting to know herself with me. She reported situations at work in which she could hold to her own point of view with less fear of being wiped out. She even began to trust that her clear-sighted intelligence and heightened sensitivity to people's moods and feelings could be precious capacities if she could find ways to filter their overwhelming quality. She could notice when she was being what she called "Asperger's-y" and when she was more "normal".

The development of this more observing and judging ego function was supported by our work. She came to sessions brimming full of all that had happened since she'd last spoken to me. Everything was reported fully and at great speed. Various anxieties would emerge. If I took up the anxieties before she had reported in full, we might get somewhere in understanding them, but she would return to her account, to the uncompleted list of events. I learnt to wait and hear the whole list through. At first it was hard to understand my role in this. I did not feel that I was offering anything much. Then it became clear that if she put everything that had happened into me, she could feel less overwhelmed by it and still hold onto it in her own mind. She realized that she had always let anything overwhelming drop out of her mind up to this point—so much so that she lived in dread of completely forgetting vital meetings. Having emptied her mind, she would fill it up with the next focus of attention. The new procedure, which involved using me as auxiliary ego, allowed her to feel that I was looking after the overwhelming aspect, so that she could go away and deal with what needed to be dealt with. Even so, she could be suddenly panicked by the thought that I had been overwhelmed by all that she had put into me, and had died. It was as if she could still not rely on my having a living mind of my own that could survive her use of it. It was a relief to find that I could go on thinking and feeling. Perhaps because of these anxieties, she was very sensitive to my mind wandering, and she watched my face carefully to see if it suddenly went dead. It seemed as though she had the burdensome task of keeping me alive while needing to use me for something that, in her experience, killed or annihilated.

Some concluding remarks

The achievement of contact—first bearable, later enriching—seems to have been the significant breakthrough in these treatments. With this came the possibility of re-starting the development of some of the most fundamental of ego functions.

What is particularly hard to bear, however, is the fact that, despite fundamental improvement, the "Asperger's-y" features do not go away. There is real ego damage—and concreteness of thinking—that does not change, and sensory experience can continue to be overwhelming. The difference, by the end of treatment, was that these were not the only features. They became features within a person who, for the first time, felt that they existed and were human and loveable, and that those aspects of their personality that reflected their Asperger's syndrome could be thought about.

I hope that, in this chapter, I have shown some of the steps that led to this point. There is a further important one: that of naming Asperger's syndrome. Sacks (1995) speaks of the suicidal feelings that people can have when they realize the nature of their condition. This is certainly true. It is a fine line between feeling understood for the first time in one's life and fearing that the diagnosis is a death sentence because of the real damage involved. The suicidal feelings can take the form of wanting to smash the damaged head open and let the brains flow out. However, the recognition of the "Asperger's self" seems, overall, to have been an important part of the development of an identity and sense of self as known and appreciated by another. Gradually the patient comes to experience a sense of self that encompasses Asperger's–type functioning and also a more integrated, developed personality that can both accept that aspect of their being and moderate it.

Notes

1. The analytic stance or attitude implies respectful, non-intrusive, and neutral listening on the part of the analyst, with communication to the patient in the form of interpretations that aim to bring into consciousness deeply unconscious processes and conflicts.

2. By projective identification I mean the unconscious phantasy of lodging aspects of the self in another person. This was originally described by Klein (1946); Bion (1962) enlarged the concept to include normal non-verbal communication between mother and infant, or between patient and analyst.

3. Harold Stewart (1992), in his exploration of Balint's work, discusses this Basic Fault phenomenon as a borderline psychotic transference. This suggests to me an overlap between these two types of presentation, with many features in common.

4. This experience of a "death gap" has also been described in the first-person account by Donna Williams (1992), aptly entitled *Nobody Nowhere*.

5. These autistic shapes are not transitional objects (Winnicott, 1951), but in their healthy aspect they seem to me to be imaginative, yet concrete, attempts to achieve the developmental step made possible through the use of transitional phenomena. Without transitional space, the patient does not have a capacity to symbolize, so the objects remain concrete. Perhaps they can be described as "failed transitional objects".

6. During psychoanalytic treatment all kinds of emotions characteristic of different stages of development are re-evoked. The baby self, referred to here, describes the feelings of the helpless, dependent baby who needs to be responsively looked after.

7. Esther Bick (1964) introduced the detailed weekly observation of a baby within its family as an essential component of training for child psychotherapists and for psychoanalysts. It is particularly helpful in understanding non-verbal and bodily forms of communication.

8. In the words of one of Tustin's patients: "What used to be my refuge became my prison" (Tustin, 1981b)

PART II

IS THIS ASPERGER'S SYNDROME?
ISSUES OF ASSESSMENT

The two chapters in this section, by Anne Alvarez and Graham Shulman, address issues of assessment from differing perspectives. Neither is concerned with the technical questions involved in an assessment for psychotherapy: most of the children in this book were assessed by a method similar to that developed by Susan Reid for use with children with autism (Reid, 1999a, 1999b; Rhode, 2000a). This method of therapeutic assessment involves work with the child and his or her family over a substantial period of time. The first aim is to help the parents to communicate better with their child, and close observation and description of the child's behaviour is an essential means of achieving this. Only after this has been accomplished is the child seen individually for some sessions, in order to gauge how he or she responds to psychotherapeutic interventions. This method means that the parents and the therapist together undertake the assessment exploration, with the aim of discovering how far this way of working is one that makes sense to this particular family. The family sessions give the parents a good idea of what treatment involves, so that they have some experience on which to base their understanding of the process if they decide, together with the therapist, that psychotherapy is an option they wish to pursue for their child. Our present, very incomplete, understanding of the processes involved in autism and Asperger's syndrome make such an extended, pragmatic approach particularly important: the child's observable response to the assessment process is the basis for recommending psychotherapeutic treatment—or not. Equally, the parents are in a position to base their decision about psychotherapy on their own experience.

The girl referred to in the clinical illustration by Anne Alvarez (chapter 6) was assessed in this way for nearly a year and later developed substantially in the course of intensive work. Alvarez does not address, except quite tangentially, the question of how to decide whether or not psychotherapy would be of benefit—and it is not of benefit to all children with autism or Asperger's syndrome. She is concerned with identifying component elements of the condition, in the hope that this may eventually lead to a sort of "periodic table" of Asperger's syndrome. Thus, she extends suggestions made in her collaboration with Reid (Alvarez & Reid, 1999b) about different sub-types and sub-sub-types of children with autism, which she links, and contrasts, with sub-types identified by Wing and Attwood (1987). Children with autism, she suggests, like children with Asperger's syndrome, can suffer from a primary deficit. They can attempt to deal with this by methods that, from their own point of view, may be essential, and indeed life-saving, but which are not conducive to ordinary development ("secondary disorder"). In some children, these self-protective devices may interact with aspects of their personality in such a way as to lead to behaviour that could be described as deviant—deliberate smearing, for example ("tertiary autism"). Alvarez stresses the importance of taking account of the personality factors specific to each individual child, and particularly of the developmental age that may have been reached by that part of the personality which is not completely occupied with self-protective strategies. Barbara, the girl whose assessment is described in the clinical illustration, was capable of great tenderness alongside a chilling coldness. Much of the assessment was concerned with understanding how some of her behaviour, which could be seen as part of a personality disorder, fitted together with her vulnerability. While Alvarez agreed with Barbara's diagnosis of Asperger's syndrome, she thought that a personality disorder was also present, and that both were amenable to therapeutic intervention. This illustrates one of the ways in which Asperger's syndrome can overlap with other diagnoses, an issue to which we referred in connection with Caroline Polmear's chapter and to which we return in the Endpiece.

Graham Shulman's chapter (chapter 7) is the story of an intensive treatment rather than of an assessment: he addresses issues of diagnosis from a different perspective. Karim, the 9-year-old boy he describes, was originally diagnosed as having Asperger's syndrome; a number of professionals later disagreed—largely, it seems, on the basis of the spontaneity with which Karim speculated on other people's states of mind. While some people with Asperger's syndrome can perform well on "theory-of-mind" tasks designed to show first-order or even second-order skills (see Chapter 2), Karim referred to his therapist's supposed intentions towards him in a way that made it quite clear that, even at the beginning of treatment, he naturally thought of his therapist as a separate person with his own individual viewpoint. In addition, while Karim satisfied the criteria related to the impairment of reciprocal social interactions as stated in the ICD–10 and DSM–IV diagnostic schedules for Asperger's syndrome, he did not show the obsessive, idiosyncratic "interests" that are the other main defining characteristic. (At one stage of therapy, he habitually conveyed to his therapist his own fear that essential components of his mind or body might go missing by the way he broke or interfered with components of the therapy-room's structure; but, as Shulman points out, this is different from the apparently meaningless and non-communicative "obsession" with body parts mentioned in DSM–IV).

Shulman's discussion illustrates vividly the bodily terrors that afflicted Karim. These were originally described in children with autism and are present in many of the children described in part III of this volume, all of whom had an undisputed diagnosis of Asperger's syndrome. Alvarez's patient had a body image composed of tubes or pipes, which is also found in the child treated by Michèle Stern and was first described by Tustin (1986) and David Rosenfeld (1984); an unusual body image is also a feature of Caroline Polmear's patients (chapter 5) and of the first-person accounts discussed by Maria Rhode (chapter 4). Shulman shows how Karim's hyperactivity and impulsive/aggressive behaviour served to communicate his own fear of bodily damage. Some very young children are sometimes thought to have ADHD before being diagnosed with Asperger's syndrome (Pozzi, 2003a), and in chapter 7 Shulman suggests that anxieties about bodily integrity may be an area of overlap between ADHD and Asperger's syndrome, just as poor motor control is an essential component of DAMP (Gillberg, 1991b).

CHAPTER SIX

Issues in assessment: Asperger's syndrome and personality

Anne Alvarez

T he impersonality of diagnostic categories can present a cruel contrast to the intense suffering and difficulty experienced by people with Asperger's syndrome (AS) and their families. But accurate description may increase our understanding. In delineating components of autism and Asperger's syndrome, I suppose we are still well behind the stage at which chemistry had arrived just before the discovery of the periodic table. It was known in 1869 that the elements could be grouped—horizontally, as it were—in terms of what properties they had in common. It was also known that they differed in atomic weights, and that they could be listed in linear form—vertically, as it were—in terms of their ascending weights, from lead to hydrogen. Yet until Mendeleyev had a dream in which he saw the periodic table and the way the two dimensions of classification were linked, the science of chemistry was stuck (Strathern, 2000). Bion used the model of the periodic table to construct his Grid for understanding the genesis of thoughts, and he also attempted to identify the elements (Bion, 1963). In the field of autism and Asperger's syndrome, however, we are still far from having identified all the elements (with the exception of neurological vulnerability (Gillberg, 1991b); and there are even arguments about the width of the definition of the syndrome itself. Yet we do have an idea of the existence of sub-types within autism (Wing & Attwood, 1987) and even of sub-sub-types (Alvarez & Reid, 1999b).

We also have some idea of levels of severity in autism through research on the Autism Diagnostic Inventory (Rutter et al., 1988) and the concept of the spectrum (Wing, 1996), and also of levels of chronicity (Alvarez, 1992b, pp. 14 and 56–57). Classification of sub-types and of levels of severity and chronicity may offer similar clarification in our understanding of people with Asperger's syndrome.

The element of personality

It is important to remember that people with AS are more than a collection of symptoms: each has his or her own unique personality, needs, preferences, will, and demands, and these deserve as much study as the symptoms themselves. Ordinary motives, for example, such as anxiety, loneliness, anger, disappointment, despair, mischievousness, and the need for attention and love may unfortunately feed the Asperger's symptoms that replace—and are poor substitutes for— psychologically life-giving social engagement. Strength of character and will can feed and unfortunately amplify the symptoms, but it can also change sides and support more ordinary engagement with the real world.

The issue of sub-types
and the boundaries of the diagnosis

Wing and Attwood (1987) distinguished between three sub-types of autism: the "passive", the "aloof", and the "active-but-odd" type. Although they suggested that the Asperger's individuals fall into the active-but-odd group, it can be seen from the present volume that a sub-classification or "horizontal" spectrum may be established within the group of people with Asperger's syndrome itself. Wing and Attwood (1987) and also Alvarez and Reid (1999b) have pointed out that individuals tend not always to stay put in neat sub-groupings. Yet distinctions between differing states of mind can alert us to the need for carefully gauged and flexible approaches at different moments.

What about the boundaries of the diagnosis of Asperger's syndrome? And the overlap with other conditions? (See chapters 1 and 2, this volume.) One boundary concerns that with high-functioning autism, but there are others. For decades it has been recognized that not only neurotic, but also psychotic or psychotic-like symptoms occur in childhood—in childhood schizophrenia and affective disorders, for example. Yet the area between neurosis and psychosis—the condition of borderline psychosis, where there is impairment in, but not total absence of ego development and of reality testing—is not included in the tenth edition of the International Classification of Diseases (ICD–10) It does appear in the fourth Diagnostic and Statistical Manual (DSM–IV) of the American Psychiatric Association, as a sub-category of personality disorder, with its main features cited as: "a pervasive pattern of instability of interpersonal relationships, self-image and marked impulsivity *beginning in early adulthood*" (italics added). Yet authors in the child field describe similarly severe disturbance in children with weak egos who experience extremes of terror, despair, hatred, or dissociation (Lubbe, 2000; Pine, 1974). There is clearly rightful concern on the part of the psychiatric classifiers to avoid an assumption of permanent damage in a person who is not yet an adult and so is, by definition, still developing. And what about a third diagnosis, that of personality disorder? There is even more reluctance to use this term in relation to a child whose personality is not yet fully formed, although the press nowadays is full of shocked reports of street children, even in parts of the United Kingdom, who develop a terrible "anomie", a soulless attitude to life and to their own and others' fate (and see the recent film, *City of God*, about the casual and brutal violence of Brazilian street children). I have previously suggested (Alvarez, 1995) that there may be a small area of overlap between autism and Asperger's syndrome and the borderline and personality disorders; this is illustrated in a recent case study (Rhode, 2001). The overlap occurs in only a small subgroup people with Asperger's syndrome—and perhaps also in a small subgroup of borderline or personality-disordered people. Issues for assessment could include, therefore, the level of ego functioning (contact with reality); the level of secondary enjoyment attached to the symptomatology; and the degree of hardening and freezing of feeling.

Some sign of more ordinary parts of the personality would also be crucial to the assessment. "Barbara", the girl I discuss in this chapter, was diagnosed as having Asperger's syndrome but presented a mixed picture with both borderline and personality-disordered features that were nevertheless, thanks to her courage and her family's love and determination, amenable to treatment. The psychoanalytic therapist who is familiar with the vicissitudes of development in even very disturbed children and adolescents would not regard a diagnosis of borderline psychosis, or of features of personality disorder, as a final judgement on a child. We would consider that treatment could produce major alterations where it was carefully calibrated to the level of severity and of chronicity of the condition. A recent plea in the *Annual Research Review of the Journal of Child Psychology and Psychiatry* is relevant here: Shiner and Caspi (2003) stress the need for research on the way child and adolescent personality is related to concurrent personality disorders and to later-appearing personality disorders in adulthood.

Links between personality and personality disorder

Certain behaviours, such as demanding, wilful, intrusive actions, defiance of discipline, of toileting routines, may lead, as adolescence progresses, to ever greater disorder: the processes of development may become ever more skewed. Parents and teachers may be so puzzled and alarmed by the oddness of the Asperger's syndrome child, as well as so sympathetic to his very real anxieties, that they become too tolerant of what may be more self-indulgent and relatively simple conduct problems. Gradual alterations in personality may build to become embedded as part of character structure. Understanding but firm support to families and carers can mitigate heavy pressures on them and help the Asperger's-syndrome individuals themselves to learn to become more friendly and to feel more likeable. They begin to feel that they can win attention, affection, and liking through less forceful methods. Left untreated and unmanaged, features of personality disorder and character formation can be very worrying in adulthood.

The issue of level of severity and chronicity

The second, "vertical", dimension, concerning degree of severity of Asperger's syndrome, is as complex as the issue of sub-types and certainly by no means simply linear. However, the issue is clarified a little by a model from the field of autism: several investigators there have begun to think in terms of primary and secondary autism (Dawson & Lewy, 1989, Mundy & Sigman, 1989) and even tertiary autism (Alvarez, 1999b). Dawson and Lewy (1989), for example, explored a complex interacting non-linear causality where a primary deficit or disorder—including neurological hypersensitivities—may lead to self-reinforcing situations and then lead on to secondary disorder. Mundy and Sigman (1989, p. 17) suggested that a baby who does not interact enough—because he finds emotional experiences with others too exciting or disturbing—may not receive the kind of lively attention that is so necessary for the development of "the neuroanatomical and neurochemical substrates of behaviour". None of these authors was suggesting that parents fail to offer what their babies need: rather, that a self-isolating baby deprives himself of emotional/social experiences that are necessary for normal development to proceed. Alvarez (1992b, pp. 186–188) made a similar plea for a non-linear causality linked to a psychoanalytic object-relations theory. Alvarez (1999b) discussed the way in which primary deficits and disorders may lead to secondary disorders, but she went further and suggested that the latter could move on to tertiary deviance. (For example, difficulties and terror about defecating may sometimes lead on to refusals and eventually even to provocative behaviour such as smearing. Anxiety about changes of schedule that lead to frantic outbursts may lead on, over the years, to a use of temper tantrums even when the anxiety is not so great. This is where the two axes, that of severity and subtypes, may begin to converge. Such downward spirals can lead to greater severity in either the more passive children or the more remote children: the more passive ones may become, as one boy put it, quite "lazy" when it suited him, and the more frantic ones may become more violent.) Alvarez and Reid (1999b) also suggested that a fourth factor, the strength of the non-autistic part of the personality, and a fifth, the nature of the child's personality itself, also should play a part in the description of any individual case of autism. Such non-linear schemas may be useful in understanding levels of severity and accessibility in Asperger's syndrome.

Primary deficits and disorders

Most of the attempts to provide an underlying explanation for the triad of impairments in autism tend nowadays to include both a concept of primary deficit and one of disorder. Some stress the deficit in desire for and curiosity about other people (Alvarez & Reid, 1999b), while others stress the deficit in a "theory of mind" (Baron-Cohen, 1988). Dawson and Lewy (1989) are interested in disorders in regulation of arousal levels, while Frith (1989) discusses cognitive coherence (see chapter 2, this volume). Still others stress the disorder of the theory of person (Hobson, 1993), or the deficit in a capacity for intersubjectivity (Trevarthen, Aitken, Papoudi, & Robarts, 1996). All of these authors assume a primary neurological vulnerability, but their assessments of the nature of the vulnerability, and of the mediating factors, differ.

Secondary disorders

Yet primary disorders affecting social engagement, communication, and the imagination tend eventually to be accompanied by further disorder. Instead of looking at faces, the child with autism grabs wrists: instead of asking for what he wants, the child may use echolalia; instead of play, the child engages in repetitive behaviours. The person with Asperger's syndrome may, instead of taking part in reciprocal, open-ended, free-flowing conversations, force the listener to attend to his "stuff". A stranger—or even an uninitiated and too kind member of the family—may think she is being asked a real question demanding a real answer: instead, the answer has been determined and foretold years ago (see, e.g., chapters 10 and 11, this volume).

A particular secondary disorder:
repetitive behaviour and preoccupations

The replacement of imagination with repetitive or stereotypical rituals has less to do with deficit than with disorder and at times even deviance. Such behaviours define what the person with Asperger's syndrome does, not what he omits to do. Indeed, the rituals replace far more than ordinary imagination: they can replace ordinary social life and communication too. Close observation of the timing and context of the occurrence of rituals can begin to provide clues to the function they fulfil. We may notice an Asperger's patient becoming less rigidly attached to his restricted "conversations" when he feels more secure and therefore free enough to be interested in something else; yet he may revert to them to calm himself whenever anxiety mounts. As well as reducing the scope for development, these rituals can serve a life- and sanity-saving function. The motive is often a kind of self-regulation, and the activity may be a way of attempting to meet deep emotional needs for security, predictability, and stability. It may also attempt, in highly indirect ways, to get attention, concern, and a strong reaction from other people.

At other times, the repetitive behaviour or talk is used merely to irritate, and this, if the compulsive and addictive motivation is not too great, is probably still functioning at the level of a secondary disorder. (Of course, sometimes the ritualistic conversations can be full of real meaning, and this can be very bewildering for parents, teachers, and therapists. Sometimes the quality of the tone of voice gives us a clue.) If the individual can be helped to find other, alternative, less Asperger-ish, methods of venting what may be at times a perfectly normal level of aggression or mischievousness, it is amenable to change. Kanner's (1944) description of rituals as the result of an "anxiously obsessive desire for sameness" therefore needs to be picked apart carefully: what kind of desire, need, motivation is involved, and can the motivation for particular rituals change from moment to moment? Much of the time, the ritualistic conversations may indeed be carried out anxiously (for example, the person with Asperger's syndrome may simply need or want some attention and is using the only way he as yet knows to get it); the repetitive conversations may, on the other hand, be engaged in a rather lazy, comfortable, even complacent manner; at other moments, they seem quite desultory, empty, and motiveless, but nevertheless the person keeps on endlessly. Clearly it is important to assess the motiva-tion—or, for that matter, the lack of it—at any particular moment so that our approach is finely tuned, just as it would be with the more ordinary children and adolescents who send out much clearer signals about their provocations or apathies or depressions.

But repetitive behaviours are not simply linked with disorders of regulation or with indirect social and emotional motives. There are other personal motives for, and consequences of, such activities. Deficit and disorder require repair, but what if something more than disorder is involved? The problem is that, as the child grows older, such "bad habits" become more and more ingrained, more and more a way of life, and may contribute to the embedding of Asperger's syndrome as a chronic condition (and see Shiner & Caspi, 2003, on the variety of ways in which personality may interact with symptoms to increase or to reduce the level of manifest difficulty). The chronicity may make the person even more unreachable, partly because ordinary develop-ment—including development of the imagination, of socialization, and of communication—is interfered with by the persistence of the symp-tom, but partly also because the preoccupations gather to themselves more and more motivations. Some of these are quite ordinary, but others may be more anti-developmental and even, eventually, deviant.

Deviance

Tustin's (1981a) concept of the "autistic object" was a revelation to psychoanalytic clinicians trying to find meaning in the repetitive rituals of their autistic patients. She showed that such objects were not full of symbolic meanings relating to live human figures: rather, they were used *instead of* such figures to shut out meaning and life. The situation in Asperger's syndrome is slightly different—other people are engaged, but in highly controlled, structured, and sometimes placating ways. Yet the more years in which the activity persists, together with the degree of relentlessness of its hold on both listener and the AS speaker, the more it is able to gather a quality of addictiveness. Here secondary disorder begins to move on to tertiary. This may be partly due to the strength of the grip with which the AS person holds on to his activities, but it is also a fact that the repetition may lead to his being as enslaved as his listeners. A patient of Tustin's said, "What used to be my refuge has become my prison" (Tustin, 1981b). The development of compulsivity is a major element in the severity and chronicity of the condition.

The repetitive activities at times exert a terrible pull and power— exactly like a drug—on both the person with Asperger's syndrome and those who try to help him. With the more chronic patients, we may have to confront this force *before it takes hold*, because obsessionality or even lazy desultoriness may easily and rapidly get terribly stuck or, worse, move on to strange states of excitement. Parents and professionals find that often it is not enough simply to discourage non-communicative talk: it is equally important to offer *at the same moment* another kind of conversation that can meet the normal social desire for contact and playfulness in a lively but ordinary way. I have found with some patients that when they were engaging in repetitive talk to provoke me and get me irritated, the best response was a sort of hammed-up exasperation, so that they knew they had got through (Alvarez, 1999b; and see Barrows, 2002, who introduced aggressive play to a child with autism with excellent results). At some moments everyone needs a good fight, some outlet for aggression, and friendly, humorous, but genuine exasperation may convey the idea that we can take the aggression. It also seems to meet some need for a certain level of lively excitement, which can be met in non-bizarre ways (see also chapter 5, this volume). Such techniques can sometimes reduce the need of the person with Asperger's syndrome for other, more strange, forms of excitement. As I shall try and show below, Barbara responded well to semi-playful but firm challenges from me.

Idiosyncratic excitements
as a consequence of repetitive behaviours:
tertiary autism

There are times when idiosyncratic excitements, thrills, frenzies, and even sexual arousal may attach themselves to the rituals and may play a large part in their perpetuation. A young person with Asperger's syndrome, who has a disordered connection to the outside world of human relationships, may be hit particularly hard by the flood of sexual feeling at the arrival of puberty. (However, see chapter 12, this volume, for an illustration of the developmental impetus that adolescence can also provide.) The ordinary outlets of interpersonal relations, and the usual adolescent peer-group flirtations, gossip, and sexual experimentation, are unavailable. The dammed-up river of feeling may begin to whirlpool around some apparently misplaced subjects or topics that would, to the rest of us and certainly to the typical adolescent, not be at all an obvious turn-on.

Kanner (1943) had referred to the fact that certain actions and rhythmic movements in autism were accompanied by an ecstatic fervour that strongly indicated the presence of masturbatory gratification, but this observation seems to have got lost in the psychiatric literature on autism. However, psychoanalysts, such as Tustin (1981b) and Meltzer (1973), did comment on the fetishistic quality of the play with some toys or objects.

Of course, the understanding of idiosyncratic sexual acts, or fantasies with unusual sexual content, has a long history in psychoanalysis. The realization, however, that abnormal fantasies may express themselves more indirectly, not through the content but through the *form of verbal presentation*, is a somewhat more recent formulation. Joseph (1982) called it "chuntering" (see chapter 8, this volume). She was discussing adult borderline psychotic individuals, but her work can be applied to other sorts of people: she showed the strange states of excitement some of her patients got into when they appeared simply to be talking about their depression and misery. Certain of their fantasies, and certain feelings in her own countertransference at such moments, began to reveal that her patients' repetitive complaining conversations, particularly where they could pull her down to share their mood of despair, were producing not despair, but excitement, even sexual excitement, in them. With the Asperger's syndrome patient, it may not be depression and misery that is the issue. *Any* topic may be brandished in this way; the point is not the subject matter, but the use to which it is being put. There probably is some sort of spectrum to be found to exist, extending from severely ritualistic behaviours in autism, through repetitive "conversations" in Asperger's syndrome, and on to the more "normal" chuntering and dwelling too long on a subject that can afflict any of us at urgent or narcissistic moments!

A fourth factor:
the non-Asperger's part of the personality

Much more account needs to be taken of the course of the condition of Asperger's syndrome over infancy, childhood, adolescence, and adulthood (Howlin, 1997, 1998). Here the issue of development is paramount, and if we are to manage and treat these conditions, we must understand the course of ordinary development as well as the course of the pathological process. The related, socially interested part of the personality in Asperger's syndrome needs as careful an assessment as does the degree of symptomatology. The trajectory of the ordinary self is hugely different from the trajectory of the Asperger's syndrome itself. It is almost always blocked and delayed (and often disguised) by the influence of the Asperger's condition. A patient, "Sam", presented with a repetitive preoccupation with Thomas the Tank Engine; yet, after a few assessment sessions, I began to comment to him on the fact that I had noticed him direct several fleeting glances towards a small Range Rover toy. Quite soon he began to play with the Range Rover, and it was not long before he began to seem nothing like so obsessed by Thomas as had at first appeared. It seemed as though he had expected *me to expect him* to show interest only in Thomas. Here, the element of healthy curiosity (see chapter 1, this volume) in something a little off his beaten track was easily accessible and only mildly developmentally delayed. In other people with Asperger's syndrome, the more ordinary part is delayed a long way behind the person's actual chrono-logical age—but it may nevertheless be available. I shall illustrate this with a moving and quite dramatic episode from one of Barbara's sessions.

I shall return later to the question of a fifth factor: the personality of the person with Asperger's syndrome.

Clinical illustration

Barbara was referred at age 13 with a diagnosis by a neuropsychologist of Asperger's syndrome. Our assessment suggested, however, that there were additional features, of a borderline condition and of a personality disorder—both of which were deemed amenable to treatment.

Barbara's parents had brought the family to England to get help for her. She was terrified of most animals and of flying on planes, and she was afraid of running or even moving quickly (Rey, 1979). Her sufferings were clearly terrible, but her rigidities, and her excessively demanding and relentlessly repetitive questions, were making their life and their younger daughter's life a misery and at times a torture. They were worried about her weird muttering—sometimes it was very private; at other times comments concerning the fate that should befall her sister were meant to be heard. Barbara seemed often to be lost in her own world, but when she emerged, she could sometimes take a cold pleasure and pride in some of her cruellest acts—roaring with grim laughter over the memory, for example, of throwing another child's beloved toy down a toilet.

She had been born with chronic diarrhoea, which lasted for the whole of her first three months. She then became a happy, healthy baby and toddler, adored and idealized by all four of her grandparents. She was still not toilet-trained when she was sent to a nursery at the age of 3, but there too she was considered a charming "little princess", and all seemed well. She changed at that point to another nursery school, which turned out to have a very different and extremely rigid regime. They demanded that she should be toilet-trained and obedient, and her fall from grace was sudden and absolute. She began holding her faeces, became withdrawn at the school, and their experts went on to suggest, first schizophrenia, then autism. A psychologist disagreed, and I have seen her video of Barbara at home at that time, looking quite normally engaged in play and with her family.

By the time of the first of a series of assessment consultations when she was 13 years old, Barbara's behaviour was odd indeed. She barely looked at me in the waiting-room; she simply continued staring at the fish tank. She said, infinitely slowly and icily, "Wha–a–t . . . a–a–are . . . fishhhhh . . . fo–o–or?" Her walk to the room was as infinitely slow and drawn out. Later, as her parents and I talked, she askcd, in the same voice, "Why was my sis–ss–tt–terrrr born?" Her unblinking stare was at times very bold and at others showed a little interest, though of a rather cool, clinical kind. Barbara chose to draw. What she drew was a cow, but one with all its orifices open and all the tubes connecting them exposed. (See David Rosenfeld's and Tustin's formulations on the body image as a system of pipes, discussed in the Introduction and in chapter 11, this volume.) There seemed to be no concept of a valve or sphincter function (Bremner & Meltzer, 1975), and I wonder if she had, somewhere in the part of her that started life with no control of her excretory processes, felt valveless, too. She certainly seemed to have no means of processing and regulating ordinary feelings, even positive ones, when they did flow through her. (See the Introduction for a fuller discussion of this state of mind).

A few sessions into the assessment, I had begun to comment to Barbara, humorously but a bit firmly, on the fact that she sometimes really enjoyed keeping the listener waiting for her—with her agonizingly slow speech—to get to the end of the sentence, or making a walking companion slow his pace radically in order to stay near her. She seemed to appreciate my knowing this, and there was a moment of warm eye contact between us: she laughed weakly as though she had been slightly moved. Abruptly she asked, "Why do human beings have two noses?" Her first language is not English, and it took me a moment to realize she meant nostrils. Her communications almost always took the form of questions, such as, "Why does gravity have to pull us down?" "Why does time have to go forward?" and so on. Although there were often deep and at times desperate meanings in these questions, she also could use them to control people and to get them to give exactly the kind of educational answer she had come to expect. And sometimes there seemed to be something even more unpleasant in them. But this one about noses fooled me for a moment, until I suddenly realized that she was looking straight into and up my nostrils and probably, in one sense, right through me. It was an unpleasant and rather chilling experience, particularly because it had followed so quickly on the heels of some real feeling between us. A bit of human contact was followed instantaneously by something that was neither desperate nor simply controlling, but which felt more tertiary and deviant: there was a cold pleasure in it. (This is not to forget that the preoccupation with orifices and their valves had probably begun as a panicky attempt to understand her own shaky start as a baby born with chronic diarrhoea. It is what it had evolved into that is the issue.)

I did a very long consultation/assessment, which continued for a year, partly because no one had a vacancy to take her on. She often spent long periods drawing the anatomy of the eye in perfect detail. We were working hard with her devoted and worried parents to set some boundaries, to help them to stop playing in with answering her controlling but really dead-end questions. We all had to learn to observe some of the deeper and more ordinary human meaning behind them and to help Barbara to find different ways of getting her emotional needs and anxieties dealt with. I could see that she was at times genuinely terrified to move quickly, but it was clear that at others she used this in a very controlling manner to make companions wait for her in an ever more frustrated state. Her parents were helping her to get a move on into life, and I was encouraging her to walk a little faster; I was also letting her know I knew she enjoyed making the listener wait for her: as I said, she seemed to appreciate the fact I knew this, and she agreed with me. I felt she respected me a little when I was firm about the fact that she could easily get a move on if she wanted to, although I also needed to show that I understood how terrified she was of losing control and returning to a valveless state. There was a terrible longing for her early "perfect" life that seemed to be hidden in the relentless questions, and her despair was real. These were not always easy balances for me to strike.

One day, after about a year of interrupted twice-weekly consultation sessions, I saw a different side of her. She made me wait in the waiting-room, at first not looking at me, then looking at me knowingly. I urged her to come on, and she got up, saying in her rather booming voice, "the brain . . . knowsss ev–er–y–thinggg. . . ." In the consulting-room she began to draw an anatomical picture of the ear, showing how sound gets in to the brain. I pointed out that she insisted on feeling that her brain knew everything, and it was so hard to acknowledge that she didn't know things—for example, the exact moment when I would come round the door of the waiting-room. She had her back turned to me, but she did say a quiet "yes" to this. (At an earlier stage of the work, on occasions when I felt she was more desperate and had no other means of dealing with anxiety, I would not have "disarmed" her in this way, in the sense of removing her defences and stressing the anxiety about not being omniscient. But by now I felt she was stronger, and a bit more grounded. In any case, her defences were not simple defences against anxiety; she was no longer so anxious with me. That is, they were not just symptoms of secondary disorder, in terms of being a means of coping with anxiety. They were also functioning at a tertiary level: she often got a cruel kick out of feeling in control and superior, and seeing other people's discomfiture or concern. Of course, when separations or changes were around, she would revert to using the behaviours in much more needy and desperate ways.)

After her acknowledgement, she started humming a tune that sounded like a folk tune from her home country—solemn, but harmonious—and started drawing how music goes into the brain. "The ear hears the music, and then the brain hears the music", she said, as she drew in every tiny component of its progression on the way through the brain. I decided to challenge this—she was humming still, and even beginning to improvise a bit as I commented on the lovely music. I said that it wasn't really true that her ear heard the music—it was *she* who heard the music, and that although she tried to get control of what happened to her when she heard something or saw something, it didn't happen slowly, like in her pictures and speech, it happened very quickly. She began to seem interested. I said things happened to surprise her, and they happened quickly, not slowly. I said I thought she was singing because she was glad to be here again, and that was a surprise, and it was quite a nice feeling, and why did she so hate surprises? She gradually improvised more in her humming. (I think I was being quite firm with a rigid and extremely powerful side of her, but also note her problem in handling and regulating the introjection of a pleasant experience. It is possible to speculate that her early lack of a solid inside self may have led to her excessive panic about any kind of free flow inside her, even when it was caused by something as harmless as a feeling. The second trauma of the change from the loving indulgent family situation and nursery to the highly rigid and severe one may have also have added to her fear and hatred of loss of control. I think on some deep level she felt she lacked regulatory valves and filters in her mind, as well as her body.)

I also commented on her turned back, and she agreed that she liked making me wait endlessly for her attention. She turned more towards me and began looking at me in an interested, almost friendly way—at least her gaze was less clinical, and I think she may have appreciated the fact I could tolerate waiting for her, even if she could not tolerate waiting for me. I saw her suddenly glance over my shoulder up at the toy shelves, and I asked what she was looking at. To my astonishment—she was, after all, 14 years old and often pretty icy—she whispered, "baby". I brought the baby doll down, and she clutched her to herself, patting her with a mixture of urgent fondness and confusion, half-laughing in her excitement and agitation. At first she spanked her and said, "she's got a sore bottom", with the same mixture of agitation and tenderness as before. She indicated that I should speak for the doll, and I started to pretend to cry and to protest that my bottom hurt, and she seemed delighted by that. Then she turned the doll round to face her and began to stroke her head very tenderly. I spoke for the doll again and said I liked it when Barbara was kind to me. These moments of tenderness continued to alternate with her picking and poking at the doll's mouth and eyes, with me protesting on the baby's behalf and Barbara laughing helplessly. The laughter seemed partly to do with excited aggression, but also something to do with relief, and real feeling flowing. At moments she was on the edge of tears, and I felt very moved too. It was very different from her usual icy control and her slow tortured sentences.

In spite of the severe personality problems, Barbara's obvious capacity for more ordinary contact with others and with herself made me hopeful that treatment was viable, and soon after, a therapist with a vacancy was found. The therapist had to work even harder with the borderline aspects of Barbara's condition—on rare occasions, early on, she might have been hallucinating—and Barbara's suffering about what she saw as the finality and irreparability of her plight was intense. The therapist also had to grasp and bridge the two extremely diverse sides of Barbara's personality: the deviant preoccupations were by now very fixed, and yet her capacity for tenderness was profound.

The family and we saw marked improvements in Barbara's capacity to show her humanity more openly. Her gaze was much softened, though still very serious, and she became, after two and a half years' treatment with her therapist—and continuing liaison with her parents and with her excellent school—much more manageable and likeable at home. She herself was gradually able to take more ordinary pleasure in life.

Conclusion

I hope that I have managed to convey that the tone with which Barbara asked her questions, carried out anatomy drawings, and stared through one, suggested neither ordinary factual curiosity nor ordinary play, but, rather, something addictive, dead-end, and quite cold. I think Barbara got a tremendous charge out of people's discomfiture at her questions and also out of their gullible willingness to answer and to get caught up in such desiccation over and over again. This deviant method of expressing aggression and, indeed, of having pleasure needed challenging, while the deeper, sadder, and indeed desperate meaning in the questions also needed recognizing. (Examples might be: "Why can't I go back in time and get all that happiness back?" "Why does gravity have to be so terrifying?" "Why is there no solid ground to catch me and my whole insides, my being?") But the other point I wish to make is how extremely young the warm, human, and genuinely playful side of Barbara was when she finally showed it to us. I should add that Barbara's parents knew this softer side of her well, but her suspicions of situations outside the family home had kept it well hidden from others.

A word more about the element of personality

As I have suggested, people with Asperger's syndrome are more than a collection of symptoms: the uniqueness of the individual's personality, his or her strengths and weaknesses, needs, and demands, all these deserve as much study as the symptoms themselves. At times, Barbara showed great courage in attempting to face and overcome her fears and her despair, and here her strength and determination played an important part (see also chapters 4 and 5, this volume). Each individual with Asperger's syndrome is different, and the way in which his personality interacts with the symptomatology of disorder and deviance, and with the developmental delay, is exceedingly complex. I have touched on only a tiny handful of the connections, those between Asperger's syndrome, personality, personality disorder, and the question of the level of developmental delay in the ordinary part of the personality.

CHAPTER SEVEN

A matter of life and death: bodily integrity and psychic survival

Graham Shulman

In this chapter I discuss a constellation of catastrophic anxieties concerning bodily integrity and psychic survival, as they featured in the intensive psychoanalytic psychotherapy of a 9-year-old boy whom I shall call "Karim". I describe the nature of these primitive anxieties and discuss their possible contribution to some of Karim's personality features and behavioural difficulties. He originally had a diagnosis of Asperger's syndrome with which other professionals later disagreed, and I consider this in the light of his clinical presentation in psychotherapy.

Family background and early history

Karim's parents, Mr and Mrs A, were of Asian origin. He was the third of four children, and the only boy. His parents reported an un-remarkable early history. Problems began when Karim started at play-group after his younger sister was born: he was unable to mix with other children and was aggressive towards them. He became more withdrawn, made less eye contact, and grew more difficult to man-age. These and other problems, including impulsive and, at times, over-active behaviour, gradually became more pronounced. They intensified further at primary school and led to a referral to a children's mental health service. Karim was eventually diagnosed with Asperger's syndrome by a child psychiatrist, though a number of professionals later disagreed.

Karim's parents subsequently referred him for psychotherapy. They felt that other approaches they had tried had not yet been successful, and they were committed to giving him the opportunity to reflect on himself and his difficulties. He was seen for an ongoing assessment over several months (Reid, 1999a, 1999b; Rhode, 2000a) before being offered a three-times-weekly vacancy. A colleague undertook parallel supportive work with his parents. Like other children with a similar presentation whom I have seen, Karim was on Ritalin. This helped him to be calmer and to make good use of his therapy.

The issue of diagnosis

From a behavioural perspective, several distinctive features were present that make Karim's diagnosis understandable. In a number of ways he appeared to fit the picture of the "highly recognizable type of child" that Asperger (1944) described. However, the ICD–10 diagnostic guidelines for Asperger's syndrome specify "qualitative abnormalities of reciprocal social interaction that typify autism, together with a restricted, stereotyped repetitive repertoire of interests and activities", and while Karim fulfilled the first of these criteria, he did not fulfil the second. Similarly, the more detailed DSM–IV diagnostic criteria for Asperger's Disorder include a number of features that seemed to apply to him (qualitative impairment in social interaction [A]; impairment in social and occupational areas of functioning [C]; no general delay in language [D]; no delay in cognitive development or self-help skills [E]), along with others that did not (restricted repetitive and stereotyped patterns of behaviour, interests and activities [B]; no delay in adaptive behaviour—other than in social interaction—[E]; no delay in curiosity about the environment in childhood [E]).

Karim's clinical presentation in the course of long-term psychotherapy suggests a more complex underlying picture than is indicated by a diagnosis of Asperger's syndrome. In my opinion, his diagnosis is understandable but open to question. What might appear to be innate deficits or impairments in social interaction and "intersubjectivity" (Stern, 1985; Trevarthen, 1979) and fixed personality features seem, in the light of clinical material, to be associated with primitive catastrophic and traumatic anxieties about bodily integrity and psychic survival. This question of diagnosis is something the reader may wish to hold in mind in the light of the clinical material from Karim's psychotherapy.

Traumatic awareness of bodily separateness

Frances Tustin (1972, 1981b, 1986, 1990) describes what she calls the elemental bodily terrors of autistic children (see Introduction). These, she thinks, are related to the traumatic awareness of bodily separateness, experienced as a catastrophic "break in bodily continuity" (Tustin, 1972) by which both baby and mother feel profoundly damaged. She proposes a two-stage theory (Tustin, 1994b) in which this catastrophic rupture is preceded by the infant's primary illusion of forming a "bodily continuum" with the mother. In such circumstances, separation experiences lead to *"sensations of helplessness, hopelessness and extreme vulnerability"* (italics added). Elsewhere, Tustin (1990) links separateness with the threat of annihilation. This, she believes, follows either from the illusory loss of a "vital part" of the body felt to ensure survival or from the presence of "illusory predatory rivals who [are] in competition for [the child's] 'thereness'". In such circumstances, life becomes a battle for continued existence or for the "thing" that is felt to ensure it.

Geneviève Haag (1985, 2000) describes various components of the "construction of the body-ego", including a primitive phantasy of mother and baby forming two halves of the body. She suggests that the infant's experience of being emotionally linked to its mother enters into the way in which different parts of its body are felt to be joined together. The physical joints, she proposes, may be understood as "a link between one part of the limb, representing the self, and another part . . . representing the [other]" (2000, p. 14). Haag observes that the junction of the head with the trunk has a special significance for babies once they become aware that thinking is located in the head. Anxieties about the head not being properly joined to the trunk may therefore be linked with a catastrophic fear of losing the capacity to think. This is presumably the source of the figure of speech "to lose one's head".

Didier Houzel (1995) describes what he calls "precipitation anxiety", a primal anxiety related to the awareness of separateness and characterized by the experience of a "precipice" and of falling. Accord-

ing to Houzel, for autistic children "every object relation, every awareness of separation from the [caregiver] reawakens fantasies of a prime-
val precipice into which [the child] . . . will be dragged down and
annihilated". This resembles Bick's (1986) ideas about early extreme
states of un-integration in infants, and the experience of separateness
in terms of catastrophic anxieties of "falling into space". Winnicott
(1949) and Tustin (1981b) have linked such fears to a traumatic experience of birth, whether actual or psychological.

Assessment: the missing links

During the assessment, my initial experience of being with Karim was
of someone emotionally and mentally impervious. He seemed not to
relate to me as a person in an ordinary way and remained absorbed in
merely *doing* things. His thoughts and behaviour appeared obscure,
disjointed, and unpredictable, though not meaningless. Superficially,
at least, he lacked a concept of the ordinary links between people or
things, as well as any sense of mutuality or reciprocity. There was no
indication of "the normal *sense of emotionally based curiosity about, and
desire for, interpersonal relationships*" (Alvarez & Reid, 1999b; original
italics). (See the discussion of curiosity in chapter 1, this volume.)

However, over the course of the extended assessment, Karim did
begin to show clear signs of a capacity to think about the feelings,
beliefs, and intentions of another person. For instance, when he asked
me to suggest something for him to draw and I did not do so, he asked
me why and then said, "Perhaps you want me to make up my own
mind." On another occasion, while discussing a recent gap in the
sessions, he spontaneously introduced the question of my state of
mind during it. "You might have felt a lot of things. . . . You might have
missed me, you might have thought about me, you might have had a
nice time, you might have had difficulties at work." Although this
corresponds to first-order rather than second-order "theory of mind"
(see chapter 2, this volume), the spontaneity with which Karim
brought up the issue of my mental state is not typical of Asperger's
syndrome. (This contrasts markedly with Kane's ascription of his own
preoccupations to his therapist—chapter 11, this volume.)

Furthermore, the initial impression of emotional absence and im-
perviousness soon gave way to glimpses of extreme underlying vul-

nerability, helplessness, and terror. At this stage, Karim did not own these feelings, though they were implied in his play and conversation. Bodily fragmentation as well as life-threatening imaginary situations were recurring themes. However, they were accompanied by emotional neutrality or absence of affect, or by an assertion that "everything was fine".

Bodily separateness, the gap, and the fight for survival

Immediately after the first weekend break, Karim, in an uncharacteristically thoughtful state, fitted together two pieces of fencing. Instead of attaching them end to end in the usual way, he joined them by the underside of their respective bases, creating a mirror effect of two "halves" with a line of symmetry along the base. He held them up by the top piece and looked at them reflectively; the lower fence soon dropped off. Karim carried on taking things out of his box as though nothing had happened and did not respond when I commented that one piece had fallen off.

Instead, he pulled apart two chairs that stood side by side touching each other, creating a gap between them of about eight inches. He laid a ruler across the gap so that each end rested on one of the chairs and said that it was "a log" that "the evil woman" had placed there. He tied one end of a length of string around the middle of a boy doll's body and the other end to one of the pieces of fencing that he had used earlier. Then he hung the string over the "log", so that the boy was hanging down in the gap between the chairs, and said that the "evil woman" had put him there.

Next, he replaced the piece of fence at one end of the string with a round lump of Plasticine, which was left dangling. I asked what it might be like for the boy to be suspended there. Karim made no response, so I described what I thought the boy might feel. As I did so, Karim began to swing the Plasticine ball on the end of the string: he said that the boy wanted to hit the woman with it to protect himself from her. I said it seemed that the boy really had to fight to keep safe. Karim then wrapped the string around the boy's body and explained that the boy had accidentally got tied up in the string while he was swinging it.

He filled the sink with water, and a long sequence unfolded in which the boy was "trapped" by the evil woman in a sack-like coating of Plasticine, fell into the water after trying to hit her, and had to hold his breath until he had reached his limit. Eventually the boy escaped, only for the evil woman to put him into a sealed water chamber, which was spun endlessly.[1] Eventually, the boy escaped again, and it was the woman's turn to be spun round in the water chamber. Karim carefully wrapped the boy in paper towels and put him in the dolls' house, explaining that the boy had "gone home to have a rest" and dry out.

Karim's play with the fences vividly conveys the experience of separateness as the loss of one half of the body. The boy doll is cruelly left dangling in mid-air, fighting for his life against a lethal persecutor. A gap, such as that between the two chairs, seems to be linked to a malign internal figure (the "evil woman"), who is felt to be a threat to survival and has to be fought off or killed. Efforts to escape or to fight back lead to further danger, followed by the malign figure's attempts at entrapment that threaten death by suffocation. The whole constellation seems relentless and inescapable. The end of this sequence, in which the boy is wrapped up and "goes home for a rest", could be interpreted as a wished-for benign ending to a catastrophic birth phantasy that includes the elements of placenta (the Plasticine ball), umbilical cord, liquid environment, and the fight for breath and for life (Tustin, 1981c; Winnicott, 1949).

Bodily un-integration:
the "extra bit", the "controller", and the super-heroes

In the run-up to the first holiday break, Karim constructed what appeared to be a primitive version of a body. First he made a rudimentary face: standing the toy sugar bowl on its side, he stuck a strip of Plasticine horizontally across the upper part of the opening, and made two holes in it for eyes. He then rested this face in a toy cup, which represented the body. Karim made noises that at first sounded feeble-minded and then became a whimper. I suggested that the figure sounded unhappy. He disagreed: "He *is* happy: he's happy because nothing had gone wrong." Karim added that the figure "is pretending to be a soldier". As he moved the figure around on the drainer surface, its head dropped off. I asked what happened, and he rejoined: "Maybe his head dropped off because he was peering over the edge".

He added that the figure was "a bit clumsy": "he can't always walk, so he made a walker for himself". This walker consisted of a piece of Plasticine stuck to the underside of the cup, with a small protruding bit at the front. Karim explained that this bit was to show the figure where it was going: it needed a walker in order not have to walk itself, as it was "too slow" and would "miss the train". Karim played out a story in which the figure missed two trains because there was not enough room in them. When the third train arrived, some people were thrown off under protest so that the figure could get on. On the way to a beach, its head dropped off, but the walker carried on regardless: "[it] nearly lost [its] walker", said Karim, and indeed the figure only just managed to catch it. At this point there were five minutes of the session left. When I let Karim know this as usual, he responded: "There's a rocky cliff but [the figure] isn't frightened".

The following week, as announced, I introduced a calendar of the holiday dates. Karim first retreated into repetitive play, then erupted into violence. He put a small ball into a cup, making a figure like the one he had previously constructed from the cup and sugar bowl. He placed this new figure at the edge of the drainer surface and violently knocked it off, so that it crashed to the floor and its head and body flew apart. Later on, other material led me to talk about his having experiences that might feel sickening, but other people told him that they were just ordinary. In response, Karim violently kicked at the metal leg supporting the drainer surface. He spent the rest of the session on the go, in a frantic spin of movement and action, repeatedly doing kung-fu kicks towards my body and throwing punches very close to my face: "*You're scared*", he said. I did in fact feel frightened and in danger: I was both shocked and shaken.

I understood the figures that Karim constructed to be versions of a primitive body-ego. The way he put them together and played with them appeared to point to early infantile anxieties related to bodily integrity and lack of coordination, along with feelings of extreme helplessness and a sense of handicap (see also Kane's "hideous idiots" and the misshapen foetuses mentioned by Caroline Polmear's patient—chapters 11 and 5, respectively, this volume). The walker seemed to be a version of the "sticking-out bit" which, according to Tustin, children on the autistic spectrum feel is essential to survival and bodily functioning—locomotion, in this case—in the absence of adequate internal structures. The play with the trains implies that there is space for the body-self only at the expense of others, as in Tustin's (1990) formulation concerning predatory rivals who, the child feels, compete for its "thereness".

Karim's comment, "Maybe his head dropped off because he was peering over the edge", makes the link between "losing one's head"—and one's capacity to think—and the fear of falling. The experience of separation as falling over a precipice is vividly represented in his association when I announced the approaching end of the session: "There's a rocky cliff, but [the figure] isn't frightened". I understand the eruption of physical violence as Karim's way of attempting unconsciously to master the impingement of the approaching holiday break, which he seemed to experience on the level of an assault threatening bodily injury or disintegration. He tried to expel this experience by means of physical action—knocking the figure off the edge of the draining board, kicking the metal leg that supported it, and directing kung-fu kicks and punches at my face and body. By violently projecting into me the fear of physical injury, he could rid himself of it while at the same time communicating to me what he could not bear to feel (Bion, 1962; Klein, 1946). Specifically, his anxieties seemed to centre on the integrity and ownership of his legs (see also Gunilla Gerland's experience of her legs as terra incognita—chapter 4, this volume): that part of his body which supported him (like the "leg" under the draining board) and allowed him to move (like the walker). This integrity appeared to be threatened by a separation that was experienced as falling over the edge, with the attendant fears of disintegration and annihilation.

At this stage, Karim did not yet possess the adequate "mental apparatus" to process and cope with such fears, and he lacked the concomitant sense of an internal "container" (Bion, 1962). Indeed, he appeared unable to differentiate adequately between psychic and bodily experience (H. S. Klein, 1965; Mitrani, 1993; Rhode, 2000b). Fonagy and Target (1999) discuss the perception of danger to the self that is felt and expressed in the body as a result of the inability to "mentalize". In the absence of psychic structures that could have enabled him to process and contain his fears, Karim sometimes retreated into schizoid states in which he seemed to be cut off and lacking in affect. In these states, he seemed to know nothing about the world of feelings or relationships. The alternative was the massive evacuation of his fears by means of violent physical action, as already discussed, which also served to communicate them to me—a process that has become known as "projective identification" (Bion, 1962; Klein, 1946). I felt bombarded, overwhelmed by fear and chaos, as though huge turbulence were literally assaulting me. In these states it was quite impossible to think.

> After the holiday break, Karim told me animatedly about a robot he had been given for his birthday (see also chapter 9, this volume). It sounded as though the head faced the wrong way and the stomach was in the wrong place or at the wrong angle. The description was confused and disorganized, rather like the body he was describing. He added that a little man went inside the robot to control it, as it did not run itself. Karim imitated the robot's arms hanging limply down at its sides (see also Kane's gorillas, chapter 11, this volume) and explained that they could not move without the man inside controlling it. He said that he had tried unsuccessfully to put the robot together himself, but he had needed to get some help. His account ran seamlessly into a story about playing a game with his younger sister, in which they imagined being members of a group of super-heroes; this in turn led into an increasingly excitable description of a computer game involving these super-hero characters. In the game, "baddies" were coming to get the super-heroes. Karim imitated these baddies, holding his arms out limply and making feeble-minded noises. He explained that the baddies could not talk, and that the super-heroes had to fight them off to stop them from taking over the world. His excitement and agitation mounted; he stopped narrating the story and lapsed into enacting it. Again he threw punches and kicks, some in my direction and one or two near my face.

> I suggested that perhaps there were some frightening feelings that he felt he needed to fight off. Karim wrapped the cord of the window blind around his neck and leaned away from the window, so that the cord tightened around his neck. He imitated the sound of someone choking.

Karim's description of the robot seemed to encapsulate primitive infantile experiences of bodily un-integration and dislocation—the head the wrong way round, the stomach in the wrong place or at the wrong angle—and also of extreme helplessness—the limply dangling arms, the need for a "little man" to go inside to make the robot work. Such extreme states are overwhelming and traumatic and consequently severely persecutory. These infantile experiences became embodied in the "baddies" who, like babies, were unable to speak or to use their arms to hold on with (see also chapter 8, this volume). These baddies, who threaten to take over the world, have to be fought off with super-human strength and skills. It seems Karim felt he had to fight off the fear of being taken over by severely persecutory feelings of bodily un-integration and helplessness.

The association of bodily separateness with levels of distress such as these, together with the idea that a bodily space for the self (on the train) comes about at the expense of others, makes for the sense of an existential battle. Apparently minor separations can then feel like a matter of life and death. Like his earlier play with the boy doll, the string, and the Plasticine ball, Karim's use of the cord around the neck to express this state of mind suggests an association with primitive catastrophic phantasies related to birth (Tustin, 1981c).

A matter of life and death

In the course of our work together, Karim's extreme anxieties came increasingly to be experienced in relation to me in the transference. This provided an opportunity for them to be worked through and modified to some extent. It was as though the therapy-room became a psychic arena in which Karim felt that he and I were locked in a struggle for survival (Rhode, 1997b, 1997c, 2000b). Aspects of this struggle, as they appeared in the sessions over time, seemed to throw light on some of his personality features and behavioural diffi-culties.

The issue of danger in the room was a recurring theme in Karim's therapy and was perhaps the main way in which the "fight for sur-vival" became manifest. The danger might concern the risk of bodily injury to Karim or me or the risk of damage to, or loss of, component parts of the therapy-room's structure. The bits of the room involved, which were nearly all detachable, came to be the focus of Karim's intense and consuming life-or-death preoccupations with possession, ownership, and control.

The fear of falling, the life-threatening cord,
and the safety harness

Karim most often communicated the danger of bodily injury or damage through physical activity that put him at risk of having an accident.
Most commonly this involved constructing "towers" or "structures",
using several chairs precariously stacked on top of each other at different angles, which he wanted to climb on. These structures were sometimes built on the floor and sometimes on the desk: in both cases they
were clearly unsafe to climb on and doing so would undoubtedly have
led Karim to fall. However, he persisted in his attempts and reacted
with complete incomprehension to the limits that I set and to my
efforts to think with him about safety. He seemed to feel that I was
trying to control and obstruct him, that I was being completely unrea-
sonable and making his life impossible, or that I was worrying for no
reason. He appeared quite impervious to any sense of bodily danger
and was persecuted by my concern for his safety.

Moments did occur when Karim could enact his bodily terrors
related to separateness without actually endangering himself. He
would repeatedly circle the room by walking on furniture arranged
around the edge, stepping from surface to surface, crossing the gaps
without touching the floor (Bick, 1986). Sometimes while doing this he
imagined being a soldier on a "Marines course", just as the precariously assembled figure he had made pretended to be a soldier. At the
end of a session he might lie on the desk with his head hanging down
over the edge—the position that had led one of the figures to lose its
head. He repeatedly looped the cord of the window blind around his
neck and leaned forward, making a choking or strangling sound, as I
have already described, but without actually letting it take his weight.
At other times, however, he passed the cord around his body under his
arms to make a kind of safety harness that seemed to be supporting
him. Depending on how he felt, the same object—the cord—could
represent a connection that was deadly or life-preserving.

Before a holiday, Karim dropped forwards over the edge of the
desk, crying "Help, Mr Shulman!" He said that he couldn't get back
up. I commented that he was showing me about a frightening feeling
of falling down into a gap and not being able to get back up again
without help, and I linked this with the forthcoming holiday. Gradually, Karim began to be able to verbalize feelings about separations and
his experience of gaps. He said that he didn't like it when it was the

holiday and he didn't come to therapy, and on another occasion before a holiday he said with feeling that he wanted to come to therapy "all day, every day".

At other times, Karim communicated bodily terrors or catastrophic anxiety about falling by means of talking about dangerous situations instead of enacting them. Such communications occurred around ordinary separations in the course of the therapy—beginnings and ends of sessions, weekends, half-term or holiday breaks. For instance, just before a summer holiday break he wanted to play a "guess what happened" game, which involved someone whom he called a "beginner flier" lying dead one mile from the airfield, with straps on but no parachute attached. The answer to the puzzle of how this had come about was that the "beginner flier" had to eject after the fuel had run out, and the parachute had caught on the plane. In the week immediately following this summer holiday break, Karim told me about an escape trick in which a famous stunt magician was tied up in a straightjacket and hung upside down, high up in the air, on the end of a rope that was on fire, with sharply pointed metal spikes on the ground far below. Karim said that this person had only very little time to escape. This was in the second year of therapy, by which time he was beginning to develop a capacity to think about experiences of falling and about the associated feelings of terror and danger. When I asked how someone in such a position might feel, Karim said that it would "freak them out".

The essential missing bit

Karim's activities involving component parts of the room called to mind Tustin's formulation concerning bodily anxieties about an essential missing bit, to which I have already referred. For instance, he might remove the metal link that joined the sink plug to the chain and place it where it might be lost down the plughole or overflow section. At other times he would yank the plug off the chain or remove the screw-bolt from the window lock. He might want to take down the removable bar for the window blind in order to use it as a fishing rod, wildly waving the bar (and flicking the looped cord on the end) so that it accidentally smashed against a hard surface and risked getting broken. On one occasion when I mentioned an impending holiday break, Karim immediately began trying to unscrew a bolt on the exposed piping under the sink. It was not uncommon for him to move from one of these activities to another within a single session. He seemed oblivious of any possibility of damage and quite unconcerned. I felt massively bombarded and also filled with anxiety that vital bits of the room might get broken or lost.

For a long time, Karim behaved as though I set limits, or tried to help him to pause for thought, in order to deny him access to things in the room or obstructively and unnecessarily to worry or disturb him. It emerged over time that he experienced any boundary, limit, or rule as dangerous and threatening. This seemed to be linked with a catastrophic infantile experience of "blocked access", where a physical boundary is confused with an experience of being emotionally obliterated (Rhode, 2000b). Karim appeared to equate rules or limits with such a physical boundary, which he seemed to experience as an impermeable barrier blocking his infantile projections of catastrophic anxiety and allowing him no space in which to exist.

It was also evident that Karim felt that I was "winding him up" by causing him to feel things he was unable to cope with—anxieties that he appeared to feel I was trying to get rid of into him by imposing boundaries. He did not even feel triumphed over so much as wiped out, and he tried to protect himself by asserting a seemingly compulsive need to be in charge and make the rules himself. Some of his material that related to removing bits from other people (Tustin, 1972) included obvious references to me in the transference. For example, Karim played at cutting off a horse's mane to make something to lie on and said that the horse would be bald (as I am), but that its mane would grow back. Acquiring things in this way, of course, led to anxieties about retaliation or about having no one strong enough to depend on. Towards the end of a session following a holiday break, for instance, Karim once again took off the window lock bolt. I suggested that perhaps I was to know about a worry about losing bits or missing bits. He dropped the bolt down the inaccessible gap in the radiator casing, laughed, and said, "You've got a bit missing!"

The fight for sanity

Karim's growing awareness of his experiences of bodily terror, vulnerability, and helplessness led to the escalation of impulsive or violent behaviour. It was increasingly necessary for me to set limits. For a while, the sessions were pervaded by an atmosphere of extreme tension and persecution, in which Karim seemed to feel that it was "him or me". Nevertheless, with the help of therapy he gradually developed the capacity to recognize and acknowledge some of his turbulent and violent states of mind, as well as his sometimes impulsive and dangerous moods and behaviour, without feeling that disaster might follow. This, in turn, brought into focus his dependency on a caregiver whose presence and support felt vital to survival and, ultimately, to sanity. He once asserted, pathetically and desperately, "I'm not mad", as though trying to convince himself. In these moods, it was hard for him to imagine that I could see and be pleased about the sane part of him, as though the battle for survival had become a battle for sanity.

Structural supports and the sense of psychic safety

Tolerating and processing the countertransference was fundamental to the work with Karim, particularly those aspects of it that derived from his seemingly relentless projections of anxiety about sanity and survival. Consultation with colleagues played an essential part in providing a triadic containing structure for myself. Technically, it was important to approach such elemental anxieties by talking about them "out there"—for instance, by asking Karim what someone might feel like in a dangerous situation, rather than locating those feelings in him. This provided a sufficiently safe distance from the danger (Alvarez, 1992a, 1992b) so that he could begin to be able to have a thought about it, as, for example, in his comment that hanging in a straightjacket from a burning rope would "freak someone out". I believe that, at some level, he came to recognize and appreciate the value of having someone think about and process these anxieties, however intolerable he might have felt them to be. After a year in therapy, he said spontaneously that Ritalin helped him to be calmer, but that there were "far reaches of the mind" that it did not influence. Much later, he was able to say that people could be unaware of aspects of their own feelings that might be plain to someone else who knew them.

Karim's developing capacity for self-reflection and self-control, and his gradual introjection of a containing structure that was felt to be supportive rather than life threatening, were reflected in his growing ability to use symbolic play as a means of self-expression and self-exploration. Omnipotent fantasies about escape and survival gave way to potent fantasies about rock-climbing with ropes. Karim now stressed the need for safety and secure fittings; this was expressed in play about "grappling" equipment that was very different in mood and quality from his earlier manic defiance of gravity. He developed a keen interest in constructing supportive structures for a winch with a holding pouch: it served to lift a variety of objects, which I understood as symbolizing Karim's infant self. These devices were tripartite in structure and often involved two chairs or items of furniture that were wedged together or interlocked in such a way at to "buttress" each other (Houzel, 2001a). I took this to represent an internalized notion of a mutually supportive parental couple, who provide the infant self with a sense of security.

Further reflections on the question of diagnosis

The clinical material that I have reported raises questions about Karim's diagnosis of Asperger's syndrome. The picture of him that emerged in treatment was of a child whose capacity for affective inter-personal relatedness (Hobson, 1993) was profoundly disturbed by primitive catastrophic anxieties. The containment of these during therapy (Bion, 1962) led in time to development and growth in his ability to relate.

While many of Karim's anxieties, including the fear of falling and of lacking an essential bodily bit, are characteristic of children on the autistic spectrum, they may be found in other conditions as well (Tustin, 1981b). He did not manifest any of the consuming preoccupa-tions that are often found in children with Asperger's syndrome, though these are not required for a diagnosis according to ICD–10. His conversations in therapy showed evidence of substantial theory-of-mind skills, while it has been argued that the absence of this capacity to understand "intentions about others' mental states" is a distinctive characteristic of people with Asperger's syndrome (Happé, 1991). From this perspective, Karim could be seen as belonging to a group of children who may have some of the characteristics of Asperger's syn-drome and may well be given the diagnosis, but who in fact possess mental and emotional capacities that are not regarded as consonant with Asperger's syndrome (Ad-Dab'bagh & Greenfield, 2001; Gillberg, 19991a, 1991b; Tantam, 1991).

Alternatively, one could take the view that Asperger's syndrome can encompass a significant capacity for affective interpersonal relatedness, combined with the presence of significant theory-of-mind skills. In her discussion of the diagnostic category of Asperger's syn-drome, Frith (1991b) writes: "The category Asperger syndrome—even when it is seen as a subcategory belonging to the spectrum of autistic disorders—has itself associated with it a spectrum of more or less prototypical cases. Just as within the range of normality there are ordinary people and eccentrics, so within the Asperger syndrome there are typical and less typical cases" (p. 31). If the range of Asperger's syndrome were defined so as to encompass someone like Karim, we could conclude that a child with the condition could benefit significantly from psychoanalytic psychotherapy focusing on emotional experience and interpersonal relatedness.

Conclusions

In this chapter I have described some of the extreme anxieties concerning bodily integrity and psychic survival that underlay some of Karim's behaviour and personality traits. He was able to make good use of his psychotherapy, so that the severity of these anxieties could be modified and they had a less severely crippling impact on his everyday functioning.

One of the outcomes of the treatment was to facilitate his acceptance at a school designed specifically for children with his kinds of difficulty. There he was able to learn in a way that had not been possible before his treatment. While he continued to have problems with behaviour and social interaction, these were less extreme, and he was able to develop friendships.

I believe that, as a result of therapy, Karim became more able to make emotionally meaningful connections, both with other people and within his own mind. In a recent session, he referred to "treasuring something from when you're a baby", and I took this as a sign of a sustained link with a good internal figure.

Notes

1. This fear of being spun in a vortex is often met with in autistic states and may underlie the characteristic preoccupations with spinning objects such as washing machines (see chapter 11, this volume). The need to master this fear may contribute to the frequently observed bodily spinning into which children on the autistic spectrum can lose themselves (chapter 4, this volume).

PART III

CLINICAL CASE HISTORIES

This section comprises six clinical case histories of children and young people with a psychiatric diagnosis of Asperger's syndrome and one chapter outlining a model for ongoing consultative support after the end of treatment. Each of the three main age ranges (5 years and under, 6 to 12 years, and 13 and upwards) is illustrated by two cases. Linda, Kane, and Adam, the story of whose therapy is told by Tanja Nesic-Vuckovic, Michèle Stern, and Brian Truckle, respectively, belong in the group who would probably have received a borderline diagnosis before the concept of Asperger's syndrome achieved its present level of currency (Lubbe, 2000). (Holly, the young person described by Margaret Rustin in chapter 14, did at one point receive a diagnosis of borderline psychosis with autistic features). These children inhabit an idiosyncratic world, and are characterized by florid behaviour and fantasies, which can make both them and the people who come in contact with them feel profoundly threatened. The other three children and young people—Olivia, described by Samantha Morgan, Marco, by Lynne Cudmore, and Jonathan, by Jane Cassidy—lack this florid element. However, they too initially had great difficulty in maintaining satisfying emotional contact with other people, showed evidence of the obsessive interests characteristic of Asperger's syndrome, and protected themselves by means of ritualized behaviours. They seemed to seek refuge in the obsessive control of other people rather than in their own private delusions.[1]

In spite of these differences, many shared themes stand out. All the children and young people seemed, to varying degrees, strangers to the ordinary world of other human beings. Linda talked about life under the ocean; Marco was obsessed by vehicles that ran on tracks; Kane insisted that he was an animal. Adam knew that he wanted to make contact but could not, while Jonathan simply could not. Even Olivia, who so quickly recognized that she needed help, for a long time resembled the Sleeping Beauty she spoke about.

This image is frequently met with in work with children on the autistic spectrum and aptly conveys something of the feeling that they evoke. All the young people discussed in this section conveyed to professionals that there was a part of their personality that desired contact with other people and could respond to it. Marco impressed the child psychotherapist who saw him for assessment with his lively, though embryonic, curiosity—a capacity that developed dramatically in the course of treatment (see also chapters 1 and 3, by David Simpson and Trudy Klauber). So did his capacity for love, as did Olivia's; and indeed, to a greater or lesser degree, this applies to all the young people.[2] Similarly, we see striking developments in the children's capacity for self-reflection and for seeing things from another person's perspective: essential components of "theory of mind" (see chapter 2). Marco's case perhaps illustrates most clearly how his own ability to pay attention to his feelings grew out of his sense that his therapist was paying attention to them; but the other chapters provide examples of the same point.

The more "borderline" children started from a different baseline: a state of confusion, not just of failure to connect. There, too, however, therapy made for striking developments in the sense of identity and in the capacity to relate to another person. This is most pronounced in Linda, the youngest of these children; but Kane and Adam made substantial gains as well, though the degree to which they would be able to maintain these was far less certain.

Taken together, such changes justify the metaphors of birth and babyhood that recur in the clinical accounts—as indeed do the images of dead, misshapen, or "ugly" babies[3] and histories of repeated miscarriages. We might mention Olivia's "awakenings", Linda's theories about her own conception, Marco's image of "coming out of the egg", Kane's play with the paper gorillas, Jonathan's budding imagination,

Adam's baby in the coracle or on the high wire. As Frances Tustin (1981c) wrote in "Psychological Birth and Psychological Catastrophe", the event of physical birth—of separation from the mother's body—is not always accompanied by psychological birth as a separate human being. For children on the autistic spectrum, physical separateness can mean extreme vulnerability and helplessness. It is through having such anxieties accepted and understood, whether in therapy or elsewhere, that the child becomes able to cope with them and to be properly "born" as a human being.

Physical clumsiness is one of the traits delineated in Asperger's original paper (see chapter 3) and is one of the diagnostic criteria for differentiating Asperger's syndrome from autism (chapters 1 and 2). The experience of bodily terrors has a been discussed in chapter 4 in relation to first-person accounts and in chapter 5 in relation to the treatment of adults. Barbara, the girl described by Anne Alvarez in chapter 6, shared with Kane the primitive body image composed of tubes or pipes that has been described by Tustin (1986) and by David Rosenfeld (1984). Similarly, Graham Shulman's chapter conveys vividly the degree of his patient Karim's fear of losing essential bits of his body, such as his head, which was equated with losing the capacity for thought (chapter 7). Terrors such as these are particularly clear in chapters 9, 11, and 12, about Linda, Kane, and Jonathan, respectively, and connect with their dislocated perceptions and experience of the world; but they are present to some degree in all these case histories. Images such as the arms or hands of a helpless infant, which hang down uselessly and cannot grasp anything properly, recur across the cases; by extension, this applies to the capacity to grasp relationships, thoughts and concepts (Alvarez, 1992c).[4] Other recurring images include robots whose hard, mechanical invulnerability links with Tustin's observations on the need of children on the autistic spectrum for "protective shells" (1990), suits of armour (1972), and other means of self-encapsulation. The image of antennae that may be up or down became part of the language evolved by more than one child–therapist couple.

Olivia (chapter 8) was in some ways the child with the fewest obvious problems, though her parents were well aware of her difficulties in relating. The account of her treatment contains examples of the cruelty and spite described by Asperger, which in her case came over as an attempt to master painful experiences by passing them on and also as the search for a person who might help her to deal with them.

Her therapist's recurrent experiences of being overwhelmed by sleep vividly convey the overpowering quality of something that fogged the mind, prevented a lively engagement and drew the child away from the world of reciprocal human relationships. Samantha Morgan retraces the moving story of Sleeping Beauty—Olivia's awakening into her capacities for love, imaginative thought, and curiosity (see also chapters 1 and 3).

Linda (chapter 9), on the other hand, inhabited a terrifying world of bodily and perceptual dislocations. She lived in constant fear that her worst imaginings would come true, and she was unable to distinguish between the content of her own mind and actual events in external reality. One of the haunting moments in her therapy concerned the "hideous idiots"—babies who were "stupid" and deformed and who were ugly in their mothers' eyes.[5] This illustrates the degree to which even such young children can apprehend the difference between themselves and other children—an issue to we return in the Endpiece. Linda's striking development during therapy is amply illustrated by Tanja Nesic-Vuckovic; after transferring to another therapist for further treatment, Linda is doing well in mainstream school.

When Marco (chapter 10) began treatment at the age of 9, he was physically uncoordinated and was obsessed by vehicles that moved on tracks. However, he also wanted to make contact with people and showed moments of genuine, lively curiosity. Lynne Cudmore describes the many episodes of mind-deadening stuckness that occurred at the beginning of therapy, as well as Marco's persistence in attempting to use her as an extension of himself. She discusses the difficult issue of balancing his genuine vulnerability against his need for firmness (see chapter 6). Marco responded well to firm boundaries and to the realization that his anger about separations had no dangerous consequences in reality. His growing ability to tolerate separateness meant that his imagination could develop. The experience of being paid attention by his therapist allowed him, in turn, to pay attention to his own feelings and to develop theory-of-mind skills and a recognition of different points of view (see chapter 2).

Kane (chapter 11), who was also 9 when he came to treatment, was a very different child. Although he satisfied all the diagnostic criteria for Asperger's syndrome, he, like Linda, would probably have been given a borderline diagnosis in earlier years. Michèle Stern has provided lengthy extracts from Kane's sessions, in order to illustrate the pull that a mad world exerted on him. His behaviour often seemed incomprehensible, but the provision of a firm therapeutic setting and of continuing careful attention to his extreme anxieties led to a substantial shift. He increasingly became able to see himself as a human being instead of insisting that he was an animal, which in turn made it possible to work on his fragile body image. Some of his more bizarre fantasies at length turned out to be based on straightforward, though painful, experiences, fears, or feelings of vulnerability. These had become unrecognizable through a process of exaggeration and of idiosyncratic associations. For example, in the latter stages of work Kane was able to represent the experience of helplessness suffered by very vulnerable creatures, which could be eased by feeling pressure against their stomachs, as is true of some new-born babies. This retrospectively made sense of his previous obsessive talk about how animals stretched out—on their back, front, or sides. He had thought of variants of a piece of behaviour that made emotional sense—stretching out on one's back or side rather than one's front—and, by dwelling exclusively on these variants, he had transformed a pressing, understandable anxiety into an apparently meaningless and obsessive rumination. Though Kane made substantial progress, the pull away from cooperative contact remained strong, and the importance of a helpful setting paramount.

Jonathan (chapter 12), like the other children, suffered from a distressing lack of physical coordination, which was greatly helped through the sporting activities he shared with his father. He tried to make things safe for himself by controlling his environment, including his therapist, and by restricting his activities and the use of his mind. The onset of puberty brought many challenges but also helped to activate what Caroline Polmear (chapter 5) has called a developmental thrust. Jane Cassidy emphasizes how much she needed to remain calm and steady and to monitor her own emotional state. As the work progressed, the shared experience of Jonathan's evident need and vulnerability was constantly threatened by a dictatorial bully-side of himself who treated his own needs and his affection for his therapist and his therapy with contempt. At the onset of puberty he became more difficult to manage at school and in his therapy sessions; however, at the point of near-despair, Jane Cassidy felt convinced that he could feel more loving, and more concerned for himself and the developments he had made already. She was able to stand firm, allowing him to manage to calm down and to be able to have a stronger sense of his own mind as a useful space. His impulsivity lessened, he became more thoughtful and did better at school (socially as well as academically) and began to think of himself as a more social being as well.

Brian Truckle—in a somewhat different key from the other histories—vividly evokes the atmosphere of once-weekly work with Adam (chapter 13), a teenager with the "borderline" type of Asperger's syndrome, who came to treatment because of the wish to make contact with other people and the realization that he did not know how to. His therapist had to bear many sessions of puzzling non-communication while working towards some kind of common language. Work in the countertransference (see Introduction) was central to the attempt. As with Kane and Linda, the distinction between fantasy and reality, between dreams and associations to them, was often blurred. Important communications emerged piecemeal, over several sessions or longer. Here again, fears of infantile helplessness were central. Like Kane, Adam appeared sometimes to turn to idiosyncratic preoccupations as an imagined refuge from the fears aroused by aspects of the shared world. As with the other children and young people, bodily anxieties were important in his therapy; and, like Marco, he used the image of an antenna in describing his ability to maintain contact. While contact was greatly desired, he also feared the impact of it, and the "force field"—the term Adam and his therapist agreed on to describe whatever it was that came between them—seemed to be both protective and hostile. Adam achieved much during his therapy, but, as with Kane, the reader is left with the realization of his continuing vulnerability and of the importance of favourable external circumstances.

These issues are addressed by Margaret Rustin in chapter 14 about ongoing consultative support to a patient whose long-term therapy had ended, as well as to her family and residential home. Holly had been helped to emerge from the kind of nightmare world that in many ways resembled that of Kane and Linda (Rustin, 1997b). However, though she had learned to differentiate between her inner imaginings and external reality, she remained highly dependent on a supportive external setting, which included the therapist's continuing survival and professional functioning. Occasional sessions provided the opportunity to review with her therapist the knowledge they shared about her development, including the preoccupations that had formerly overwhelmed her. Distinctions between her own perspective and another person's were confirmed and strengthened through the need to explain what happened in the intervals between sessions, and Holly's development as a separate person continued to be validated and supported.

Notes

1. The children described in this book were unrepresentative in that there were more girls than is true of people with Asperger's syndrome in general. This is not true of all children who receive and do well in psychotherapy: it arose out of the wish to select clear, extreme examples of the two sub-groups.

2. It is important to repeat that the ability to love is bound up with the child's relationship to his or her caregivers, which may have become overlaid with conflicts related to a variety of external or internal factors. When these have been addressed in the course of therapy, the child is able to be more in touch with the loving side of his personality.

3. Meltzer (1988) has described poignantly how the grief of giving birth to an impaired, unresponsive, or "different" baby can interfere with the mother's response and in this way contribute to problems with the baby's developing self-image. Psychotherapy can address this and initiate a virtuous circle, even in the presence of physical impairment (Emanuel, 1997; Sinason, 1986).

4. Although this image was important in Olivia's case and seemed to connect to her mother's illness, its occurrence in other cases where maternal illness was not a factor is a salutary warning against premature causal theorizing.

5. See note 3.

CHAPTER EIGHT

Sleeping beauty:
the development of psychic strength,
love, and imagination in a 4-year-old girl

Samantha Morgan

W hen she was 4 years old, "Olivia" was referred with a diagnosis of Asperger's syndrome. Her GP enclosed a letter from her nursery teacher, which gave a closely observed account of Olivia's behaviour. She was described as having intense and unusual preoccupations, and as forming inseparable attachments to a particular object. She avoided eye contact, responded "inappropriately", and did not appear to listen. She was insistently demanding and bossy, had fixed ideas, and hated change. She was also described as intelligent, with a sophisticated and impressive vocabulary and advanced verbal and imaginary abilities. I saw Olivia for three years, including a period of intensive work.

Olivia's parents were highly intelligent professionals. Her mother, Mrs Katie B, became physically ill in Olivia's early infancy, though this was not diagnosed until Olivia was 7 months old. It was possible that her condition had been triggered by pregnancy. She was at times exhausted and physically fragile, and although there were periods of recovery, her condition slowly deteriorated. After an early miscarriage, Mr and Mrs B went on to have another child, a boy, who was robust and lively. Olivia was initially very jealous of her brother but subsequently ignored him. A succession of live-in nannies helped Mrs B to look after the children.

Olivia was born after a straightforward pregnancy and a protracted delivery. Her mother said that she had cried excessively for the first three months, but this ended the day breast-feeding stopped. Feeding difficulties continued with disrupted sleep, both of which produced frequent conflicts between Olivia and her carers. Olivia was described as unable to mould to the body when she was a baby, so that she was difficult to hold. Her motor milestones were normal, while her language development was extremely advanced. She started at nursery when she was 2½ years old. She found separations extremely difficult, and it was not easy to help her with them.

Once-weekly psychotherapy

Following my initial assessment of Olivia, it was agreed that she would begin once-weekly psychotherapy. The main themes in the first year were: Olivia's feeling of being fundamentally "different" and of something not fitting; her assertion that she was already grown-up and independent; repeated play about things being buried; and my own recurring feeling of overwhelming exhaustion.

Olivia seemed to have a strong sense of something that would not fit, both within herself and in her relation to the world and other people. In the second assessment session, she spoke about the Mummy doll holding the baby, but, despite trying very hard, she was unable to make the doll hold it. It was striking that she did not think of bending the mother's arms. She finally gave up and swiftly and without difficulty bent the father doll's arms to hold the baby. Olivia accompanied this play with endless chuntering, which Betty Joseph (1982) refers to as a "secret world of violence" that is torturing to both patient and analyst. It seemed to reduce everything to a uniformity without gaps or differences and also without end. Her voice was at times sharp, neither engaging nor modulated. She used language in a flat, unbending way that did not capture my mind, very much like the straight arms of the first doll that could not hold the baby.

It was as though Olivia had a heightened sensitivity to difference that easily led to a feeling of mismatch or miscommunication between us. If my meaning were not precisely the same as hers, then it was all wrong. For example, in an early session:

Olivia drew a human figure with a baby inside it. I commented, "Perhaps it's a baby in a Mummy." Olivia said, correcting me, "It's not a Mummy—it's Katie." I asked, "Who's Katie?" Olivia said, "Mummy".

My meaning had to be just the same as her meaning for it to be acceptable, with the same depth and emotional tone and with the same timing. Her conception of things was literal and ungeneralized, as though her Mummy, Katie, did not belong to the class of "Mummies".

Another striking quality in Olivia was her fantasy of having a prematurely independent state of mind—a mixture of Peter Pan and Tinkerbell. The value of Peter Pan seemed to be that he was "forever young", someone who never had to grow up and face any painful reality such as the birth of siblings. Tinkerbell, by contrast, was "already a fairy", already grown up, who had no need for a Mummy. Olivia seemed to imagine that it was possible to be born and to grow up without needing a mother and also that it was possible to live in a "forever everness", a timeless–placeless state. The wish to maintain this was particularly strong in the face of separation: the material about Peter Pan appeared just before the first holiday break in the psychotherapy, and Olivia returned to it when we came back to work. However, Olivia also said that Wendy was in a dangerous place, high up in the sky with pirates and crocodiles below, and that it was necessary for Peter Pan to rescue her. She seemed to be aware that the state of "foreverness" was in fact a precarious one and that she needed someone to give her some grounding.

However, Olivia treated the idea of the "rescuer" or helper with great scorn. Towards the end of the second term, she repeatedly mentioned "Sleeping Beauty"—for example:

Olivia was speaking about Sleeping Beauty, how roses were growing high around her, and how there was a prince with a bow and arrow trying to get through to her. Olivia drew a castle with Sleeping Beauty on the top floor and chuntered on. It felt impossible for me to get through to her, and I felt increasingly exhausted. In an attempt to rouse myself, I exclaimed, "Sleeping Beauty!" I felt wide awake—as though a spell had been broken. Olivia went on to describe a floor in the castle being the floor in my room. I linked Sleeping Beauty's room to my own room: perhaps I was Sleeping Beauty and she wanted me to go to sleep? Olivia said emphatically "no" and pointed to Sleeping Beauty. I felt confused as to who was supposed to be Sleeping Beauty. Olivia promptly spoke about the prince coming all the way up the stairs. It seemed to be a long and arduous journey. I wondered aloud whether perhaps I was to be the prince who came up all those stairs to reach Sleeping Beauty at the very top, but it was so difficult. The tone promptly changed, and Olivia started to chunter on again, listing all the animals and things that had gone to sleep. Almost immediately it became impossible to maintain my interest. . . .

The identity of Sleeping Beauty, who is put to sleep in a kind of a living death and who needs rescuing from her predicament, seemed to shift: one moment I felt it was me, and the next it seemed to be Olivia. However, as soon as I raised the possibility of rescue, Olivia switched off. She returned to a state of stuck repetitiousness, in which she was not only hard to reach but also seemed indifferent to the psychic danger of remaining "asleep". Perhaps I was not yet sufficiently trustworthy for her to risk depending on me to help her to wake up.

Indeed, from the beginning of my work with Olivia my capacity to stay alert was strikingly disturbed. At times I could feel engaged, with a mind that was thinking thoughts and discerning meaning. At other times, however, I felt disengaged from Olivia, inert and incapable of thinking. At such times my mind felt empty and flattened, lacking any sense of time or urgency. It seemed to be an apt complement to Olivia's empty and tireless chuntering. I did not find myself dipping in and out of contact: I was either "there" or "gone", and the "goneness" felt unbearable and impossible to process. Interestingly, the experience of "going" was absent, as though there were no transition, no bridge between the two—for example:

> I felt shut out and tired by Olivia's constant chuntering and solitary play. After trying to think about this, I said to Olivia, "You want to be in your own world and keep me far away." Olivia turned to the whiteboard and drew a huge hill with a tiny house on the top. She said, "There is a little girl a long way up", and then added some steps running up the hill. I said, "It's so difficult to reach this little girl, but she does want me to reach her." Olivia added a banister and said that there was a woman there too.

I struggled with this tiredness that could rapidly come over me and disable my thinking. As the work developed, I began to think that she was conveying to me the exhausted state of her internal mothering person but also her own cut-off states of mind. Furthermore, by the third term of work it was becoming evident that these feelings of mine seemed to be connected to flashes of aggression and sadism in Olivia, which had until then been hard to grasp. For example, Olivia frequently played at submerging something or someone, but she strongly denied that this might be unpleasant. She insisted the animals were moving easily through the sand when they were clearly buried up to their necks, or that they liked being force-fed and entombed in wet, sticky, play-dough. At times it was hard to know who was doing the burying and stuffing the animals' mouths and who was the passive recipient. Similarly, it was unclear whether the aggressor was aware of what they were doing or whether the victim enjoyed what was done to them.

After a year of once-weekly psychotherapy, Olivia had improved. She was becoming more emotionally available for longer periods of time and was more able to protest when something annoyed her instead of retreating into a cut-off state. Mrs B reported that Olivia was more aware of other people's needs, related more directly to others, was less isolated at school, and had more friends. Since it was felt that Olivia had been able to benefit by psychotherapy but still remained cut-off for long periods, it was agreed that she should come three times a week. Olivia herself said that this would "help a lot".

Intensive psychotherapy

With the intensification of the work in the second year there were three major themes: the continued repetitiveness and dullness to the stories and play, a development of some spontaneity and liveliness, and increasing moments of spitefulness and cruelty.

Olivia continued to repeat stories and games while chuntering for long periods, often in a controlling and bullish manner. She set me tasks in handwriting, maths, and spelling, and she created a "behaviour book" and a set of "rules". She insisted that I carried out these tasks exactly as she said and quickly became agitated and bullish if I did not comply at once or made an interpretation. Any resistance increased rather than decreased her dictatorial manner. The only approach that led to a slightly different response from Olivia was one of wry humour. It was as though I had to side-step her defences, to confine myself to describing what she was doing and allow what she was depriving herself of to remain implicit. Anne Alvarez has described this technique of wry humour, one that has a certain muscular strength to it but without being rigid or weak (personal communication). For instance, I might comment wryly, "Oh no, it's bossy Olivia again." There would be a momentary pause, possibly a rueful smile while Olivia considered her behaviour, and sometimes she would respond in a similar tone, as, for instance, when she said, "No, there will always be a bossy Olivia, and there will never be a not-bossy Olivia". It seemed that she was slowly developing an internal presence that noticed what she did and made it possible for her to notice herself, as well as a playful one with which she could, in turn, begin to play. For instance:

> Olivia began to form bubbles in her mouth in an earnest and serious way. I commented "Oh, that was nearly a bubble." Olivia repeated this a number of times, and I talked about her "making bubbles" and also "having fun making bubbles". I used my voice as a way of reflecting her actions: raising it and lowering it in response to her leaning forward, creating the bubbles, and then withdrawing (Stern, 1985). In contrast to this Olivia was serious and unsmiling, as though making bubbles were hard labour. Then she stopped and said, "Right: back to work". I said lightly, "Oh, it's so hard for Olivia just to have fun, you have to get back to work and make me work." Olivia grinned.

Olivia easily got stuck repeating facts, without imagination or emotional depth. An initially interesting idea could turn into a turgid lesson, just as blowing bubbles became "work". In this vignette, though, she responded with humour to my comment that I was supposed to work: we both remembered times when she had delighted in describing how she could fly while I had to trudge along.

By the second year of therapy, some of Olivia's play and contact with me was becoming increasingly spontaneous and lively, with moments of shared humour and enjoyment:

> Olivia asked me to help turn the low table over. I did. Olivia then stood on the up-turned table, hesitated, smiled, and then danced. Smilingly, I said, "Olivia is having such fun". Olivia grinned. She then asked me to have a go. I hesitated, but feeling it was important for Olivia to see me as someone who could have fun, I stood on the up-turned table and danced. I grinned broadly at Olivia, and Olivia watched me and said, "It's good." Then she said, "We can both do it", and we danced together. She told me to click my fingers and clap my hands, which I did. There was a tremendous feeling of warmth and spontaneity by this stage. . . . Olivia then made a

camp. She got into it and said warmly, "It's the best camp, it's so cosy." It felt very touching.

At shared moments like this, there was a refreshing and warm quality to Olivia's play, which was in contrast to the frequently earnest and laborious atmosphere.

Olivia was also beginning to protest and show some healthy aggression. At the same time I found myself more able to tackle her stuck states of mind. As I got to know her better, I was more able to identify those times when Olivia went on repetitively out of habit as opposed to need and to pitch my response accordingly. For instance:

Olivia took a long time to leave her book in the waiting-room. By the lift, I commented dryly, "You don't need to do that any more." Olivia immediately grinned and began to squeal. In fact, she became so noisy I then had to try to quieten her down. In the room, she became calm and said, "Brakes on a bike don't stop quickly, but take some time to slow down." I answered, "Just like you." Olivia nodded. I said, "I think you don't just need slowing down after getting excited: you also needed winding up to leave your book downstairs."

Olivia was becoming more accepting of a certain robustness and firmness and could often be lively and even humorous in response instead of being aggrieved. She was taking more frequent and longer breaks from being imperious and beginning to show a lively imagination that was more attuned to the external reality around her. She could pretend to be a fierce, biting lion:

Olivia said, "I'm chewing you, I'm taking your bones out and I'll feed them to my babies." She went to "feed" her babies and then leapt vigorously back on my lap and said, "I am a fierce, roaring lion" and set about trying to chew and suck my arms. I had to work surprisingly hard to keep my arms away from her. Olivia then said that she was going into her den and told me that I had to walk past her noisily so that she could then "get" me. I walked past and Olivia rushed out, "caught" me, and pretended to chew me. Olivia said, "You're caught, you can't get away, wherever you go I've got you." I said "Oh, Olivia's got me. Wherever I go Olivia's got me." Olivia grinned and repeated, "Wherever you go in the whole world I have you."

It seemed that Olivia was taking in and identifying with a lively and robust object. Alvarez (1980) writes that the internalized caregiver needs to have "a backbone", to be vertebrate both literally and metaphorically; to be both firm and resilient, bony and muscular (Alvarez, 1993). It seemed that Olivia was quite literally eating and digesting such a resilient person—a fantasy of concrete incorporation, as was described by Abraham (1924) and by Melanie Klein (1932). She was developing a sense of ownership and possession as opposed to omnipotent control. At this stage, the me she was incorporating in fantasy was still left weakened by the fierce removal of my bones.

By this stage, some of Olivia's play and her treatment of me had become more clearly wilful, sadistic, and imperious. For example, she spoke of a "cross gorilla" who was shunned for being cross because he was "born different". When I naively commented on the unfairness of this treatment, Olivia responded, "Oh, they don't think it's unfair, they think it's all fair and square". There was something quite chilling in her judicial sentence. There also seemed to be a real bitterness in Olivia, which made it hard at times to shift some of the repetitive, stuck patterns in her. For instance:

> Olivia repeatedly put pieces of furniture around a little girl in the dolls' house. She said that the little girl was "locked in" because "others didn't like her" and that she would be there "a long time". Unable to bear the full, despairing implications of what Olivia was saying, I far too hastily tried to introduce an idea of a rescuer. Olivia took this up and described a Mummy who had come to the rescue, but then set about tangling her in string and saying that she did not want to help the little girl who was "ugly and awful to people". Olivia said icily, "The Mummy forgets the little girl." She then bashed the mother doll with relish and threw furniture at her, at the little girl, and then at me.

> Four sessions later, Olivia re-played the scene of the little girl being "locked in", this time "forever". She used the mother doll and various animals to bash down the walls but then repeatedly and with delight re-built them. She said, "They tried their best, but the best in the world would still not be enough." Olivia swung around and said with relish, "You're the little girl."

By the second year I was more aware of the contribution of this quality of cruelty to Olivia's chuntering and what felt like repeated wilful misuse of people's attention. Her mother once said in a review that Olivia "demanded your attention without your engagement", which, I felt, was a very accurate description. There was an uncomfortable feeling that Olivia took pleasure in my discomfort, which at times felt torturing. As the work progressed, I became more alert to the moment when my interest waned and when something more deadly and repetitive took over in what Olivia was saying, which impeded rather than facilitated communication. Perhaps she felt encouraged by my increasing ability to address this. By the third term of intensive psychotherapy, Olivia was repeatedly playing at being a beautiful crowned princess, at times a Queen, dressed in fine clothes with gold, rubies, and sapphires, while I was the ugly, poor servant dressed in rags and tatters who "ate poo and drank wee". As she once said, in a very imperious tone of voice, "I don't care for the poor." One of the objects of this game seemed to be the conscious wish to impoverish me and to bore me by the mind-numbing repetitiveness. At one point, Olivia asked me, "Are you bored?" I was taken aback and asked her what she thought. She said nothing, so I ventured, "Perhaps you feel I should be." "Good", she said emphatically.

Often when Olivia behaved towards me like someone imperious with the power to torture, I felt cut off from my resources, as though I had lost any possibility of having an alive and capable mind. I would feel completely exhausted:

> Olivia drew a picture of me with "ice bags" under my eyes and useless arms, an exhausted-looking figure who was held up by a chair. She added herself looking rather menacing; then, sounding close to tears, she pointed out another little girl she had drawn: "I don't know who it is". Strikingly, this second little girl had no arms.

Olivia seemed to be making a despairing connection between me as an ill mothering person with impotent arms and legs, incapable of holding herself up or of holding anything else—like the mother doll in the second assessment session—and the condition of this waif-like little girl who did not have arms to reach out and grasp her mother. It seemed a telling representation of what happened when my mind shut down and, lacking enough muscularity and strength, I did not reach out to Olivia while Olivia mentally did not reach out and grasp me.

Working towards an ending

After a year of intensive psychotherapy, Olivia's parents requested to reduce her sessions with a view to ending. Although Olivia could have used more work, bringing her was a very real burden for her family, who had shown great commitment to the work over a substantial period. It was agreed to work towards ending, on the understanding that Olivia would probably need further help, particularly in adolescence. We decided to reduce to twice-weekly sessions at the end of the following term and to end two terms later, which would come to a total of three years' work.

Shortly after the term began, themes concerning separations, returns, and endings became prominent in Olivia's material. She was ambivalent towards me in a healthy and vital way: both angry and not wanting to see me, and also wanting to get close and wishing for five-times-a-week therapy. When I told her that we would be cutting down to two sessions at the end of the term with a view to ending two terms later, Olivia cried and raged at me for three sessions: she emphasized her lack of "choosing".

However, in the following two terms she began to symbolize the experience of saying goodbye. For instance, at one point she used my legs as a slide, and together we played at letting her down slowly. Olivia was also strikingly more engaged with me. If my interest began to wane, she would recover it by changing her play or getting me re-involved. When her behaviour became repetitive or bullish, she was at times able to desist and to re-engage with me. There was a real sense that, in the face of real external difficulties, she was trying to hold on to what she felt could help her:

> I asked Olivia to show me the picture she had drawn. She corrected me: "It's not a picture, it's a map." I commented dryly, "Oh, silly Samantha for getting it wrong." Olivia turned to hug me, and said, "No, nice Samantha, trying Samantha." It was the first time that I had heard Olivia use the word "trying". She had come to realize that I might get it wrong, but that I was still trying to understand her. This was in stark contrast to a month earlier when, in response to her play, I had wondered about the possibility of forgiveness. Olivia had said, "Oh no, we don't do forgiveness."

Olivia seemed to be struggling to hold on to her feeling that I was someone who tried to help and understand her, while she also felt that

I was abandoning her without her "choosing". Towards the end of the term she called me "norrid Samantha" and explained: "horrid and nice Samantha". In turn, she felt she was "norrid" for being both nice and bossy. In another new development, a princess was stuck in a castle, but this time the King and the Queen were arguing about how to rescue her. Olivia directed me, as the King, to negotiate various difficulties in order to rescue the princess. She was reaching out to help and guide me so that I could help her. She seemed to feel that it was incredibly painful to be dependent on someone else, and yet that it was even more painful to be lonely, like the sad, lonely tortoise she described in the following session who was locked in, unfed, and so might "even die".

> Olivia drew a circle in blue and then another circle in green on top. "What a lovely colour it's become", she said. Immediately she turned to me, saying, "Cuddle", and put her arms around my waist and embraced me. I said gently, feeling very touched, "You feel now that if you get a little mixed up with someone like me, that it could lead to something rather lovely." . . . Towards the end of the session, Olivia pretended to pick up an imaginary baby field mouse. She said that it needed a Mummy and pretended to collect a Mummy to look after the baby. She said, "I know it's a Mummy, as it hasn't got a willy, it's got a breast." She whispered the word "breast". Olivia sat down and pretended to nurse both of them. She then put them under a sieve and said that they were in a cage but that they got out at night. Finally I suggested, "perhaps they didn't like being in a cage, but it's so painful if they're not, as they could go away". Olivia then made a house out of paper and tissue, making sure there were gaps for the mice "to go in and out". She said, "If you were a field mouse I would make you really comfy and make it full of love." . . . A few minutes later I alluded to her feeling that I was the Mummy who was looking after her, the baby. Olivia corrected me, "No, it's the other way around." "In what way?" I asked. Olivia answered, "Because I love you." I said, "You want to make it up to me for all the hard times in here." Olivia then lay down on the sofa and wanted to make sure that I was comfy sitting on the sofa. She said, "I want you to be comfortable too. I hope you are. . . . I do hope you're snuggling down."

It seemed that loving feelings were developing and a real wish to take care of someone who was alive and different from herself. The therapeutic work was beginning to impact on some of the factors that had previously prevented Olivia from accessing fully the capacity for love that derived from her relationship with her parents. It was loving feelings that made Olivia want to make it up with me, to keep my interest, and to treat me kindly. She hoped at this point that I was left comfy and full, rather than depleted and exhausted. Olivia's experience of togetherness was beginning to be strikingly different from her often bullish and one-dimensional stance: "You are my servant." Instead, it felt like a shared, alive adventure, with a sense of intimacy, where my mind could be free and three-dimensional. As Olivia said in another session, "It's true love", adding "I'm loveable Olivia too." In the transference relationship she was in touch with an internal mother whom she loved and to whom she was loveable.

Towards the end, Olivia came twice a week. She continued to improve: in the therapy, at home, and at school. Her mother reported that Olivia was getting on much better with her brother and was able to respond to his robust but loving treatment of her, and that she continued to have many friends. Mrs B's physical condition continued slowly to deteriorate. In her sessions, Olivia was more able to recover from cut-off states, and when she retreated, it was for shorter periods. She would say lightly, "Enough about that", or "I'm fed up with being fed up". She was less imperious and more friendly. When she sometimes drew me as a servant, she gave me "quite a pretty" dress or "fine livery". She was also more articulate about her feelings, in particular her angry and loving feelings. At the start of the penultimate term, Olivia managed to tell me very sadly, "I'm angry with everything", and at one point she said that she was feeling "lonely". She could now appropriately direct her anger at what had caused it; she showed less grievance and contempt, and she was more able to tentatively put together her angry and loving feelings.

Towards the end of the last term, Olivia drew "a love monster". It had three eyes and big lips. I commented dryly, "All the better for kissing you with." Olivia smiled and kissed my arm. Four sessions later, when some of this was replayed, she said, instead, "I'm angry." As the ending approached, she was concerned with loss, separation, and, in one session, with death:

> Olivia said thoughtfully, "When Mummies are ill, they give birth to dead babies. It's quite sad." I felt shocked and pained. After stumbling through an unhelpful response, I steadied myself and said quietly, "You want me to know how sad that is." Olivia said sim-

ply, "Yes." She then went on to speak about her Granny, who had died. Olivia talked about missing her, and that she had had such a special dolls' house. . . . She drew her Granny in a coffin on the whiteboard. . . . She said there were flowers and a will, because Granny knew she was going to die and had taken care and had lots of thoughts about it. . . . Olivia then drew in bells, writing "ding dong" repeatedly in big letters. She said the bells brought the people to the church. I spoke about her wanting me to hear and also about this being a way to remember. At this point Olivia drew in herself, her mother, and her brother. She added her father and some other people and another family. She then talked about her own family: "my family". At the end of the session she said of the drawing, "It's a shame to rub it out." I asked what else might happen. Olivia tapped her head and said, "Remember it."

Olivia could begin to explore in a symbolic area what "goneness" and loss meant: that it was possible not only to remember her lost Granny, but to include others, and for them to be linked in a wider human circle, to be "family". By this stage she had increasing insight into her predicament: that sometimes she was lonely and isolated, that the way she was with other people contributed to this isolation and sense of difference, and that the feeling of being different had begun to matter.

Olivia drew on the whiteboard a round, sad face, which she said was me. Then she drew various people with square faces, whom she called the "Box-bif-alien" family: she said they were "different" and "odd". She went on and on in a superior tone of voice and drew more and more family members. At various points I interjected that she was getting stuck and wanting to bore me, but Olivia continued with relish. Finally, I said directly, "Your wanting to bore me when I'm telling you you're boring me is odd." Olivia sat back and stopped and said, "Oh, I see now."

The pull towards "odd" squareness continued to be strong. Sometimes it was a great struggle for both Olivia and me to generate softer, more contoured experiences. She seemed to need me to hold on to the idea of something softer and rounder, but with an equal measure of firmness and strength. This, in turn, supported the strength and courage she needed to give up eccentric squareness without feeling mocked for it and to become rounder and softer herself.

After the ending

Three months after finishing I saw Olivia for a follow-up session. What was striking was that at one moment, just before my interest waned, Olivia, of her own accord, stopped her perseverating behaviour, first by encouraging herself ("Let's play now"), and then by asking me to play. She used her imagination creatively: there were not enough dolls and beds for her game, so she imagined an additional bed and baby-sitter. She flew two girls through the air as she had before, but this time she said they were attached to a rope that prevented them from flying too high or getting away. She seemed to want to keep them grounded. She also said that they were doing a finale, that it was a finale here with me today. Shortly afterwards she added, "They have had enough practising of the finale", and changed the play. I felt that we had been repeatedly practising saying goodbye, both last term and again in this session, and it felt healthy that Olivia was measuring the usefulness of this and saying "Enough." Alvarez has pointed out how important it is to forget if new experiences are to happen (Alvarez, 1992b, p. 210), and that there can be a reparative quality to such forgetting (Alvarez, 1990, p. 33).

Olivia then spoke of people going far away, to Africa, and she put a girl and a boy on an elephant. The girl was hanging on to the trunk, and the boy was hanging on to the tail. There seemed to be a lively, dynamic, vital quality to this image, which had been added to the internal structure, the bones. Something phallic and muscular was now providing strength and support at this stage. Olivia also thoughtfully noted differences between the dolls and between the size of the toy ostrich's two eyes. Differences seemed no longer to provoke panic or persecution, as they once did, but to merit attentive consideration.

Conclusions

At the start of the therapy, Olivia was a fragile child who used hard, inflexible methods to protect herself from a world that frightened her. Over the three years she laboured valiantly to resist the pull towards sterile repetition, to become less superior and imperious, to feel self-respect without triumphing over the sufferings of other people. She gained insight into some aspects of herself that were "odd" and began to feel that this sense of difference was painful rather than special, but equally not something that should be mocked. Towards the end of therapy she was able to grasp a multi-dimensional point of view. Describing her little brother's temper tantrum, she did not just focus on what he looked like, as she would have done earlier, but talked about what she had felt and what she thought her mother felt. This remarkable little girl's sense of psychic strength developed together with her imagination and her capacity to acknowledge her love as well as her hate. In our three years of work a softer side grew in Olivia, associated with muscular strength and flexibility. Increasingly she had the capacity to reflect on her situation and, according to what she felt was good for her, to decide to be open or shut.

CHAPTER NINE

Out of the nightmare: the treatment of a 5-year-old girl with Asperger's syndrome

Tanja Nesic-Vuckovic

When she was referred for assessment, "Linda" was 5 years old. At school her behaviour was unmanageable, and she was considered to be odd and difficult. She could not play with other children, respond to their initiatives, or enter into any kind of ordinary exchange with them. She often collapsed in uncontrollable distress and was impossible to comfort. Adults could not understand what had brought on the collapse: there seemed to be no obvious link with preceding events.

Linda's teachers agreed with the educational psychologist that she was intelligent, but she seemed unable to learn in an ordinary way. Instead, she garnered facts that she assembled into random collections of information that others found difficult to relate to. She might tell people, a bit pompously, the Latin name of a particular plant or an animal, but she was unable to assimilate more ordinary, age-appropriate knowledge. Early on in her treatment, she asked me, "Where does the letter k come in the word, please?" The question seemed bizarrely lacking in context but still conveyed a genuine confusion. Sometimes she would say, "I'm going to play now", but her play did not unfold: it was as though the announcement had been made by a different person.

Family life was ruled to a great degree by Linda's uncontrollable and unpredictable fears. Extremely complicated preparations were necessary if other children were to be invited to the house, and even then Linda could not interact with them. Equally complicated rules had to be observed if she was to manage the daily routines of eating, sleeping, and playing.

Linda was initially seen by a child psychiatrist who made the diagnosis of Asperger's syndrome and recommended intensive psychotherapy. Her parents were seen fortnightly by a colleague and brought her regularly and reliably throughout.

Linda's mother was originally from Latin America. She had suffered bereavements, financial hardship, and political persecution before coming to Britain, where she met and married Linda's father. She never felt accepted by her husband's family and was lonely and isolated. She could not give me much information about Linda's babyhood: she thought that her development had been "normal and ordinary". Later she recalled perinatal complications that could have been fatal. It was as though she expected adversity and did not at first think it worth mentioning. She was determined and eager to get help for her daughter, and we arranged that I would see Linda three times a week. This chapter is an account of some aspects of the first two years of work.

Learning Linda's bubble-language

Linda was a sturdy child, dark-haired, blue-eyed, and good-looking. In her school uniform she seemed an ordinary 5-year-old. She habitually parted from her mother in the waiting-room without difficulty and followed me to the therapy-room with no sign of unease or anxiety.

The first time I collected Linda from the waiting-room, I offered her my hand, and as she took it a slight electric shock passed between us, which neither of us referred to. On the way to my room I thought that something about her hand felt unusual. It did not feel solid, and also there was something on one of her fingers that felt unpleasant. In fact, as I discovered when we had got to the room, it was only a plaster. This episode made more sense later on, as I hope to convey.

Once in the therapy-room, Linda's presence was powerful and rather unsettling. She did not speak, but she drew compulsively, as though her life depended on it—12 or more pictures in a session. However, she did not allow me to use her drawings as means of establishing contact between us or to attribute intention or meaning to them—if I ventured a comment, she told me to shut up. It turned out that I was supposed to understand without being told anything and never to interrupt her "flow". If I did, Linda's thin layer of tolerance would crack, and an angry outburst would follow.

When Linda did speak, the effect was disturbing. She did not use one voice that was recognizably hers: instead, she interrupted her activities to comment on them. "I am playing now", she announced, or "I am drawing now." It sounded as though there are two children involved—one who was performing an activity and the other who monitored and directed this. In fact, Linda's play lacked purpose and direction, and she could not follow through on what she began.

Sometimes she used the toy telephone to imitate an adult having a conversation, but without using real words. She relied on the rhythm and music of her voice to create the desired effect, very convincingly. She seemed accomplished at disguising those characteristics that defined her own identity—perhaps she did not really feel that she had one. At yet other times she spoke in an incomprehensible jargon, and I was "allowed" to hear only a few disconnected words. Only very occasionally at this stage of our contact would she speak in a way that I felt I was meant both to hear and to understand. It was at these times that I learnt about her urgent preoccupations. For instance, she allowed me to hear that she was preparing to leave planet Earth and go to "beautiful Jupiter". For this journey she needed the right provisions, oxygen most of all; but she also needed to protect herself from insatiable dragons that breathed lethal fire. Linda was obviously terrified of what she was saying; she would speak quietly, almost whispering, as though speaking her thoughts aloud could make them come true. At yet other times she would jumble the words up, so that I needed to make a special effort not to miss the ones that might be meant to reach me.

In those early sessions I felt very easily dislocated in Linda's presence, taken by surprise, bereft of thought or speech. But most of all I felt that my expectation and wish to make contact with this child was out of place, as was my wish to play an active part. Much later, I was to understand these feelings as a reflection of Linda's sense that she had no place in the world of human beings. They also helped me to realize the sense of irrelevance that the parents of children like Linda have to bear in attempting to get through to their child.

I was also struck by Linda's apparent inability to apply her mind to straightforward tasks. The box that I provided for her had a small lock and key. She asked me to open it for her: "I'm not good at opening boxes." When I encouraged her to try, she struggled for a while, fiddling both with the key and the lock, and she finally tried to undo the lock without using the key. At this stage, she seemed to have very little idea of how ordinary objects fitted together, even after watching me unlock the box. In another example she held the spout of her toy teapot to her eyelid, as though looking up the spout with a closed eye. This made sense as I came to understand how frightened Linda was of exploring the inside of anything or anybody.

Another noteworthy feature of Linda's early sessions was the way in which she used her body. Over and over again, she compulsively traced circular movements in front of her chest with her index finger. All she could tell me about it was "... germs ...". At other times she would shake her body as though shaking something off it; or else, with painful concentration showing on her face, she repositioned each limb as though putting her body back together (see review of Geneviève Haag's work in the Introduction). This was either introduced or accompanied by sounds very similar to those that people make when they are shaking because of a chill. I did not understand then what Linda was doing, nor did the context of the session make it clearer.

Very early in the therapy I realized that I did not know when was the right time to speak to Linda, let alone what it might be helpful to say to her. A word, a whisper, the look in my eye, even my taking a breath before speaking could—and often did—provoke an uncontainable, violent outburst. Very occasionally, when she was feeling less threatened, she would instead shut out my voice by plugging her ears with her fingers, or would make noises to drown out my words. The only way forward seemed to be to keep quiet.

Gradually, however, as my quiet and—as I thought then—ineffectual presence became more tolerable, Linda dared to use words to describe her drawings. As I mentioned earlier, she drew at a frenzied pace—she could easily cover a dozen sheets in a session—but little by little her drawings began to depict events that were horrific but understandable. For example, she drew houses in which everything had been smashed to bits by a train speeding through; or people who lit a fire while trapped inside a whale, risking destruction to the creature that was carrying them as well as to themselves; or, again, the inside of what she called a "bloated" dragon filled with the corpses of children and adults it had devoured. The other main class of her drawings depicted rockets and space shuttles. These were either being launched into space or were looking down at the earth from the stratosphere. They were always manned by one solitary person whom Linda described as an astronaut, who invariably wore a very thick helmet.

Linda stressed how important it was for the astronaut to have a sufficient supply of oxygen to breathe.

After a while it became possible to speak to Linda—very gently, a little at a time—about the places that seemed to be so frightening, in which devastating things could happen. I said that she appeared not to believe in safety anywhere except in outer space, the furthest place mankind had reached. Linda would reply that the spaceships were going to Jupiter: "Jupiter is a gassy planet." I pointed out that a gassy planet was impossible to land on, and that she did not seem to believe that she could touch down on safe, firm ground. Linda repeatedly played at circling high above the earth, looking for a safe place to land and never finding one.

As well as the astronaut in space (Bick, 1986; Briggs, 2002), Linda drew a little girl who went deep below the sea in a variety of vessels. The little girl was alone in the dark depths, except for the sharks that surrounded her. She could not try to call for help, Linda said, because she only spoke "bubbles"—an instance perhaps of Tustin's "autistic shapes" discussed in the Introduction.

These various drawings conveyed powerfully to me the absence of any reasonable, safe, and liveable habitat for ordinary human beings. In this world there was nowhere to go, nothing to attach oneself to, no people who could understand one's language or pull one to safety. All the living creatures in Linda's drawings were destructive. Godzilla crushed cities; dragons spat fire; drivers crashed their cars into each other.

These violent scenes felt very real to Linda. She crumbled in fear and needed to be taken to her mother in the waiting-room. This was particularly so if a toy mother animal had come to harm during a game. The mother kangaroo, for instance, was often ferociously attacked, and the rescuing ambulance would have an accident on the way to hospital.

Linda had not yet established the security that comes from negotiating what Melanie Klein (1935) called the depressive position. Children normally come to feel that their love and their wish to put things right are stronger than their hostility, and that caregivers are strong enough not to be damaged. Linda was reassured by seeing that her mother—a real, external, separate person—was all right. She could then return to the therapy-room, but she remained frightened of this place where she had given shape to her internal imaginings. She would enter it as though walking into an unknown space that was treacherous and full of danger. She moved slowly and gingerly, touching the walls (Bick, 1986), looking towards the window with trepidation, as though something or someone might intrude. She always insisted that the light must be switched on, no matter what time of day was. She behaved as though she were in a nightmare place.

With the repeated reassurance that exploring these states of mind did her mother no harm, Linda found the courage to tell me more about them.

LINDA: This ship is at the bottom of the sea. This is an anchor. . . . And look who is on the anchor—a girl! The anchor is hooked onto the pirate's ship. The girl is talking bubbles and can't ask for help. The fish can't understand her.

ME: The girl is talking bubbles. Sometimes I can understand when you talk your bubble-language, sometimes I can't understand all of it yet. This girl is shouting for help because a big, dangerous boat is pulling her down to the bottom of the sea. The girl is frightened.

LINDA: The girl is lonely. She's seen something. . . . Pirates' swords. Pirates are cutting the boat in half with their swords. This pirate has goggles because his eyes were poked out. The pirate has cut the boat in half.

As Linda drew, she leant forward, and the lid of her box fell on her head. In surprise and sympathy I exclaimed "Oh!" She said: "It didn't hurt me".

ME: You are talking bubble-language now—it would have hurt me, it would hurt anybody—it must have hurt you.

LINDA: I am not talking bubble-talk, I'm on the surface now.

There are many thought-provoking aspects to this communication, including the recurring theme of a ship that should be a place of safety but has been cut in half (Haag, 1985). In this instance the damaged ship drags the child down with it. Even feeling "anchored" meant being anchored to a dangerous object. The little girl knew that she needed help, but the fish could not understand her and the pirate, though he belonged to her own species, was both damaged and frightening. Linda and I had shared feelings about her story, which may have contributed to her saying that she was back on the surface and not speaking bubble-language. On the other hand, the reality that she and I shared did not yet include the crucial fact of her physical pain. It may have felt less upsetting at this point to remain dissociated from it than to feel that I had failed to keep her safe.

The structure of reality:
distinguishing "myth" and "history"

There were times when Linda wished for the world to contract to the size of a box. "I live in a box", she would say; or "the world is a box". I thought she was referring to her inner world, which the toy-box allowed her to represent, but also to a wish for the boundedness and limits that she could not find in the stratosphere or in the depths of the ocean. She needed walls she could touch in order not to feel that she might fall forever into a terrifying infinity (Bick, 1968, 1986; Tustin, 1986; Winnicott, 1949).

Gradually I came to understand the extent to which Linda lived in a flimsy world with no firm, supportive structure. She might walk the length of the corridor between waiting-room and therapy-room leaning against the wall and still gingerly touch the part of it in front of her as though it might crumble at any moment. If there were the slightest delay in my dating her drawings when she asked me to, she "fell" into a state of anger and despair, as though I had compromised the supportive structure of the session on which she relied. Linda's hold on reality was correspondingly precarious. She repeatedly checked whether my head was properly attached to my shoulders (Haag, 1991) or whether she could pull it off, reminding me of her previous habit of seeming to assemble all the parts of her body. At times, as I have described, she seemed to feel that the room had actually become the bizarre and frightening place of her imagining—whether the moon, an underwater world, or a fragile surface that could crack dangerously under her feet like thin ice. The world in which Linda lived was not just physically insubstantial and precarious: it was arranged very differently from the world most of us inhabit. Linda mentioned "airports under the sea"; she described spoken words as being "invisible"; she said that "underwater plants need to be watered to be able to grow".

Not surprisingly, Linda did not feel that she could trust her mind to help her in orientating herself. "I don't have a mind", she said; "a tiny, tiny mind perhaps. . . ." "The pirates", she told me one day, "have taken the treasure chest—the most precious thing of all". "What is that?" I asked her. Linda answered, "My mind."

Linda was conveying poignantly what it was like to live without being able to think properly. She frequently drew a robot with a very thick helmet. I felt that this was meant to protect its head from outside impingements, but also to keep inside its head the things that belonged there, so that they would not leak out and contaminate outside reality—turn the therapy-room into the bottom of the ocean, for instance. She seemed at this stage to feel that it was safer to be a robot than a feeling, vulnerable human being.

Sometimes Linda thought that she was the source of destruction and chaos. For example, she drew a cyclone sucking up everything in its path, and breathing mightily she said, "I am the cyclone!" On another occasion she drew a wrecked ship drifting on the ocean. Only part of it had sunk, but the bit that was still afloat was struck by lightning. We both agreed that this represented Linda's own experience. Then a whirlpool pulled the shipwreck down. Linda said that a wicked witch had made it happen. Then she caught sight of a mole on my neck and immediately said, "I did it." It seemed that she either held herself delusionally responsible for any imperfection through being all-powerfully destructive, or that the alternative was to feel completely helpless in the hands of malevolent figures. It is perhaps not surprising that she often built a machine-like "construction", which, she said, was herself: seeing herself as a machine may have felt like a way out of the dilemma.

Linda tried desperately to establish reliable criteria that would always let her know what was real and what was not. She emphasized the difference between what belonged in the category of "myth" (the Loch Ness Monster) and what belonged in the category of "history" (Queen Elizabeth I). This effort to keep fact apart from fantasy was unsuccessful because the historical "facts" that impressed Linda enough for her to remember them were largely determined by her own anxieties and preoccupations. For example, she was fascinated by the "fact" that the alphabet for the blind was invented by Braille to help his son, who had been blinded by burning leather.

The following, uttered at panic-stricken speed, is an example of Linda trying to master the frightening "myths" that crowded in on her:

"The shark has gone through the boat. The sea was stormy. The squid has eaten the crab. The skyscrapers in the city exploded. The rocket landed on the wrong launching pad. The bus has turned into a cake. The sunflowers are sad. Baby Jesus died. The flowerpot was happy. The seeds grew from a

woman's hands. The cushion grew eyes.[1] *The china exploded. The train
run through the wall. The spoon stumbled down the mountain. The owl
flew to Mexico."*

Even at such moments, I did not feel that contact between us was ever
totally lost. I tried as best I could to make shared sense of these idiosyncratic "myths":

LINDA: The bugs are eating my hair.

ME: Maybe you feel that bad bugs are bad thoughts, eating your
good thoughts.

LINDA: My brain. The cockroaches are eating my hair. They think I
am a flash.

ME: I know you are not a flash, you are you, a person, Linda. It's
scary if you think things want to eat you.

[There was a sudden noise from somewhere near the therapy-
room].

LINDA: I told you the earth wasn't safe.

Linda's fantasy experience coloured her perception of the physical
world and also her capacity to relate to me. She often felt compelled to
kiss me: this felt like a placation—of a shark or a monster perhaps—
rather than a sexualized enactment. As our relationship deepened, she
naturally drew me into her system of myths. She would refer to "all my
myths, Miss Nesic": since she knew that I was Mrs Nesic, calling me
"Miss" was itself mythical, not factual. This suggests that one aspect of
her myth-making was not just an alternative system to historical fact,
but actually stood in opposition to the truth and was directed against
the idea that I formed part of a parental couple.

I have already mentioned the degree to which she was distressed
by the mole on my neck, which she was frightened she had caused. At
times and under pressure of this distress, Linda interfered sufficiently
with her own perception to convince herself that the mole was not
there. At other times she believed that this mole was something that
had come from inside me, and that it was a sign of how black, damaged, or wicked I was. I was reminded of David Grossman's novel *See
Under: Love*, in which no one is able to explain to a little boy that his
grandfather had been in the concentration camps. The boy tries to
wash the tattooed number off his grandfather's arm, but nothing he

can do is any use. He concludes that the numbers must come from inside: "There must be somebody there inside Grandfather . . ." (p. 19).

The structure of bodies: conception and birth

Linda found the rules governing bodily existence—both hers and mine—a puzzling and unsettling mystery. Sometimes she moved her body in slow motion, as if convinced that she could float, "hovering" just above the surface of the furniture as though she really believed she was not standing on the floor. At such moments I could not get through to her at all. However, in these states of mind she was particularly interested in my body. She would sniff me, or try to see whether she could detach parts of my body such as my head or my toes. She shook my hands, as though to check whether they would come off but also, I thought, to try to understand what the binding force was that held me together. She was particularly interested in the apertures that she thought led inside me (see also chapter 6). For instance, she put her index finger into my ear, then looked at the finger and said, "Monster"; she would also crawl under my chair as though looking for a way in from underneath. On the other hand she avoided my eyes, which would have provided the most direct possible access to my inner self; but eye contact still felt dangerous to Linda, so much so that she covered my eyes with her hands. Indeed, she was generally frightened of transparent objects, such as the window in the therapy-room door. It was as though transparency left her feeling that there was no protective barrier that could keep her from invading or being invaded (Rhode, 2000b). As Sodre (2002) has suggested, transparency implies the possibility of a "look inside" a space in which something frightening may be occurring.

From very early on, Linda showed me that she was concerned about how her own insides were put together, and that she felt that her internal structure was different from other people's. She genuinely believed that she was different from the rest of humankind, even in respect of her internal anatomy and the way her body worked. This was another emotional burden that she had to contend with.

As I have already mentioned, at the beginning of therapy Linda did in fact use her body in unusual ways. She shook it as though she literally wanted to empty it out; at other times she moved parts of her body as though she were trying to assemble herself or things inside herself in a way she found acceptable. She was very worried about things that could get into her body—I have described the magical finger movement that was, it turned out, supposed to protect her from germs. At other times she would show great anxiety if anything came out of her body—if she broke wind, she would try to get it back, and she would eat any mucus that came out of her nose. She was preoccupied with the faeces that she thought her body was full of, and sometimes she described them as "dead".

Linda often felt that explosions were going on inside her: "Fire is coming out of my mouth, my ears and my nose", she said. Sometimes she seemed to believe that these explosions fragmented her into countless tiny particles that might get lost, and, not surprisingly, she panicked. "Oh, come back, you runaway space particles" was the way she experienced a bad bout of tummy-ache.

Linda's attempts to understand and control her bodily functions were closely linked to beliefs about her parents' sexual relationship and her own conception. More often than not, as I have mentioned, she did not feel a member of the ordinary human race. She felt so different in comparison with others, so greatly at odds with them, so incapable of sharing their experience, that she was convinced that something must have gone very wrong when she was conceived to make her the way she was. Her daily experiences with classmates reinforced this feeling. She did not fit in at school; she felt different from the other children and could not make contact with them in a way that felt rewarding. (Indeed she once described school as a dark tunnel, with just two lights—"our two dinner ladies".)

Linda often talked about how she thought her life began. Her first descriptions were brief: "When I was a sperm, an asteroid hit the earth." A later version is more elaborate but still devoid of ordinary human relationships:

> LINDA: This is the London train . . . this is the London train . . . this is the London train. . . . It's going to X [the Latin American country where Linda's mother had come from; her father, it will be recalled, was English]. "It will go through a Channel, like the English Channel. The English Channel is under the sea, but it's not dripping, its only muddy. This is X, underground. There are fireflies underground . . . at the bottom. . . . Now two people are underground. . . .

Linda spent the rest of the session crashing the toy cars together, as though enacting a violent coming together of the "two people".

Later in treatment, Linda's accounts of conception and birth became less bizarre and more recognizably human, partly thanks to the pregnancy of Linda's paternal aunt:

> Linda crashed together two cars and an ambulance. She kept attacking the ambulance directly, but she insisted that the two cars were "evil". I asked in what way. She said that they were born evil and wrong. She crashed the cars into the box and said: "They've crashed into the bed now. The two evil cars have an engine malfunction."
>
> ME: Two cars with an engine malfunction have crashed into the bed together? It sounds a bit like a Mummy-car and a Daddy-car that have gone to bed with their equipment not working the right way, maybe to make a wrong sort of baby.
>
> LINDA: Yes. [She farted emphatically.]
>
> ME: That sounds as though a "wrong" sort of fart came out of the bed where the Mummy-car and Daddy-car with the malfunctioning engine were together.
>
> Linda got up and spat on the windowsill. I asked her what it was, and she said, "Come and see."
>
> ME: It's a spit.
>
> LINDA: Yes. . . . A shark.
>
> ME: You seem to feel you can see a dangerous shark in your spit.

The confused implications seem to be that two parents with malfunctioning reproductive equipment and "evil" intentions crashed into one another and produced a "wrong", smelly, dangerous shark–baby. As yet, Linda had no realistic concept of loving sexual reproduction.

In the following session the theme was developed further:

> Linda took two cars and an ambulance out of her box. "Now you'll see the chase", she said. She chased the cars around the desktop and finally made them fall off the "cliff". I reminded her that on the previous day she had said that the two cars were born "evil" and "wrong", and I asked why and how that was.
>
> LINDA: The sperm got into a wrong egg.
>
> ME: Why was the egg wrong?

LINDA: Because the Mummy's body forgot to make it good . . . to make the baby good . . . to grow it into a good person. . . .

Linda spoke with a great sense of sadness and loss. She looked at me, and could see that I was visibly moved. She carried on staring at me with an expression of complete disbelief. Struggling to find adequate words, I said that sometimes she felt she was completely bad and did not believe that she could grow into a good person; but that she and I knew there was more to her than just bad things.

Linda came close and touched me on the shoulder. She said, "May God be with you." This sounded like something off the television, but the emotion in it felt genuine. I thought Linda did not know what to do next: whether to persist in this new gentleness or to revert to her habit of being violent. I said, "Maybe now you're not sure whether to give me a hug or push me."

From then on in the session Linda was lost to me. She seemed unable at this point to bear her recognition that I felt for her, and she reverted to talking impenetrably about space and sharks. I wondered whether I could have supported her better by talking about the overwhelming newness of the way she had just felt.

At the very core of Linda's personality was her belief that she was created bad by two "malfunctioning" parents (Meltzer, 1988). She seemed to connect part of this "malfunction" with the fact that her mother was foreign, just as she herself so often felt a foreigner among people. She called her mother's South American country of origin "an old land" and said that this side of the family had reached Britain on "a Granny-ship whose propeller wasn't right". On the one hand, she seemed to be implying that her grandmother's equipment was faulty, just like the malfunctioning engines of the two "evil" cars, and that this was the reason her mother felt "foreign"; on the other hand, she also appeared to think that babies did their parents harm: for example, she said "infantstation" when she meant "infestation", as though infants were a plague of vermin. Not surprisingly, she was often worried about her mother's health.

Linda was shocked by the idea that I might see her as a desirable, "good" infant or child, with whose pain I could identify. It was an idea she seemed unable to grasp. In a session soon afterwards, we learnt more about her fear of grasping:

Linda asked me to look at the hairs on her arms. As I did so, she said:

LINDA: These aren't prickles . . . or poison. . . . I'll touch you now. . . . [She touched me.] "You see? not prickles, not poisonous. . . ."

ME: I can survive your touch, it's not poisonous. . . . It's only poisonous in your mind, in your thoughts.

Now that she felt more confident, Linda could show me that she had thought of herself as literally "untouchable". She was just beginning to dare to touch and to allow herself to be touched, both physically and emotionally. It is in the light of this session that I now understand my sense of recoil when I took Linda's hand in the waiting-room the very first time we met.

I wish to conclude with two contrasting vignettes: one from the beginning of Linda's therapy, the other after nearly two years' work. They illustrate the development of Linda's capacity to relate to me as a human being rather than a bizarre figure out of a nightmare.

The first exchange, at the beginning of Linda's treatment, took place just after I had collected her from the waiting-room:

LINDA: Electricity—the fish shoots electricity and immobilizes the other fish.

ME: When I say Hello in the waiting-room, you can't believe I'm not shooting electricity at you.

LINDA: The big fish opens its mouth and swallows the small fish.

ME: When I come to pick you up in the waiting-room, it's as though I opened my mouth to swallow you and bring you in here.

LINDA: There are poisonous fish that have prickles.

ME: Sometimes you don't believe I'm Mrs Nesic, you think I'm like a poisonous fish that has prickles—my words.

LINDA: The green African snake is green like a leaf.

ME: That means a dangerous snake looks like a leaf. You don't think you can tell whether I'm dangerous like a snake pretending to be an innocent leaf.

The second extract is from the last term of Linda's second year of psychotherapy:

Linda was sitting on the edge of the couch.

LINDA: I am sitting on a cliff, looking at the sea. No, it's an island. [She stretched out her feet towards me.] It's a bridge.

ME: It's a bridge between us.

LINDA: Hold my feet.

I did so:

ME: It's safe now.

LINDA: Make sure you don't let go. You are protecting me now.

ME: I'll do the best I can.

Later on in the session:

LINDA: I'll fly to the Antarctic now.

ME: Sometimes being with people is so hard—maybe penguins seem a good option.

Linda's plane crashed on the way to the Antarctic, and she phoned me from there:

LINDA: I am in trouble, I need help.

Linda's new-found capacity to allow herself to be helped has continued to stand her in good stead. She transferred to another therapist when her parents moved house and the journey to the clinic where I worked was no longer practical. She is doing well in mainstream school, has friends, and her life is no longer dominated by nightmare experiences.

Notes

1. This is an example of what Bion (1957, 1958) called a "bizarre object", in which part of the self has become lodged in and confused with an external object. In the present case, Linda's eyes have been lodged in the cushion, which, she might then feel, was watching her.

CHAPTER TEN

Hiding and learning to seek: becoming a somebody

Lynne Cudmore

When "Marco" came to psychotherapy, he had very little concept of being a "somebody". Discovering that he was somebody, that he could be separate and a person, was the central achievement of our work together.

Marco loved playing hide-and-seek, but for long periods his version of this game was about hiding, not seeking. He did not want to be found, to emerge into what felt to him a very unpredictable world. The idea that he possessed a mind of his own was inconceivable, because while he remained under cover, he could not discover anything about himself. This chapter describes the often painful and frustrating process for Marco and his therapist of discovering that he was somebody to discover.

Marco was 7 years old when he was referred by a child psychiatrist who had seen him at his parents' request. He described a child with an "excessive pedantic persona", a rigidity to his personality exemplified by an obsessive interest in tramcars and an enormous dislike of any change. He agreed with the diagnosis of Asperger's syndrome suggested by the educational psychologist at Marco's primary school. However, the psychiatrist also described a boy with a lively and imaginative side to his personality and was impressed by his evident curiosity and zest for life (see the discussion of curiosity in chapters 1 and 2).

Marco's parents were concerned about his consuming preoccupation with all sorts of vehicles that moved on tracks—trains, trolley buses, underground trains, and tramcars. He talked about these endlessly, and even when they made it clear that they wanted to talk about something else, he had the greatest difficulty in "changing track". While he seemed impervious to the effect he had on them, they felt he had a real grip on them and controlled them. He was particularly possessive of his mother and had always had great difficulty leaving her. This lack of any sense of reciprocity affected Marco's relationships outside home too, and he had never made a friend.

Mr Andrews, the child psychotherapist who assessed Marco, described his body and posture. "A boy with a physical frame that seemed so slight and scrunched up, as if crouched in a tiny corner where there was no space and he didn't dare give himself elbow-room." He noticed that Marco had a tendency to "play stupid", endlessly asking the adults questions to which he really knew the answer. He made others use their mind for him, instead of using his own. Yet Mr Andrews was encouraged by Marco's progress during the assessment. He began to play much more freely and imaginatively, conveying the energy and vitality that the psychiatrist had commented on. Mr Andrews recommended three-times-weekly psychotherapy, and Marco's concerned parents were keen to take up this offer. Marco was keen too as he had enjoyed his assessment sessions. I began work with him two months later, by which time Marco was 9.

History and first impressions

Marco's family moved to this country from Spain when he was 4 months old. He was the oldest of four children, all boys, who were each born two years apart. Following the move, his mother noticed that Marco cried continuously, and in his second year she began to worry that there was something wrong with him. She noticed that he had never babbled. At 2 years of age he attended the local child guidance unit and was diagnosed as dyspraxic. When he started primary school, his specific learning needs were recognized, and he received extra help in class.

I met Marco for the first time with his parents and Mr Andrews. First Marco and Mr Andrews met alone to say goodbye, then they joined his parents and me. As he came through the door, his smiling,

curious little face, "looking" for his new therapist, immediately engaged me. He was excited, full of anticipation, and as we all sat down
and started talking, he clearly enjoyed being the centre of attention
among all the grown-ups. This meeting felt a big occasion, a special
day. He was holding the cars he had been playing with in the other
room, and he spontaneously handed them over to Mr Andrews. He
was both acknowledging saying goodbye to them and accepting the
transfer to his new therapist. His generosity and his capacity to adapt
to this changeover impressed me. I had written the times and days
when he would be coming to see me on a piece of paper, and he
reached over to take it and proudly put it in his breast pocket. He
whispered to his Mum that there was something he wanted me to
know: she should tell me that when he grew up, he wanted to drive a
Land Rover on a farm. It felt as if he were letting me know the agenda
for his therapy. I was there to help him to grow up and "to be"
somebody.

When we started work, Marco was in a hurry. When I went to
collect him, he hurtled off to the therapy-room, barely glancing at me
or looking back at his parents. His physical presence had a marked
impact on me. His step was desperately uncoordinated: there was no
rhythm to his gait. He appeared almost bodiless, as though there were
nothing of substance at the centre of him that could anchor his head,
arms, and legs. He seemed a ragbag of appendages.

He showed a young child's delight at the contents of his box—
particularly the pens and pencils, because he liked drawing. He asked
me what each item was, though I was sure he knew, much as he had in
the assessment. This questioning had a kind of automatic "tumbling"
quality, as if he could not pause for a moment to look at a toy and think
about what it was. Metaphorically he "handed over" his mind. It felt as
though I was with a very young child who looked to a parent to name
something so that he could then repeat and sound the word and build
his language and his knowledge of the world.

His speech was characteristically indistinct, broken up, jumbled up.
He tripped over words, and he rarely spoke in sentences. His mouth
had a slack and floppy look; he often dribbled without noticing, the
saliva pouring out of his mouth. He could not form the words, shape
them, and contain them, so that they, too, spilled unformed out of his
mouth. I found myself studying it, wondering what it was that didn't
seem to work. Could a mouth that seemed so floppy and slack have fed
at the breast or bottle? Could he have had the experience of his lips and
tongue closing around the nipple or teat to create an enclosed space?

His dribbling and his unformed words gave me the impression that he had little concept of an inside place that could hold his bodily fluids and words, or a place inside his head that might contain thoughts. He presented as simple, even stupid, and very immature for his age.

At first he played with the Plasticine, making a series of little yellow ducks with blue scarves that waddled along the windowsill. I thought he had taken rather like a "duck to water" to this new therapy situation. Although he was clearly able to keep in mind the previous therapist, his room, and his toys, it felt as though he had somehow bypassed a beginning with me. There was no "paddling in the water", no tentative tasting of this new situation, no palpable anxiety about my being a new therapist for him. He seemed to have no concept of a threshold that would mark a boundary between outside and inside, between him and me. I remembered his father telling me in the introductory meeting that Marco couldn't use a knife and fork: he had to eat with his hands, as though asserting that he was one with his food. My experience of him at the beginning was similar to this. He just moved in, as though he had always been there with me and I were not a separate person.

However, the content of his play and drawings revealed an internal world dominated by scenarios of natural disasters and catastrophic anxieties. His first drawing was of a huge black tornado curling up the left-hand side of the page and looming overhead, threatening to break the lines of communication, the telephone wires. It graphically portrayed impending doom. In the middle of the picture he drew a little car, rubbed it out, and then made three attempts at placing it at different distances from the tornado. In the third session he ran around the room whipping up a terrible wind, shaking the cars in his hands. The cars ended up upside down on the couch, their wheels in the air. He told me that the tornado had broken everything, including the bridge, so he couldn't get home, and no one had heard his cries for help. At the start of each session he went straight to the dolls' house, which, he said, had been shaken by an earthquake in his absence. His drawing and play suggested difficulties with finding a perspective, a position at a manageable distance from the whirlwind of sensations inside himself that broke his links with the secure base of home and shook him to pieces. These breakages meant that he had no trust in the lines of communication to a caregiver, so he could not trust that any one could hear or respond to the cries for help of his baby self.

The transfer from Mr Andrews would have stirred up powerful feelings associated with the earlier disruptions in his life, but I believe that he was also communicating an internal disaster scenario, whereby links were broken, catastrophe loomed, and parental figures could not be relied upon to rescue. As I watched him enact these disasters, I was very conscious of the broken-up feel to the pattern of our appointments. They were on Mondays, Tuesdays, and Fridays, so Marco's therapy week had two two-day breaks. I talked to him about the days he came to see me and the days away, attempting to map the pattern of my presence and absence. I tried to establish an idea of a rhythm to our contact, a sense of which he seemed to desperately lack internally as he so graphically conveyed in his disjointed walk and talk. He repeated the days after me, and very slowly the idea began to emerge that presence and absence formed part of a process, as distinct from break-ups with disastrous consequences. He returned each time to check whether the baby ducks "were drying", again implying an ongoing process to our work. At length he drew a train with a smiling face steaming over a bridge held up by three supports. The support of the three sessions, of a "rhythm of safety" (Tustin, 1986), was in place for him.

Against this background, Marco represented the "stuckness" of his developmental difficulties. Cars ground to a halt and sank deeper and deeper into the mud. It required a double rope to pull them out, but even this broke. There was little sense of a reliable lifeline.

Marco reacted to the announcement of the first holiday break by excluding me from his play. I felt very put aside: he had communicated very effectively the feeling of being cast out. The hurt of the separation was also somatized. He developed a tummy-ache and woke up crying in the night. In the following session he told me his first dream: *The blue car*, which he called his "baby car", *had fallen off a cliff*. I told him that I was here to make sure that he did not fall, and I would return to him after the holidays. He put his head on my shoulder and rolled the car in my lap, and then he told me the pattern of the sessions in the week and the two-week gap at Christmas. Despite the disruptive holiday news, he had retained the pattern of our meetings in his mind and an idea of the "therapy lap" that was there for him.

Subsequently his play became wilder: cars skidded along the windowsill in an excited frenzy, unable to keep any grip on the road. There was no story line, and no properly mental activity. The play was mindless and almost unbearable to watch. I placed my hand on the cars and said that they needed help to calm down. I linked the cars that had lost their grip on the road and their sense of direction with Marco's feeling that he had lost his grip on Mrs Cudmore when his routine was going to be disrupted by the holiday break. I was not sure if he heard my words and the meaning of what I said, but he responded to my gesture. He said, "Hold them tight, the sun is shining in their eyes and they want to sleep." I thought he was letting me know how urgently he needed me to keep a firm grip on him and just how tenuous his own grip was. Following this, he talked about his feelings, "the states" he got into when his brothers went into his room and he felt invaded.[1]

Marco played that the cars were arguing: they wanted to go in different directions. I talked to him about the argument he might want to have with me over our separate directions at Christmas. He drew three planes that were all under attack from a warship: his time at the clinic felt under threat, and he was angry. Yet amidst all this he showed signs of believing that he could emerge into the light from a dark place. A drawing depicted a train disappearing into a tunnel and then reappearing, as though returning from the holidays.

In the last session before the break, Marco covered his hands with glue and then stuck his palm onto mine, surface to surface. I talked to him about his wish to stick us together in the face of the holiday separation, his way of keeping us connected (Bick, 1968). He then cut up a paper wheel into little bits and placed them into my hands. I talked to him about his cut-up feelings, his upset, and how he needed Mrs Cudmore to know about these feelings that he placed in my hands for safekeeping. I said that I would be holding onto Marco in my mind, remembering him in our time apart.

In this initial phase I was very struck by Marco's capacity to convey his very primitive anxieties through the medium of his play and drawings. He said very little, he hardly ever talked about himself, and he never began a sentence with "I". His problem seemed more than just the lack of an emotional vocabulary. It felt as though he had little awareness of himself as a person with emotions that emanated from a place inside him and little concept of a mental space, of a mind of his own that could think. He handed his drawings to me as though handing himself over, so that I would think about what he drew and discover the meaning for him. At this stage I did not know whether thinking himself was something that he could not do for lack of the basic building blocks, or something that he would not do. On the one hand, he behaved as though there were no meaning in the drawings he mechanically churned out. On the other hand, he sought me out as though he had an idea that I might "make" something of his drawings or his play. Similarly, from the beginning I talked to him about my understanding of what he did, but I often felt that there was "no place inside" him where my understanding might lodge. He felt as thin and two-dimensional (Meltzer, 1975a) as the paper on which he drew. My words seemed to trickle over his surface. I was often not even sure whether he had heard what I said, let alone understood it or realized that I was talking about him.

Holiday anxieties and hide-and-seek

After the break, Marco sellotaped three cars together and then joined them to a truck, which he asked me to hold in place on the table. He said that he needed to see whether the truck could hold on to the cars and prevent them from falling into the jaws of the crocodile waiting below. I said that the holiday gap had made him frightened of becoming unlinked from his three sessions and left to drop into a dangerous place where a crocodile might eat him. I said that I thought he wanted to test whether Mrs Cudmore was strong enough to hold the link with him, to hold on to our three meetings and prevent him from falling and being devoured.

Similarly, he tested out whether I would search for him and for things that mattered to him. He hid the cars for me to find, but he could not bear the suspense of waiting for me to do so. He did not trust me to persist in this task that felt so vital for him, so he told me immediately where the cars were to make sure I found them. I was still an extension of himself, not yet a separate person with whom he could play.

For many months Marco drew pages and pages of artillery: repetitive pictures of battles between armies who were often stuck in the mud. He possessed an encyclopaedic knowledge of army equipment and was fascinated with vehicles encased in their metal shells. He did not seem to notice my presence, so encased was he within his own shell (Tustin, 1972). When he did notice me, he hated my attempts to talk to him and think about what he was doing. He just wanted "to do it", he told me angrily, as though he could not understand the idea of a mental link. He felt as impenetrable as his armoured tanks. The aim of the battles in his drawings was to possess territory, and I experienced him as engaged in a take-over of my mind, as though I were to have no thoughts of my own and there were no space for two of us.

He related to my body in this same rather tyrannical way. He often wanted to sit on my lap, kiss me, or lick me or demanded that I touch his feet. He would get into a frenzy if I did not comply. These approaches did not feel like affection, more like an assertion of his rights in which my body was an appendage to be appropriated.

In one session he placed the toy-box on his head and tried to force my head inside it too. He often threw the rug over my head and tried to kiss me under it. This degree of intrusiveness and my resulting claustrophobia made me want to fend him off. It could be hard to find a sensitive way of suggesting that we could get close by talking together. Sometimes he seemed absolutely deaf to this; at other times, his sensuousness seemed motivated by affection, making it difficult not to sound rejecting.

After some months, Marco made up elaborate rules for another version of hide-and-seek. I was not allowed to look down or to enter areas of the room that were out of bounds. He barricaded himself under the chairs and ordered me to touch his feet, but if I managed to discover him, he shrank from contact with me. This was not a game about being found, with the attendant excitement and relief: it was a parody of hide-and-seek, an activity that led nowhere. I tried for hours to understand what he might be communicating, but again this enraged him: "Just do it!" he screeched. He could not yet tolerate two perspectives. When he let me get a word in, I described what he was doing, how he shrank from being discovered, how he ordered me around. At other times I just said firmly that enough was enough, and I was not going to take part in this activity. This firmer approach did seem to reach him. In one session he shouted "I'm stuck, I'm stuck. I need to be pulled out. I can't get out." I too often felt stuck and sinking into mindlessness.

Helpful limits:
private places, shared references, and self-reflection

With hindsight I wonder whether I endured this game for far too long. Trying to understand the content might have side-tracked me from focusing on the interaction between Marco and me and the mindless state I could get pulled into. It was difficult to get the balance right between helpful firmness and sensitivity: I did not want Marco to feel prematurely stripped of the protection, however illusory, that these rituals provided. When finally I did feel able to be firmer and began to resist his tyranny, he became a child who was much more frustrated and angry, but also much livelier. He grew aware of strong feelings, often feelings of hatred, and he began to express these feelings directly. Destruction and anger were no longer confined to the battle scenes he drew: they were part of our living relationship.

We began to develop shared references. I once used the term, "putting your receivers down", to describe how he covered his hands with his ears when he did not want to hear what I was saying—that way he could tune out when he felt cross with me or that I was not attuned to him. He was very taken with this metaphor, possibly because he understood it literally, as though he were a radio with receivers. I noticed that after this "aerials" appeared in his drawings of battleships or aircraft carriers. He proudly pointed them out to me, directing my attention to his receptive state of mind. He pretended to pull his aerials down over his head (turned off) or to put them up (turned on), as a way of letting me know whether he felt like listening. In this way, he began to notice when he was in a receptive state of mind and when he was not, and this became something we could think about together. He was beginning to be able to take a step sideways to pay attention to himself, just as I paid attention to him.

His drawings also began to feature windows, from which people looked out. He seemed now to have an idea of an inside place, from which there was an outlook. He began to have a view, and sometimes he would move alongside me to see what the view was from my angle. He realized that I could have a different point of view, and he was interested in it.

Tornadoes and earthquakes had disappeared from his drawings, along with the battles and armoured cars. Instead he drew domestic scenes: semi-detached houses where a little boy kicked a football in the garden. A little butterfly with a smiling face sometimes hovered in the blue sky. The roots of the trees were firmly embedded in the earth. These pictures were more colourful and lively, and Marco began to tell me about them, as though he had realized that they belonged to him. Sometimes he linked his drawings to events that were happening in his life outside the therapy. I felt this was an important new development.

Marco was able now to describe his own drawings, to make his own explorations, his own discoveries, to think for himself. I encouraged him to do this, though sometimes he hated it: the effort of it seemed too great. He often wanted me to do it for him, but I was beginning to realize that what he wanted and what he needed were now very different. It was time to "hand over" to him while remaining available if needed.

Doing more for himself helped Marco to develop a sense of his own potency, his own capacity, the idea of growth. I was struck by the preponderance of flowers in bud and then in bloom in his drawings. He drew two rather splendid express trains that he labelled Mr Marco Flying Scotsman Perez and Mrs Lynne Inter City Cudmore in which he really captured the movement of the trains. In another drawing, set in New York, he was the driver of a yellow cab, and I was the passenger sitting in the back, while he showed me the sights. This did not come over as bossiness, but as part of him taking charge, executive and potent. He really did seem to have started to "sight-see" for himself. He was shy at the different Marco represented in his drawings—"only pretend", he would reassure me hastily. It felt as if he were daring to wonder whether this really could be he. This self-consciousness was another new development. His imagination was beginning to flower.

I believe that these developments were related to his feeling more firmly rooted in the therapy. The primitive anxieties of falling and spilling and being swallowed up, so much a characteristic of the first year of his therapy, were no longer in evidence. Now, men tumbling out of a plane were drawn with parachutes attached. When he rolled the cars on the table, he asked me to place my hand at the edge to keep them safe. There was the beginning of a sense of an enclosed space. Traffic lights often featured in his drawings. The red light, the stop sign, seemed a recognition of the regulatory importance of my firm-ness. This acknowledgement placed a curb on his omnipotence and made him feel much safer about taking risks. I noticed that he became more physically adventurous, and with much encouragement— greatly resisted—he began to enjoy jumping by himself off a low surface. He seemed more physically robust; the bodiless little boy, that "ragbag of appendages" that I had first met, was changing. The sessions were often fun.

Coming out of the egg: growth, time, and change

Marco had mixed feelings about the notion of growth. Growth implies progress, but also change and the concept of time. Time implies the future, and with it the possibility of an ending. He told me that he was in Year 6; then he would move to big school, and after that to college. He attacked my watch, trying to pull off the winder: he said he wanted to change the time. He asked whether he would still be coming to see me when he was a hundred? He began to doubt it.

His social life outside therapy was widening too. In the first summer holiday he made friends at a play scheme, and for the first time in his life had children over to tea. He could now enjoy their company instead of seeing them as rivals, and he drew a bird feeding "all the babies" in the nest.[2] For the first time he let himself realize that I might see other children and was able to describe feelings about this: "horrid". The idea of a future had made him aware of his past, and he began to distinguish between his "old ways" and his "new ways". I felt very aware of the opposing forces in him: a push towards development was often accompanied by a wish to return to familiar routines. It made him anxious when I pointed out that he was doing something new, and I learnt not to do this. This fluctuation happened even in the course of a session, so that he could appear unstable. I noticed that Marco was more likely to resort to ritualistic activity at the start of the week or as breaks approached. The separations really mattered to him, and I think his rituals felt life-saving at these times.

At this time he played an ordinary version of hide-and-seek. He excluded me from the room at the beginning of sessions, then I was to come inside and look for him. I took my time finding him, dramatizing the situation, and he emerged from his hiding-place laughing. Then, just when I felt more confident that he was developing, he introduced what seemed like a regressive version. Lying on the couch under the rug, he asked how much of him I could see. He revealed a tiny bit of himself and withdrew the moment I glimpsed him. He repeated this endlessly. It felt as though he were luxuriating in the warmth, in the soft sensuous feel of the rug. However, he complained that he could not straighten his legs and still keep them covered. I pointed out that this was because he was growing. He was indignant.

From underneath the rug, Marco watched me watching him. I said perhaps he could not believe that he could hold my attention without fixing it on himself like this. After all, when he was right inside and covered up, it was not only he who was hidden. He could not get a view of me either, and we could not talk and find out about each other. Following this interpretation, he often begged to play hiding "one more time". It seemed important then to tell him that it was time to come out; that he had been underneath the cover long enough. Sometimes he was able to do so of his own accord: "I'm getting out", he shouted, "I'm coming out of the egg, I'm being born."

Being born meant facing new situations. Marco was visiting possible schools with a view to secondary transfer. He remained hypersensitive to change: even when he acknowledged an improvement, the fact of difference worried him. By this time things were different: he was able to make mental connections with me. When I named his fears, he was able to talk about them. He was aware of himself now as somebody who could have a whole range of feelings—loving and hating, happy and sad—which could be named and thought about.

Marco's new recognition of our separateness brought the first signs of real curiosity about me and, inevitably, frustrations, worries, and pain. He began to scan my face for my reactions—but without the intrusiveness of the "in my face" approaches of the early months. He questioned me about whether I had a family, where I lived, what I had for Christmas. He really wanted to know, but he could sometimes bear the frustration of not knowing without flying into a rage. Just as he had struggled to recognize that he could not commandeer my body, he began to realize that he could not force himself into my mind and know all its contents. He had a notion of privacy for himself too. He chose not to tell me what he had for Christmas: "it's a secret". There was a slight retaliatory tinge to this, but, more importantly, he had discovered that he did not have to tell me everything. If he were to modulate his feelings so that the "disasters of living" did not over-whelm him, he had to be able to shut things out (Alvarez, 1992a; Rustin, 1997a). The curtains in his drawings began to be opened in the morning and shut at night, which also implied a sense of rhythm and pattern.

Marco was much more settled, less manic, but increasingly lively. He could now be naughty and rebellious with his mother and myself. He started to tease me. From the beginning of therapy he had pressed the lift buttons on the way to my room. Now, as he approached them, he watched me watching him, as if he were registering that I was wondering what he would do. He realized that I had a mind and was interested in what went on in it. Instead of being stuck, he could move between different states of mind even within the space of a session.

His growing awareness of himself as "somebody" brought worries about what kind of somebody he was. He was more aware of being different from other children. For many weeks he laughed and pointed at me, mocking and contemptuous; I felt that he was treating me as he was treated at school, where his mother had told me he was bullied. He once brought a toy bat to his session and told me how he would love to take a real bat into school for everyone to admire. It felt very poignant. Later that week he told me that he could not imagine what he would be able to do when he grew up. He was worried about ever having to leave his Mummy and he wanted to stay the same age, like Peter Pan.

Growing meant having to fend for himself without being able to, and it frightened him.

One day at a tender moment he blew a kiss across the room to me. This was very touching, as his gesture acknowledged both our separateness and the link between us. It was very different from the insincerity and intrusiveness that sometimes accompanied his expressions of affection. A few sessions later, he made two chairs into a bridge, stretching the rug between them and saying that it that it needed to be anchored. At first the "bridge" flopped and his cars fell off, so he folded the rug in half to make it firmer. He moved his car towards me and wanted me to guide mine back to him: there was a coming and going, a to and fro, a reciprocity. The floppy bridge had reminded me of his floppy, slack mouth at the beginning of the therapy, when I had wondered how he could have held on to the nipple or teat. Normally a feeding baby would experience the nipple or teat as a link to the breast or bottle. Marco's floppiness and lack of grip might have impaired this sense of a potentially firm connection, leaving him exposed to catastrophic anxieties.

Now he realized that a bridge had to be firm and properly anchored, but he still wanted it to be as smooth as possible: "no bumps". I said that there were often bumps along the road when people travelled from one place to another, just as he would have all sorts of different feelings, which he might experience as bumps and disruptions, when he moved from one school to another. Marco placed a chair underneath the bridge to support it. He went under the rug "for a little rest", then said that he wanted to play at being born. He emerged from the rug, crawled like a baby, then practised standing and showed me how a toddler who was learning to walk would stagger as he risked his first steps. "This is growing up, all the different stages you go through", he told me. I talked to him about these important milestones, all of which he had negotiated, and about the next big step for him—the move to a new school. With a very determined look he leapt across the room. He seemed ready to take a big step forward.

* * *

After some two years of therapy, Marco's first session after a holiday seemed to encapsulate his achievements as well as his continuing struggles.

Marco studiously ignored me when I went to collect him, and I had to insist on his coming with me. He shut me out of the therapy-room; when I went in, he was hiding under the rug. I said that he might feel that I had been hidden from him over the holidays. He started to peep out, and I remarked that now he was back with me, he might be able to risk looking at me. The rug had slipped off; he got up and told me that it was a dinosaur game. I said I thought it was, but as this was his first time back and he was rather over-whelmed by lots of different feelings—shy, angry, excited when he saw me again—he just wanted to be safe under the rug. He asked if I remembered when he used to hide under there. "How old was I then?" he asked. I asked why he thought he used to do so much hiding. He answered, "so you could find me". I said that I thought he knew now that I would come and find him after I had been away. He asked how many years it was since he used to hide. He said he couldn't fit in there any more: "When I first came I could fit in there, but I can't now." I said that he had grown too big, but he was also letting me know that he didn't really need these dinosaur games any more, that he could do different things now that he was growing up. He was also showing me that he could know about a "then", he could look back at a Marco who did things in a particu-lar way and he could know about a "now", when he was different. I thought this sequence illustrated his developing capacity to ob-serve himself and to think about himself.

Marco wanted to massage my feet and felt very rejected when I said that he knew that was not allowed, but we could talk about his feelings. He said he was an aeroplane, and he fell on the floor with a bump. He seemed to be enacting a fantasy of being dropped.

He then questioned me about my holidays and was cross when I did not give him information. "Why don't you ever answer my questions?" he demanded. I said it made him cross when I didn't do as he wanted, but I was interested in the ideas he had and in what he imagined. "I'm not interested in my mind. I'm interested in your mind and what you're doing. I'm turning my mind off." He turned an imaginary switch off at the side of his head. "There we are, it's half off now." I said I was glad it was only half off, but I had noticed that the moment he switched off his own mind was when he was cross because he couldn't get into my mind. He said that if I asked him now what two and two were, he would say three. I said that was what happened when you switched your mind off. He said, "If I turned it on again, I could tell you that it was four." I said that I thought he switched his mind off quite a lot because he wanted to hear about my mind instead, to get inside it just as he had crawled under the rug, so he could get me to think it all out for him. . . .

Marco lay on the floor and looked up at the light; he asked why the lights were not working. He said that there was still a screw missing from the light, there was a hole. He went over to the switch and turned the light on: "It works." I asked if he knew of the expression, "a screw missing". He giggled, pointing to the side of his head and turning his finger round, then laughed, a slightly brittle, chilling laugh. I wondered if other children had taunted him with this expression, and I also thought of the mocking part of him that laughed unkindly at himself but also played the fool. I said that there had been something missing lately: I had been missing because of the holidays. I reminded him of what he had said about switching off his mind, getting rid of his own screws, preferring to rely on mine, and I thought there were times when he needed my "screws", my thoughts, to help things make sense.

Marco said he was going to put the screws back in, and he mimed a screwdriver doing so. He thought this was very funny. I said I thought he could often forget what he could do for himself. He went to the table and drew a heart. Inside he wrote "I love Mrs Cudmore from Marco." I said there was a very good feeling now about being back with a Mrs Cudmore whom he liked very much.[3]

Marco asked whether I had noticed that his voice was different, and that sometimes it squeaked. I said that I had noticed that his voice was changing, another sign of growing up perhaps.

Hearing a noise in the car park, he went to look out of the window. He wanted to know which my car was and then wondered where I lived. "Do you live over there?" (pointing to some houses). I said he was beginning to have an idea of a Mrs Cudmore who was not always at the Clinic. He sometimes thought of her being with other children, going places in her car, someone who could be with him and with other people too, who could do other things. . . .

Marco counted the black cars, the white cars, and the red cars. I said he was sorting the cars according to their colour, putting them into groups, noticing the differences. I said it made me wonder whether he was thinking about the differences between him and me. "You mean that I'm a boy and you're a girl?" he said. I agreed that that was one difference. Several times today he'd drawn attention to his growing size, his voice, his body: he was beginning to change from a boy into the man he was going to become. "Into a teenager", he said firmly. I said he had much more of an idea of a changing Marco. He said, "Now I'm in Year 7. Next year, Year 8. Goodbye to Year 7, Hello Year 8." He carried on listing the school years until he went to college or perhaps got a job. When he grew up, he wanted to be a fireman.

I felt that this session encapsulated many of Marco's developments during therapy. When I had met him two and a half years previously, he could not make connections, whether to me, to his play, or to his drawings. He had little awareness of himself as somebody, or of me as someone separate and different. This session illustrates the abiding lure of the "undercover" life and the pull towards living inside my mind. He oscillates between wanting to know more and turning away from knowing. But he also clearly demonstrates that now he knows that he does have a mind of his own and can use it: to feel, to observe, and to think. He connects with me and is more connected to himself. He has developed into a "somebody" who can be lively, engaging, and fun to be with.

Notes

1. This is an example of the way in which emotional impingement can be experienced in terms of sensory hypersensitivity, as discussed in the Introduction and the Endpiece.

2. The "nest of babies" fantasy is commonly met with in autistic spectrum disorder (Houzel, 2001b; Tustin, 1990). The child often feels overwhelmingly threatened by inchoate persecutory "entities". It is a measure of Marco's improvement that his feelings about imagined rivals were no more than "horrid" and that he could verbalize them.

3. This illustrates how working on the distress and anger stimulated by separation can put a child in touch with his capacity for affection, which ultimately derives from his relationship with his parents.

CHAPTER ELEVEN

The lure of a mad world: supporting a 10-year-old boy's capacity for ordinary contact

Michèle Stern

When I first met "Kane", he was 10 years old, a sturdy, slightly plump boy with dark eyes that hardly ever met mine. At that time, he insisted that he was an animal. He drew Disney cartoons with great speed and accuracy, and when he was in one of his "mad" states of mind, he behaved like a cartoon character. His eyes rolled in their sockets, his hair flew to right and left, furniture was sent crashing: there seemed no possibility of a sense of balance, let alone perspective. He appeared not to know where he was, where the therapy-room was, or even whether he was inside it or outside.

Kane's behaviour was making life a misery at home, and his primary school had not been able to cope with him. Although a psychological assessment had established that he was of superior intelligence, he was underachieving in all school subjects. He interfered with assembly by squealing and rolling about, he damaged his school equipment, and he objected strenuously when anyone used words that he had banned. Since these included words like "a" and "and", conversations were seriously disrupted. In class, he shouted out "rude" words like "poo" and "smelly feet". He lifted girls' skirts in the playground to look at their bottoms, and on once occasion he did the same to a teacher.

Kane was diagnosed with Asperger's syndrome by a clinical psychologist, and then by the child psychiatrist who referred him to me for intensive treatment. They noted his obsessive patterns of play, which never developed into a meaningful sequence, the equally obsessive quality of his ban on certain words, and the fact that he never referred to himself as "I". He was preoccupied with the spinning motion of the washing machine, which he watched for long periods and talked about compulsively. As I have noted, he avoided eye contact. His mother said that he had never had a friend, and this was confirmed by reports from the nurseries and schools Kane had attended. At the same time, the psychiatrist felt that Kane wanted to make contact but lacked the necessary empathic skills. Throughout the meeting Kane consistently interrupted the adults' conversation.

In his sessions, Kane revealed many of the catastrophic anxieties that have been described in children with autistic spectrum disorders, though it was difficult to focus on these because of his stream of confused and confusing talk. It took time to appreciate the level of anguish in this child, who was tormented by so many fears and talked about them in a non-communicative way, as though by not taking them quite seriously he could prevent catastrophe. I felt bombarded and found it extremely difficult to think. In the midst of this there were occasions when Kane showed that he was capable of good sense, insight, and reflection. My aim will be to illustrate and discuss his preoccupations, as well as some of the changes that were achieved in the course of our work together. In order to convey something of the effect of his stream of talk and the quality of our interaction, I shall quote at length from some of his sessions.

Background and history

Kane's family were descended from English and Scottish emigrants who had settled in Argentina many generations previously. They had continued to give their children English or English-sounding names, and Kane and his mother both remarked on the fact that his name sounded the same as Cain's in the Bible, though it was spelled differently. Kane's parents left Argentina at the time of the military junta, and Kane was born in Britain. There was a history of severe mental illness and marital breakdown on both sides of the family.

Kane was born somewhat prematurely, though his birth weight was not unduly low. He had had to remain in hospital for some weeks. Breastfeeding could not be established, but he took well to the bottle and was a good eater, though as an infant he was often irritable and did not sleep well. These sleeping difficulties worsened after a year, and Kane could never be put down to sleep alone. His motor milestones were very slightly delayed; he began to speak at the age of 1. He had a very brief stay in hospital for an infection when he was 2 years old.

Kane always found it hard to separate from his mother, and this contributed to a difficult time at nursery school. From an early age, Kane had loved listening to music, as do many children on the autistic spectrum. Sadly, he was too disruptive to take part in group activities of any kind. He did not listen to the teacher's instructions or imitate what the other children were doing; instead, he wandered off and "did his own thing".

At nursery school he was described as a loner, not joining in or playing, and talking to himself. His hearing was checked by the health visitor and was found to be normal. The other children called him naughty, but he did not seem aware of this or interested in them. However, he does appear to have been very tense, grinding his teeth and hitting things with a stick. At this stage he began to scream when frustrated in any way. This worsened and became a major problem at home.

When Kane was 3, he started at a different nursery, where he was described as "strange" and as not conforming. He did not communicate or join in, he did not obey instructions, and he made no eye contact. He began to be aggressive towards other children, hitting, pulling hair, and screaming if they came too near him. He generally appeared to be angry and cross. Separations became increasingly difficult, and a few months later he started to refuse school.

Kane had a keen eye for detail and often latched on to information in a way that fed the obsessive interests that are characteristic of Asperger's syndrome. He learned all kinds of facts about edible animals, especially about their internal organs. He also took on the identity of various animals and loved dressing up as one. This went beyond imaginative make-believe, since he insisted at primary school that the teacher should treat him as whatever animal he was being at that point. Adults can feel particularly disconcerted by the disjunction between behaviour that is normally playful and the child's driven quality. In my experience with other children who identified with animals, this can contribute to their carers' sense of bewilderment and helplessness.

Kane's mother seems to have felt torn between being worried by his increasingly bizarre behaviour and seeing it as a sign of talented eccentricity. Indeed, many of the professionals involved with Kane emphasized his intelligence and quickness, particularly his high verbal ability. The family history of severe mental illness would have made it difficult for his parents to be ordinarily and constructively worried by Kane's behaviour without immediately thinking that he must be going mad. Kane was in fact sensitive to other people's opinion of him; it distressed him not to be liked by his classmates and their parents. At school he would attempt to separate other children who were holding hands, but he would also try for a while to curb his behaviour. However, mother and father disagreed over how much firmness was appropriate. In particular, mother seemed concerned that an occasional smack might escalate into serious violence. The parents had separated some years before Kane was referred, and mother lived with a partner whose attitude towards Kane was understanding and paternal.

Throughout my work with Kane, I made a point of keeping in touch with his mother by means of weekly telephone conversations, as well as termly reviews together with the colleague who saw her regularly. Both my colleague and I visited Kane's special school and spoke to his teachers on the telephone. This degree of contact was essential in promoting cooperation between all the adults concerned with Kane's welfare. Without it, a child whose behaviour is so puzzling can easily create a situation in which parents and professionals all feel that they are struggling alone and unsupported. This can mean that the child receives inconsistent messages. At best, this increases his confusion; at worst, he may blame himself for setting the adults against each other.

Kane's first session: "hideous idiots"

One of Kane's chief preoccupations—about living at other people's expense—was prominent in his first session.

When I met him in the waiting-room, he avoided eye contact with me. In my room he explained that there was something I ought to know: sometimes he liked being an animal, and then he liked being called by the animal's name. At the moment he was a badger. He had toy animals that came from the house he used to live in: some of them carried things in their mouths, wasn't that sweet? I said these animals from the old house were precious animals, and he agreed. He examined the animals in his toy-box and said that the calves did not like being touched, as they had been hurt when they were little, so children were not allowed to touch them. All the while he was looking past me rather than at me. I said that perhaps it felt strange being here with someone he didn't know, and that this might make it hard to have a good look at me. Kane explained that he had a problem looking straight at people; he preferred to look at people and things sideways. This did not really sound like an explanation that was meant to help me to understand him: more like a fact about his identity that was not to be explored further. In fact, when I said that perhaps it could feel a bit easier to look at people sideways, he talked over my words and drowned them out.

He said that the calves had been called "hideous" when they were babies—he pronounced it so that it sounded like "idiots". Now they were in a new place where they would be safe. I said that perhaps he was wondering whether this place was safe, and he said that the other lady (the psychotherapist who had assessed him) had been kind to him, so it was a safe place.

Kane made a dog out of Plasticine and said it had the same name as one of his toys at home. He got out all the other animals in the box and was particularly pleased with the baby kangaroo. The doll children got hold of the baby animals, and the animal parents intervened fiercely to get their offspring back. They seemed to be suspicious of what would happen between the children and the baby animals. The baby piglets were feeding from their mother. Kane looked agitated and said he was thirsty. I said it was as if the baby piglets drinking from their mother had made him think about his own Mummy, and wish for a drink himself. He agreed, and repeated urgently that he needed a drink. He asked doubtfully whether the beakers in the box were clean, and he looked relieved when I said that he could use one of the cups from the tea set if he preferred to. He filled it with water from the tap and drank, sucking thirstily from the cup. . . .

Kane found the male lion and said that he didn't like him, because he was King of the Beasts and he didn't like the idea of the lion being king over the dogs and badgers. One of the doll children went to play with a lion cub, but the father lion killed it, then was killed in his turn, though Kane said he had only fainted. He decided to feed some meat—red Plasticine—to the lion; then he said that the meat was actually a baby otter. The lion savaged it, and Kane asked me quite provocatively whether I felt sorry for the baby otter?—but the lion did have to eat, after all. He smeared the red Plasticine on the lion cubs' chops. Then he showed me the baby otter again and again asked whether I was sorry for it, pointing out the lions' tooth marks. I said that something quite savage seemed to be going on, something to do with life and death: the life of the baby otter as against the life of the lion cubs, who needed food. Maybe he needed me to know that sometimes things felt very savage to him. He said that the baby otter was coming back to life, and it did, but was savaged to death again; this was repeated several times. I said it was like a nightmare, being killed again and again. Kane agreed and said he had had a nightmare the previous night: about *his favourite ball, which he took to bed with him, his "tomato ball". He was crying, and the more he cried, the smaller the ball became, and that made him cry even more.* I said that that meant the ball hadn't been there to comfort him when he needed it most. He agreed but quickly said that then *the ball was inflated and got bigger and bigger,* and he added, somewhat hesitantly, that he liked that. It felt a bit like a magical solution to the sadness of the dream.

I wondered whether he thought I would be able to manage if he ever felt sad here, or did I just want to see a happy boy. Kane ignored my words but made a mother otter out of Plasticine. She attacked the lion, who completely destroyed her. Kane held both the otters right in front of my face and asked me, again quite provocatively, "What about that, then, do you feel sad for the two otters?" I said it seemed a terrible situation, and he agreed. He found the fences and arranged them vaguely around the animals, but without consistently separating the lions from the otters.

In this session Kane showed me his pleasure at the idea of a baby kangaroo with a place in its mother's pouch. The theme of vulnerable creatures who have been hurt as babies is linked to their supposed "hideousness", which in turn is confused with "idiocy". This suggests that Kane was aware of being different, and it makes one wonder about whether other children had taunted him with being an idiot. The statement that the calves had been "hurt as babies" does not, of course, imply that this was Kane's actual experience, though his stay in a special care unit after birth could well have left him with a degree of vulnerability (Cohen, 2003). What it does indicate is that in his personal attempt to make meaning of his condition he linked being an "idiot" with infantile vulnerability and the feeling of being ugly.

In his play, parent animals looked after their babies, sometimes at the cost of their own lives; but they also prevented them from having relationships with the doll children. It was hard to tell whether this was sensibly cautious or destructively possessive. Kane's urgent and agitated need for a drink in reaction to the toy piglets being suckled indicates how precarious was his hold on the "pretend", symbolic aspect of play. Indeed, while play is generally children's preferred medium for working through their anxieties, Kane's play sequences with the lions and otters did not lead to a resolution of his worry that one baby's growth meant another baby's death. This is the kind of anxiety that is often met with in youngest or only children, who can hold themselves responsible for the fact that no babies were born after them; the more general theme of living at someone else's expense has been described in children with autistic spectrum disorder (Rhode, 1997b; Tustin, 1972) as well as in some anorexias (Rhode, 2002; Tustin, 1958, 1981b). It is a theme that recurred throughout Kane's therapy.

One of the most striking features of this session is the way in which Kane related to me. Those comments that seemed to get through to him were comments about the animals—for instance, when he agreed that the otters were in a terrible situation. This way of speaking to some extent defused the provocativeness of his question as to what I thought of the killing that was going on: I felt that he was both communicating to me what it was like to be helpless in the face of torture and also setting me up to condemn the lion, who was, after all, acting according to his nature and looking after his cubs. Either way I would be neglecting an essential point of view, and Kane may similarly have felt that any choice he made was bound to be wrong.

Kane easily launched himself into narrations that were a way of keeping me at a distance rather than a meaningful communication. An example was the way he picked up on my use of the word "nightmare" and seamlessly incorporated it into his own train of thought. It had the effect of keeping me out, but by means of devices that Tustin (1981b) termed confusional and entangling to distinguish children who used them from the "shell-type" children of classical Kanner's syndrome. He half agreed with my reflection on what his dream must have felt like but quickly moved on to a magical way of dealing with it. It may be that the feeling was too painful, or that he did not yet trust me enough to allow me to get through to him. The way he talked over me when I tried to explore the reason he did not make eye contact was another instance: he had presented me with his preference as though it were a fact about his identity, not something to be thought about.

In the course of our work together, Kane became able to risk contact for longer periods, even though it meant communicating some very painful feelings. I will illustrate some of these developments by quoting from three sessions. The first took place before the first holiday break; the second, 15 months later; and the third, just before we stopped work after some three years because Kane was going to boarding-school.

Before the first holiday:
in and out of contact

Kane was about to go on a plane journey by himself, to visit his father, whom he had not seen for some time. He had been very frightened of making this journey, saying that the door lock on the plane might fail and he might get sucked out and fall to his death. The extracts I quote illustrate something of the oscillation between ordinary contact and bizarre confusion that was typical of Kane at this time.

> The waiting-room was very crowded and chaotic. Kane was standing in the middle of it making a lot of noise; he had thrown pencils and large plastic bricks all over the place. He shouted, "Oh no" when he saw me and violently threw a teddy-bear onto the floor. His mother soothed him, and he came with me; it all felt a bit as though he had been going through the motions of misbehaving. Kane giggled to himself, looking a bit mad, with his eyes all over the place. I had to point out to him that we had reached my room.

> Kane seized his box in both hands and swung it across the room, screaming loudly, "motorcycle sidecar" (this is what he had always called his box, possibly because of its shiny plastic surface; he tended to think of it as a world in which confusing and cruel things happened). The box fell on its side, and he paused so that I could unlock it. He said that he had something to talk about today: what really worried him was that some people might say that animals always stood up, or only stretched out on their backs or sides. He knew that wasn't true, they also stretched out face down some-

times, but he was worried that some people might say they didn't. Kane's voice trailed off, and I felt that he was miles away. Then he said, "That's something that's the trouble with me." I acknowledged that he felt troubled. Hoping to help him re-connect with me, I asked whether shouting "motorcycle sidecar" and throwing his box about had been meant to show me that he was troubled?

Kane giggled, making crazy faces again. "No, it wasn't." The only trouble concerned the position in which animals stretched out. He had a thing about that; maybe he hadn't told me? I said indeed he had, many times in fact (it was something he talked about in most sessions). Perhaps, I suggested, he thought that was what interested me, not thinking about him and how he felt, and what his shouting might mean, both here and in the waiting-room.

Kane tried to answer but seemed to be confusing the therapy-room with the waiting-room. I pointed this out, and he agreed that he was confused about which was which. I talked about the chaos in the waiting-room. Kane said he had not thrown the pencils on the floor, but he had made the bricks crash. He sounded quite frightened. I said maybe the waiting-room had felt like a crazy place today, with all the people in there and the things all over the floor. "Yes", he agreed, sounding more steady.

He returned to the animals, but I persisted in talking about his own feelings, in the waiting-room as well as here, and said that that was what really mattered. After a while, I mentioned the approaching holiday: could he believe that he had a place in my mind and that I would remember him? Kane immediately talked about the space in his own mind: his step-father said it was 50% filled up with nonsense. There was a pause, and he said he knew what I was thinking: that it was time to stop now. I said no, it wasn't, not yet, and wondered aloud why he had thought that. What did he think was happening in my mind when there was a silence? He said that I was either counting to ten so as not to get angry and say silly things, or I was thinking about animals, or I was thinking about . . . (his voice trailed off again). I said maybe it was difficult for him to believe I was thinking about him and his feelings.

Kane started quizzing me: would I feel sorry if an animal got killed? I felt that he was trying to get me to join in his obsessions. I said that perhaps what he really wanted to know was whether his own feelings were more important to me than these animals. I added that it was he I was concerned about: that he was my patient, not the animals. Immediately I felt I had made a mistake by not taking the animals as an aspect of himself: he was slipping again into being silly, with a slow, "stupid" grin spreading over his face. I said how difficult it was for him to hear that I thought his feelings were important. He agreed, again sounding more firm and grounded.

He then made a Plasticine wolf, very rapidly and skilfully. I commented that it looked like his drawing of the wolf howling to the moon. He answered that that was what it was: could I read his mind? I said no, I could not read his mind, but I remembered that he had drawn it many times before. He was slipping again into being silly and talking nonsense. I spoke about how it felt to stop for the holiday, what his feelings might be about seeing his father and missing his mother perhaps.

Kane took two Plasticine "monster" creatures he had made during a previous session and linked their tails. On the one side was a very thin wolf, on the other a little mouse, both without hind legs. They were pulling in opposite directions. Kane said they couldn't do anything good because they were stuck together. Then the big wolf bit through the linked tails. Kane said that now the thin wolf and the mouse could grow back legs and start looking after themselves. He added scornfully, "Like Mummy and Daddy, when they grow up." I said perhaps also like Mummy and he; and maybe he was worried about being stuck like that with me in the therapy, too. He did not answer but quickly and very skilfully made the animals' hind legs.

Then the big wolf brought food for the thin one, "so that it gets stronger and fatter", he said. They went hunting together and killed an otter, but Kane said they were not being cruel: they were killing it quickly because they needed to eat. I said that I understood that they needed the food in order to survive. He then asked me whether I felt sorry for the otter. I thought that Kane was confusing eating with cannibalism. As in the first session, it seemed impossible for him to get what he needed without feeling like a murderer. He slipped the little mouse down the spout back into the teapot—for safekeeping, it seemed.

Then he said, "But the wolves have killed a little boy, ten otters . . ." followed by a whole list of animals. He started giggling and seemed to be slipping again into a mad flight of ideas. He became "sillier", saying that the therapy food I gave him had gone all bad, the eggs had gone bad, the sausages had turned to poo, and so on.

I said that he was worried that the things we talked about would turn bad for him. He replied, sounding more sober again, that things always turned bad. It was nearly the end of the session; he said it was difficult to stop. I agreed that it was difficult to think about holidays and stopping. He said he was not scared any more about being sucked out of the aeroplane during the journey to his father, and I agreed that that was progress. Immediately he reverted to silliness. I said how difficult it was to stop this session. When it was time to go, he didn't move. When I got up, he sat in my chair, saying he wanted to be me for a while. He parodied my words and accent, with quite a touching quality. Then he got up, saying that he was going to be himself again. He was silly and giggly, and I asked whether that was what he meant by being himself—going back to his nonsense? Yes, he answered: that was being himself. I said it was sad that at the end of the session he felt he had to back into nonsense. He shrugged and giggled.

This session illustrates the ebb and flow of contact between us, as well as some of the factors that made it easier or harder for Kane to stay in touch instead of veering off into a world of his own. He responded well when his feelings were addressed straightforwardly (for example, that he had experienced the waiting-room as a mad place, and that it was hard to believe I really cared about his feelings). On the other hand, he could feel frightened when I understood him, since it felt like a magical process of having his mind read. The theme from the first session about living and growing by killing others was still present. This was obviously something that Kane was really worried about, though he attempted to deal with his worry by setting me up as someone who condoned killing ("They've killed a boy, ten otters, etc.") He spun off into mad-sounding talk both when he was frightened by the chaos in the waiting-room and when he was worried about murderous eating, although he was sometimes able to explore the extent of his own responsibility (he had made the bricks crash, but hadn't thrown the pencils).

Kane was showing himself to be capable of an impressive degree of self-reflection—for instance, when he said that he was no longer frightened of being sucked out of the plane; or that it was hard to end the session and that he thought being me might feel easier; or that things always turned out badly for him. This was a serious, painful statement, and not surprisingly he could not tolerate such extreme distress for a whole session. Viewed from this perspective, his mad talk could be seen as a way of distancing himself from painful feelings while at the same time conveying to me a powerful sense of confusion, incomprehensibility, and helplessness. There is only one instance, however, of the device he relied on much more in his first session—that of incorporating something I said seamlessly into a story of his own. This instance involved his taking what I said about a space in my mind and immediately applying it to his own mind. Similarly, when he thought of what I might be thinking when I was silent (counting to ten, and so on), he attributed his own obsessions to me and eliminated the fact that we were separate people.

Separation, as he showed at the end, was extremely painful to Kane. On the other hand, being physically linked—like the wolf and mouse—prevented independence and development. Kane was scornful of his parents, which left him in the position of having no adult internal presences to support him. The mouse and wolf linked by their tails could be seen as representing two aspects of his personality at odds with each other—the vulnerable mouse (like the calves or the baby kangaroo of the first session) and the predatory wolf. Kane seemed to feel that the alternative to being completely vulnerable was to be destructive, and then turned to "mad" behaviour to escape from guilt. His moments of insight were often followed by a relapse into silliness.

At this point, trying to understand the meaning of Kane's "animals stretching out" would have felt like getting drawn into the mad world of his obsessions. Later in our work together, some of the meaning became clearer. As I have said, early in treatment Kane still insisted that he was an animal. Indeed, he told me how horrified he had been to look in a mirror and see himself reflected as a boy, though he thought he could hear the swish of a tail behind him, which meant that he must be an animal after all. We might speculate that the animal's tail would have fulfilled the same function of a bodily link as did the tails of the thin wolf and the mouse—a link that was both a reassurance (against falling out of an aeroplane, for instance) and an obstacle to development and independence.

Kane did, however, increasingly develop fantasies concerning the body image of human beings—both himself and me. He drew a picture of me with a tummy full of babies with smiling faces, a fantasy that is generally conscious only in much younger children (Klein, 1932). He also drew pictures of his own body as a system of pipes. Tustin (1986) and David Rosenfeld (1984) have both written about patients with such a body image, which they considered to be the most fundamental and primitive of any described.

Helpless babies and the hole in the mother

The following session, 15 months into treatment, shows how the animals with tails have evolved into gorillas with many human qualities. By this time, Kane still made a token show of mad behaviour in the waiting-room but sobered up very quickly in response to a firm tone of voice and to my insistence on entering the therapy-room and opening the box in an orderly way.

> In the previous session, he had cut gorilla shapes out of paper and clamped them between his box and the lid, so that the bottom half was inside the closed box while the top half hung out. He immediately began to talk about the poor gorillas who had spent all that time—since the last session—stuck in the box. He said they were very unhappy hanging down like that—you could tell by their faces. He drew more sad-looking gorillas, one with a prominent tummy-button. I described their sad faces, and their arms hanging down, not holding on to anything. He said it was because of the weight of the motorcycle sidecar lid on their chests. I said, "It's so heavy they can't do anything, they're like helpless little babies." He laid them on the table and said they were lying down on their tummies now. During the first part of the session he repeated everything he said, as though echoing himself.
>
> I reflected that the gorillas were lying on their tummies: they couldn't look at anything, their arms were hanging down, they seemed to be feeling bad. I mimed how they looked and how I thought they might feel. I compared them to little babies coming out of their Mummy's tummy and feeling there was nothing to hold on to. Kane agreed: he said the sheet of paper was a Mummy-sheet, with a hole in it where the baby gorillas had been. I said the

gorillas seemed to imagine they had left their Mummy with a hole in her when they were born. Kane listened very attentively.

I said we knew he found it hard to leave things: the waiting-room when he was playing with something, and the therapy-room at the end of the session. Did he feel that he left a hole in me? He said the motorcycle sidecar was a trap, where motorcycle-sidecar creatures were to hurt the gorillas. I said perhaps the gorillas felt sad about leaving the Mummy with a hole, and now they felt trapped: no good time for them, no good feeling that things were OK, that they were allowed to be born and to enjoy life. Kane spoke kindly to the gorilla in the box: "Don't stay like that, making yourself upset, come and enjoy what there is to enjoy." He explained that a friend had said that to him.

Kane explained that the gorillas liked each other—and him too, they *had* to like him, otherwise they would feel so jealous. He said that he wouldn't want to be a woman having a baby and have pipes and things coming out of her vagina; much better not to grow up. He was still echoing himself at the end of sentences. I reminded him of a time when he had said there was a big mess inside tummies. This seemed to be the mess the baby left after being born, so that things did not connect up properly and function as they should—liver, kidneys, intestines, and the rest. Kane found a gorilla whose arm was coming off, and with my help he mended it with Sellotape. He remarked on the mess in his box.

Kane said again that the gorillas were lying on their tummies. I wondered whether that helped them not to feel the absence of the cord that used to link them to their Mummy. Perhaps the strong, steady ground made their tummies feel all right, not empty or wounded around their belly button. After this exchange, Kane stopped echoing himself. He explained to me that the box had interesting things in it after all, though they were mixed up with the rubbish, and that the gorillas would go and explore.

They spent the rest of the session exploring, and Kane discovered equipment he had not realized he had. He asked me where I had bought the box—had I gone to a shop? I said maybe he wondered whether I thought of what he would like when I had got the things together. He stopped quietly when it was time and walked calmly back to the waiting-room.

Children on the autistic spectrum often suffer terrors concerning bodily mutilation of various kinds (Haag, 2000; Tustin, 1986), which tend to be expressed in terms of a physical link to the caregiver that has been torn away. Tustin's patients felt that they lost part of their mouth (Tustin, 1972); that they had left a hole in the mother when they were born (Tustin, 1990)—similarly to Joyce McDougall's (1986) idea of the "cork child"—or that their body had come apart down the middle. This idea has been developed by Haag, who has also described the children's experience of losing limbs. Some children, like Kane, seem to experience the rupture in terms of a lost umbilical link (Rhode, 1997b, 1997c). It is interesting that Kane stopped echoing himself after we had talked about these feelings of the gorillas: as though he no longer needed to compensate for the sense of bodily truncation by doubling up his words (Haag, 1984).

Kane's gorillas are not unlike the tiny baby described by Cornwell (1983), who was comforted by the feeling of a firm mattress against her tummy but seemed to fall apart when lying on her back. While the stretched-out animals of Kane's obsessions seemed to belong to an incomprehensible, alien world, gorillas are closely related to human beings, and their experience is easier to grasp. Kane's choice of gorillas in this session is a measure of how far he had moved towards joining the shared human world: he no longer needed to dress up his extreme vulnerability in a disguise of "madness".

It turned out that one reason for Kane's wish to be an animal concerned his fear that he was responsible for messing up the whole world, including his parents' relationship. His father had told him off for making a mess shortly before his parents separated, and Kane was convinced that there must be a causal connection. He became preoccupied with dog mess on the street, thinking it must be human mess and that there was so much of it in the world that there would be no clean grass for cows to eat. He often dwelt repetitively on these obsessions in the early months of treatment. It was not until much later that he felt safe enough to make plain the fairly ordinary, though intensely painful, human anxieties that underlay them.

Ending treatment

Kane increasingly wished to join the world of shared human experience, and more and more often felt safe enough to do so for a time. He made efforts to adapt at school, which paid off in terms of his peer relationships and his academic performance. At home, however, he still required his parents to adapt to his version of reality; often this meant going through rituals designed to humiliate them. As he grew bigger, they became increasingly alarmed by his verbal and physical aggression and no longer felt that they could enforce order. It became clear that it would be better both for him and for them if he were placed in a specialized residential setting.

Inevitably Kane felt that I was abandoning him. We did a lot of work on what I felt was his justified hatred of me for leaving the job unfinished; acknowledging his point of view allowed him to say that he did hate me, but not all the time. He felt despair about what there would be time to sort out, and often reverted to silliness, which, he agreed, felt safer. Sometimes he touched objects compulsively. When I asked him why, he explained that there was a voice in his head telling him that if he did not do as he was told, he would become "what he did not want to be". It seemed that he was turning to compulsive acts to protect himself against this destructive voice, instead of obeying it at once by becoming "crazy" as he had done previously.

> In one of his last sessions, I found Kane in the waiting-room covering sheets of paper in large letters: "I am the King"; "I am the Queen"; "Mrs Stern is a fucking bitch". After we had negotiated our way to the room, he became involved in sorting out and reviewing his old drawings. "In those days", he said, "I drew lots of teeth, and poo". He found a drawing of a badger and said that he used to think he was lots of different animals. I said I remembered: he had found it very difficult to be himself. He agreed. I said that maybe he felt that he had changed since then, and we talked about his having found it so hard to just be himself. He said he used to think there was a monster in the washing machine that made a noise—"rrrr". He wasn't scared of that any more.
>
> Then he found a little book, which we both identified as being the first thing he had made in therapy. On the back cover was the picture of me with lots of smiling babies in my tummy. He opened it and looked a bit shocked when he saw "I am not Kane" scribbled all over the page. After a while, I said yes, that was just what we were saying: in those days he did not want to be a person. He agreed, adding, "I have changed quite a lot." At once he corrected himself: "In some ways I have changed—a bit."

I said it was true that we also needed to keep in mind the part of him that did not really want to change, that found it too difficult and painful: that part of him was important too. Specifically, he might feel that he had left a part of himself in the waiting-room— the one that had written all those angry things on scraps of paper. It was important for us to think about every part of him, good bits as well as not-so-good bits, because all of them needed to be thought about—the whole of that was what made up Kane.

He cupped his cheeks in his hands, looking me straight in the eye. His own eyes were full of tears. I said gently how hard it was to feel that there were some things that were not yet right. He carried on gazing at me while seeming to block his ears. I felt so moved by the look in his eyes that I stretched out my hand and touched his shoulder. He said, "I can't hear a word you're saying." Then he began to shout. Other people understood, but not me: maybe I didn't want to, I was useless. "How come you don't think? You must be brain-damaged. I won't even miss you—anyone can see you're no good."

In my wish at the end of therapy to help Kane as much as possible with his feelings of despair, I may have been asking him to remain in touch with them for longer than he could tolerate. He reacted by blocking me out. I became the one who could not think, who was useless and "brain-damaged".

The ending was hard for both of us. I could only hope that living in an orderly environment with a high level of individual attention would provide him with the security of knowing that he could not wreak havoc, and that this would allow him to stand up to the under-mining voice in his mind and to show that he had indeed changed more than just "a bit".

CHAPTER TWELVE

"I need my scripts": A boy with Asperger's syndrome entering adolescence

Jane Cassidy

This chapter focuses on the treatment of "Jonathan", a pubertal boy with a diagnosis of Asperger's syndrome. He had psychoanalytic psychotherapy for nearly three years, three times weekly, during the course which his behaviour changed markedly.

It has been noted that puberty and adolescence present opportunities for useful work with young people who are diagnosed on the autistic spectrum (Howlin, 1997). The relationship with his psychotherapist at this time of Jonathan's life seemed to afford him the opportunity to take a somewhat different developmental path from the one he had been set on. Finding that difficult situations could be managed, and that his very strong projections could be responded to helpfully, were significant factors in enabling him to begin to feel differently about himself, and, most particularly, to feel more secure in the face of his anxiety and aggressive impulses.

Whatever Jonathan's underlying neurological difficulties may have been, his improvement in a number of areas suggests that he had some interest in the unconscious meaning of his behaviour, which changed through his relationship with his psychotherapist.

In Jonathan's case, early family trauma may have contributed to the feeling that the world of relationships was dangerous and to his need to take control. His controlling behaviour, in turn, elicited anger from adults; this fed into a view of himself as different, unacceptable, and of little worth. There was evidence from early meetings with the family that he misinterpreted his parents' anxiety and concern as disapproval and that he had internalized this view as fact.

The result was that Jonathan was both unskilled and unpractised at managing separation and change. He saw separation as dangerous, and his behaviour showed extreme anxiety about being abandoned. This highly agitated state of mind left him unable to distinguish between small and large changes—all appeared to him to be disastrous. His attempts to manage his anxieties seemed to take up all his mental capacity and to contribute substantially to inhibitions in his cognitive development as well as in his emotional life. He kept his mind out of touch with what could be thought of as everyday change by means of self-distraction and disruptive behaviour. The lack of concentration did not allow much integrated mental activity and seems likely to have contributed to his literalness and his apparent lack of imagination.

Referral, diagnosis, and early history

Jonathan was referred at the age of 9 to his local Child and Adolescent Mental Health Service (CAMHS), where he and his parents were seen for nearly six months before he was referred on for intensive psychoanalytic psychotherapy. His complex treatment and clinical history included a diagnosis of Asperger's syndrome by a child psychiatrist. Jonathan suffered from sub-clinical epileptic discharge at night, which interfered with restful sleep and was controlled with medication. The hospital believed his pattern of difficulties to be of a neurological origin, and they investigated the possibility of brain lesions when he was very young. He had specific learning difficulties and dyspraxia, and poor relationships with teachers and peers, and he appeared not to notice pain in himself or in others. His parents thought that he hurt other children because he did not realize what it felt like for them. Both parents were puzzled that he should laugh when he saw people stumble or fall and said that he simply did not understand.

Jonathan was born nearly two months premature, and he spent his first weeks of life in the special care baby unit. Both parents were professionals who had been hit hard by the distressing circumstances of his birth. They saw him as organically impaired and devoted themselves to finding all possible resources to support him. Early consultations revealed the all-too-familiar pattern of parents worn down by the struggle to understand their child and to find appropriate services to help them (Klauber, 1998).

His mother had a miscarriage when Jonathan was 2 years old, and by the time he was 6, they had given up any thought of a second child. His mother was struggling to maintain boundaries at home. Father described himself as calmer and more forceful with Jonathan, while mother depended on her husband and mother-in-law for support. Beneath an apparent acceptance of their situation, both were angry at the perceived lack of help from professionals and were eager to tell their story and to communicate their distress. They were, in fact, themselves divided in their approach to Jonathan, who treated his mother badly. He was better behaved, though placatory, with his father. In early meetings, he showed how sensitive he was about his father telling him what to do. Though superficially he appeared to be obedient, he rebelled covertly, for example by secretly damaging a table top in the consulting-room. He was like a toddler, seeking affectionate cuddles on his father's lap while simultaneously telling tales of hitting and parental arguments.

Beginning treatment:
"stickiness" and fears about space

I would like to convey the atmosphere at the beginning of treatment by quoting from a family session when a colleague and I met Jonathan and his parents just before I began seeing him for three-times-weekly psychotherapy.

At the age of 10, Jonathan was a slim, attractive boy. His parents seemed anxious about what he might do, as though they feared that he might get out of control. Everyone seemed to be watching each other in a tense atmosphere.

His parents began by describing the current crisis at his primary school, which had rejected a support assistant for Jonathan so that he could be just like the other children. Jonathan tried to disentangle two pieces of fencing from the toy-box, then asked in an incredulous tone whether the pens worked. He began to draw and to cut out triangles, and marked the vertices *a, b,* and *c,* while his mother described the difficulties at school in a whisper, as though he would not notice that she was talking about him. When we encouraged her to speak in her normal tone, since Jonathan was undoubtedly listening, he angrily tore into pieces a large rectangle he had been cutting out. Then he appeared to try to change the subject by asking me what colour certain pens were; he said the colour he wanted wasn't there. He had begun to draw shapes reminiscent of the marks on the toy giraffe. He began to put crosses through them and said that he disliked his teacher and wanted to leave the session. When we told him it wasn't time to go, he asked to play football with his father (something they both enjoyed and which was used as a reward). When I took up how much he might dislike changing from the old clinic to here, he rapidly revealed, with only a little encouragement, how much he had enjoyed those sessions, that he liked feeling understood and agreed with me that he didn't like all the talk about his difficulties and did not want to change to a new place and new clinicians. Then it seemed that everything got too intense for him, and he began to throw a soft ball around with increasing force, until it hit the light, and he became very excited. He threw it at my colleague, just missing her, and both his parents tried to stop him getting anxious. He was furious when my colleague took away the ball and said that that was enough: she said that she thought it could be very frightening for him to continue to do these things without knowing when or how to stop.

Jonathan made a strange noise, half laughing, half crying, and seemed to be trying to produce tears. He fell silent and looked sulky. His mother denied he was sulking and implied that this idea was unfair and too harsh. His father said that he ignored Jonathan when he was like this: after a few minutes, he would come and apologize and ask for a hug, and then they would talk about what he had done wrong.

Jonathan hid behind his mother and said that he wanted to go home. There were still ten minutes left. We discussed practical arrangements for his sessions, and Jonathan recovered to ask my colleague whether she would be there, looking disappointed when she said that I would be his psychotherapist. He immediately got into a battle about whether he would come by taxi or train and announced that he wouldn't come if it weren't by taxi.

This early family session served as an introduction to some recurring themes. I shall refer later to the "sticky" quality of Jonathan's eye contact: there was a first glimpse of it in the way he looked at me and, perhaps, an indication of the entangled feelings in the family that went with it. His unwillingness to be different from the adults, and his need to control their decisions, are also clear. His difficulty in remaining focused on a subject that evoked difficult feelings emerges in the way he threw the ball around, distracting everyone and also, I thought, trying to locate any discomfort in other people. Such distractibility on Jonathan's part, and his reliance on distracting tactics to avoid situations that he did not like, were probably an important component of his learning difficulties.

Learning from experience, and being able to concentrate step by step, always entails some degree of uncertainty and anxiety. If these cannot be managed, the child can feel increasingly alienated and "different". Jonathan's sulky cajoling, and the sense of menace he emanated when he was prevented from leaving the room, are subjects to which I return in connection with the impact of puberty.

I focus on three main themes from Jonathan's therapy. These are his "stickiness" and difficulty in negotiating time and space in a realistic way; the nature of his learning difficulties; and, finally, a number of developmental issues linked with the onset of adolescence.

Difficulties in distinguishing self and other

Jonathan formed a rapid attachment to me, which felt somewhat uncomfortable. He showed no normal wariness and came physically inappropriately close, apparently unaware of my real existence as a separate person. He leaned against me in a way that would be acceptable in a toddler but not in a 10-year-old; he trod on my feet without seeming to notice. He behaved as though there were no space between us. When he made eye contact, his gaze felt as though he were clinging to me and he was having to tear his eyes away rather than simply looking in a different direction. This was the "sticky" quality to which I referred earlier. Esther Bick (1968) has described the way in which babies, and older people in a vulnerable state, can use vision in order literally to "attach" themselves to other people or to things—a theme that Tustin (1981b) developed in relation to what she called the "tactile" use of vision, which is more properly the sensory modality suited to relating to objects and to people across a gap.

This "sticky" looking linked to Jonathan's difficulty in believing that he and I could continue to exist as separate people when we were not in actual or apparent physical contact (Bick, 1968; Tustin, 1972). In his first session he asked where the therapist he had seen in the other clinic had gone—did she stop because she had retired? Then he interjected, "I don't like talking", and asked about my colleague in this new clinic. "She said she'd come." (She had been clear that she would not.) He avoided eye contact with me, concentrating instead on sticking a label to his chest, and he insisted that he could take the label away with him at the end. In his second session he wanted to play football but then acknowledged that he hadn't liked not being able to take the label with him. He stuck it back on his chest and asked about the "rules of psychotherapy", as he called them, so that he could write them out and stick them on the wall. He refused to include one "rule" (or fact): that there would be breaks at Christmas, at Easter, and in the summer, just like at school. "No" he said, "I don't think I'll put that on the list". Then he said that he would write it down, but very quickly, and he immediately asked whether my colleague would come to tell him off for sticking the paper on the wall. Was he wasting the sticky tape? Then he hesitated over how to describe my role: he wanted me to be his friend rather than his therapist, as though a relationship that allowed for differences between the generations must mean that I was not friendly or on his side. He did not want to leave at the end of the time and grimaced as we walked down the corridor. Then he hurled himself along to the waiting-room and at his mother, as though obliterating the fact that he had ever been away or that he and she were separate individuals (Tustin, 1981b). The enmeshed twosomes he formed with me and his mother co-existed with a developing relationship to my colleague in his mind. He often referred to her as Mr and not Mrs, and he was both enraged and sometimes relieved by the idea of her representing part of an adult couple with me. At this point his idea of this couple was certainly not benign.

It seemed to me that Jonathan spent a lot of time obliterating evidence of the space that existed between himself and others, a space that could be crossed by ordinary looking or by verbal communication. (See also Zara's "death gap" in chapter 5, this volume, and Donna Williams's, 1992, description of this experience.) He did not really look, and I think he did relatively little listening, which made managing beginnings and endings, partings and reunions more difficult for him. He remained desperately anxious or, as often happened, furiously indignant that the world did not actually operate in the way he said that it did or should (Tustin, 1981b).

Jonathan's behaviour was often over-excited, and he reacted to most experiences as though they were "larger than life", whether for good or ill. There were no half-measures. I had to learn, over time, that I needed to be very steady and consistent in order to enable him to calm down, though I often felt pulled into the drama and provoked into premature and thoughtless action. I frequently felt anxious, powerless, and frustrated, and my initial liking for Jonathan began to give way to ambivalence. He was so determined and insistent that we did things his way that my frustration easily turned to moments of dislike, and I began to sympathize with his teachers and to understand why they found him so difficult. I had to keep reminding myself that this excessively controlling behaviour, which could often leave me feeling wiped out, was a communication of his own extreme anxiety whenever he was not in charge.

Frances Tustin described autism as a "psychobiological protective manoeuvre" (1981b). She identified a distinct group of children whom she called "confusional children" to distinguish them from the "encapsulated shell-like children" who had Kanner's autism. These "confusional children" have much in common with those originally described by Hans Asperger (1944) (see Introduction and chapters 2, 3, and 4), and many of the characteristics of both groupings apply to Jonathan. Confusional children were clumsy, made strange eye contact, and responded to people in an undiscriminating way, nuzzling up like pets or "sinking into people". They were not the quiet, gentle, beautiful children described by others (e.g. Meltzer et al., 1975); rather, they were hyperactive, odd, and seemed often to be extremely disturbed. On all these counts, Jonathan resembled Asperger's boys.

Frances Tustin came to think that the confusional children's way of dealing with the terrors they associated with separation was to become enmeshed with their mothers and with other significant adults. She described an over-sensual relationship between mother and infant in which mothers could not think of other ways of comforting their child. Tustin noted that this kind of excessive sensuality did not encourage the development of the infant's internal capacities to manage separation. Such children found it hard to believe that relationships could continue (in mind or imagination) in the absence of actual physical contact. The result was a concrete, enmeshed attachment and an inability to tolerate separation. She explained that the confusional children she treated used the image of a hole to convey the experience of bodily separateness, which for them felt traumatic, like a physical wound. It was this traumatic experience of separateness, she thought, from which they had to protect themselves. Asperger, too, commented on his patients' inability to tolerate separation, as shown by their extreme homesickness (see chapters 1 and 3). Children like this devote so much effort to fending off the awareness of bodily separateness that there is very little opportunity to help them get used to it. At moments when it does impinge, they can feel devastated. They may react with panicky impulsiveness, expressing their feelings physically and concretely.

Jonathan's headlong run from me "into" his mother, at the end of his session, had this quality. Such concreteness in relation to separation has a profound effect on the development of mental activity, including thought and the use of the imagination. It is the imagination that helps to surmount the experience of separation and loss. Instead of the sense of catastrophe that loss can bring with it, particularly for a helpless and dependent infant, the mental capacities, which have grown within the mindful relationship of mother and baby, allow us to *imagine* the existence of the other person. We realize that, though they may be absent, they continue to know about us, care for us, and keep us in mind. This imaginative capacity was not yet developed in Jonathan, who could not play imaginatively when I first saw him. Separation therefore actually was a catastrophe for him, since he experienced it as a complete loss of contact without being able to imagine a loving reunion. Instead, he entangled himself with his mother—and with other people—in the belief that this could keep him stuck to them and therefore safe. Naturally, this was transferred onto Jonathan's relationship with me: he could not manage an appropriate distance between us (Rey, 1979; Rhode, 2000b). Indeed, at those times when he invaded my personal space, my thoughts would become chaotic and sometimes panic-stricken. On reflection, I think that I was beginning to sense his terror about separateness, which might endanger his very survival. From the beginning of our work, he was extremely anxious lest any third party should intrude, which to him felt like coming between us. He seemed to hope that sticking to rules, sticking on labels, would somehow help him to feel that he knew where he was—a much more extreme version of the reassurance we can all derive from predictable routines.

This phase of the therapy was pervaded by a striking sense of hostility. I have wondered how far this might have reflected Jonathan's very early experience of being born before he was ready (Cohen, 2003) and of then being subjected to invasive medical procedures. These were necessary to his survival but could well have been misunderstood as the impingements of a hostile environment. His parents' complaints about inadequate support and resources may well have been accurate, but they also conveyed the degree of their own traumatization. This would have interfered with their capacity to contain and process this particular baby's pervasive sense of anxiety and fragility.

Concentration: the capacity to play and to symbolize

Jonathan had some learning difficulties, but he maintained his position in mainstream school, with partial attendance at an on-site unit. Perhaps, as Bruce Perry (Perry et al., 1995) writes, ". . . dissociation allows one to maintain or even diminish internal states of physiological hyper-arousal, thereby allowing cognitive activity and problem-solving at a higher level of capability than would be possible in a state of absolute terror." (See also Caroline Polmear's description of her patient's better ability to perform mental arithmetic when less emotionally integrated—chapter 5.) Cognitive tasks such as arithmetical computation may have taken Jonathan's mind off his states of anxiety and could therefore have become a way of cutting himself off from awareness of his feelings (Youell, 1999). However, he was left foundering when he attempted anything other than highly mechanical repetitive tasks, particularly if this involved sophisticated language. He seemed unable to comprehend such language or to tolerate the degree of uncertainty implicit in any but the most basic questions.

Jonathan had little belief in his own ego strength and frequently denigrated some of his genuine abilities. This lack of self-esteem was combined with a refusal to do much for himself. As he settled into his therapy, the more cruel and demanding side to Jonathan's personality began to emerge: he became more aggressive and controlling, imperiously bossy and contemptuous. I began to wonder whether he became nastier when he was more frightened, but it was hard to keep this possibility in mind when he behaved in a way that provoked dislike rather than sympathy.

Jonathan frequently claimed to have forgotten how to do things. When I was able to react in a cool, neutral manner, he usually acknowledged that he could remember what to do. If I seemed exasperated, or too eager to encourage, he would become stubborn and refuse to try; it was as though, at such times, he felt that he had to be able to manage for my sake, rather than for his own.

He filled his sessions with endless and monotonous "games" of football, which served as a means of avoiding contact with me or with difficult feelings. These activities seemed to be used in the same way as "autistic objects" (Tustin, 1981a)—that is, as a means of denying physical separateness and as a source of reassurance. (Similarly, Paul Barrows, 2001, has described an autistic child's use of stories as autistic objects.) I began to think that I was colluding with something noncommunicative, although at times Jonathan may have felt the predictability to be essential. I noticed that if I joined in, he could become very excited—and, I now believe, frightened of it. I seemed to have become caught up in something that prevented me from observing and thinking. As I ceased to join in, I came under greater pressure from Jonathan, who attempted to persuade, bully, or negotiate to get me to agree to join in for a bit of time. When I continued to resist, the games finally began to develop: he became able to use words to describe a game of football that he seemed to have pictured mentally. The feeling in the room changed. It was clear that something new had been created, and that he was not merely repeating some activity ritualistically. (See also the discussion of this issue with respect to Olivia and Marco, in chapters 8 and 10, respectively.) My attempt to create my own mental space to think about whether or not his activity was meaningful seemed to have led to a small but significant development (Bion, 1962).

Gradually, sessions began to include occasional moments of fun, when Jonathan's spontaneous actions took him by surprise and he enjoyed himself. He hated the moment ending, he and tried desperately to get it back by repeating the same actions again and again. Sadly, of course, the more he repeated the game, the more deadened it became. The lively spontaneity had thrilled him, but he had no understanding that such moments come unbidden into the mind when it feels sufficiently free and safe to allow space for an idea or thought to emerge (Alvarez, 1992b).

Relatively early on in the treatment, Jonathan introduced an imaginary companion into his sessions—an important proto-imaginative development. This character was called Manninger, after an actual goalkeeper. In Jonathan's mind, he seemed to be both goalkeeper and manager—a pun on his name perhaps, and certainly an emphasis on the executive capacities of a male figure. Manninger appeared in sessions when Jonathan seemed to be feeling vulnerable. He would tell me that Manninger had arrived and would sit having an inaudible, imaginary conversation with him at other end of room in a way that ostentatiously excluded me from this private dialogue. As I endured the exclusion, Jonathan felt provoked and began to be bossier in his determination to be the one in control. His ability to cut off from feelings about my significance to him and the fact that I came and went and had other relationships—sessions only on three days of the working week—was being challenged, and his defences were working less well. This more ordinary oedipal situation, and the recognition that I was part of a couple, could not be addressed until much more had developed.

At length there came a session when he told me what to do, clearly *pretending* to be my teacher. The feeling of playfulness in the room was quite different from his previous need for control. He was playing. I commented on this—"Oh, you're the teacher now"—and he responded with a delighted smile. As these tiny seedlings of imaginative and playful life appeared, so did an arrogant bully persona, also sometimes in the guise of a teacher, who was harsh and who treated his student—me—very cruelly. The bully had strong views about a weak and "little" child/student. Working with Jonathan was extremely difficult, and my energy and patience were easily exhausted. (I later came to think that this corresponded to one of his fears: namely, that he wore out his parents and teachers and made them give up on him.)

"I need my scripts":
conflicts in the face of development of play and imagination

After several months, Jonathan was a little more able to tolerate that I knew that he did not understand everything and that, like other people, he might need help. The disabling limits to his imagination became increasingly clear. He brought some homework: he was to write a play based on scenes from C. S. Lewis's *The Lion, the Witch and the Wardrobe*. He was very worried about not being able to do it. Although he had brought the problem, he did not really believe that I could help him with it or understand his fear, and he became very anxious.

Jonathan went to the door and pretended to open it. He said flatly, "We're in Narnia." He walked across the room, turned, and looked at me, completely lost and stuck. I said, "So. This is Narnia. Brrr, it's cold, isn't it?" and I pretended to shiver. Jonathan smiled and repeated in a monotone, "Brrr, it's cold", and tried to shiver too. . . . I asked him what he could see. Again he looked paralysed and blank and shrugged helplessly. I suggested, rather too enthusiastically, "Maybe trees and snow?" He repeated without conviction, "Trees and snow. . . ." I wondered where the witch would be. He shrugged. . . . He asked me to read from the script, and I said that perhaps he wanted to know what was coming next in this pretend game, so that he knew what to expect. (This was by now a familiar process. He would suddenly freeze, fearing that whatever pretend activity he was engaged in had become literally real and terrifying.) Jonathan nodded . . . he picked up all his pieces of paper, and the dolls and the lion. "I need my scripts", he said, but he could not manage to hold them all. I wondered aloud if he could make up the words as we went along, but he clutched the papers: "No", he pleaded, sounding panic-stricken. I said he seemed to need to hold onto everything tight, to help him feel safe in this new, strange place. He nodded and went through the door, saying, "Brrr, it's cold, isn't it?" This time, he said he could see trees and snow. I waited a bit, then wondered if he could see anything else.

"Swings and slides!" he cried triumphantly after some time. He turned back and then hesitated, as if lost again. He looked at me, suddenly worried: "Can we play football now?"

It became increasingly clear from my countertransference that there was a recognizable moment that could be identified just before his flight from a new, imaginative game. This enabled me to take up his anxiety and to find ways of helping him to notice that such play might be less frightening than he feared, and that he could stay with it if he could imagine I could be helpful. In this way, I was assisting a process of building experiences of play. These could begin to lead to the realization that his mind was capable of lively activity—something to which he could turn when he was in a panic or alone; and that this, perhaps, was a better and more interesting resource than the repetitive lists of team members and scores that had previously constituted what he called "playing football". There were many moments of panic and retreat when he believed the play was real, and I actually became a witch in his mind; he would feel overwhelmed and take flight into obsessional play again.

Jonathan was developmentally at the emotional level of a toddler, and, as such, he desperately needed an adult with him who would not panic, or retaliate when toddler omnipotence and control threatened a safer sense of the adult being in charge. It felt intensely important to maintain the right psychological and physical distance and to be aware that my facial expression and tone of voice were being monitored for any signs of rejection, intolerance, or disapproval (Alvarez, 1999a).

Change continued to be extremely problematic for Jonathan, as it can be for toddlers. He behaved as though separation were a catastrophe: he had had little practice at it and therefore did not expect people and things to continue to exist in his absence, to return or be returned to. Recognizing his own need for a predictable adult presence did not please the part of him that was convinced that the world was full of cruelty and that adults sought to humiliate children—a view with which he readily identified as the bully in his sessions.

As I have mentioned, Jonathan's fear of separateness often led him to intrude into my physical and mental space to a degree that could make me feel like running out of the room. It took time to be able to think about this in a way that increased my understanding of him. One aspect of this was the degree of Jonathan's attunement to my state of mind. He knew, for example, the exact second when my concentration was not fully on him, and he would react to this, usually by demanding something of me. Having his back to me seemed to make no difference: it was as though he had antenna-like eyes and ears in the back of his head. (See also Marco and Adam, in chapters 10 and 13, respectively, and Endpiece.)

Jonathan's invasiveness short-circuited any possibility of developing ways to maintain contact across time and space. This requires some tolerance of separateness and the realization that it does not imply a cruel or deliberate exclusion. I felt considerably challenged by the intrusiveness, which foreclosed on the possibility that separateness could be borne or could bring with it the joys of reunion or the pleasures of the imagination. Sometimes there seemed to be something deeply cold about his view of relationships. At other times, his vulnerability was more obvious: he seemed to confuse anxiety with being bad and could only look for confirmation of his fear of being hated, rather than for evidence that he was likeable. All this took place against a background of the onset of puberty and of the move to secondary school.

The concept of the third dimension:
adolescence, aggression, and excitement

Bringing Jonathan into contact with his emotions meant facing the pervasive anxiety that he so desperately avoided. Alvarez's description (1999b, p. 62) of tiny temperature changes causing the melting of a glacier, bringing " . . . great cascades of ice, sometimes twenty storeys tall, crashing down", provides a vivid image of what it felt like. Jonathan was changing school, entering puberty, and, with the progress he was making, his old strategies for avoiding anxiety were working less well.

He began to make sexual "jokes" and occasionally to ask questions in a way that suggested some curiosity (see also chapter 1). It was difficult to be sure, since he diverted himself by getting excited by feelings and information that he did not understand and which disturbed him. He naturally felt vulnerable and exposed and found it difficult not to revert either to his obsessive games or to the familiar role of bully.

Puberty was accompanied by the challenges of the final year of primary school, where, like his peers, he had to wait for an appropriate secondary school place. He was due to take SATs (statutory achievement tests) and was terrified of public failure. At school he appeared to be wild and uncaring, causing mayhem, just as he seemed set on provoking me. It was as though the uncertainties and the fear of change and loss led him to provoke me, as well as the school, to exclude him. Perhaps this felt like achieving some sort of control over an uncontrollable process.

Alongside the almost unbearable challenging behaviour, there were some tender moments when he could acknowledge his vulnerability and neediness, and I was in touch with feelings of protectiveness and warmth towards him. However, at moments of closeness I frequently felt a sudden chilling sense of alarm. This feeling invariably heralded a physical attack, as though Jonathan did not know how else to regulate emotional closeness. It was not clear whether any feeling of dependency made him fear rejection or whether he was resisting a pull towards fusion, which could mean a loss of identity. He may also have been confused by intense infantile feelings becoming sexualized and feeling out of his control.

There was one difficult session, near to a planned break, when he got physically close to me after being very cut off and began to look very sad. I was feeling warm towards him, and suddenly he lunged at my foot with a pencil—I was wearing sandals, and a bandaged toe was visible. The only warning that allowed me to avoid injury was a sudden sense that the sad atmosphere felt quite coldly creepy. The attack felt full of calculated hatred. His attack on my "weak spot" may have stemmed from a fear of any weakness in himself; alternatively, he may have held himself responsible for anything wrong with me and tried to disprove this fear by eliciting a firm reaction (see Endpiece).

Jonathan had always had a tendency to become over-excited. With the onset of adolescence, the situation became more complex, as he began to get excited by fear, pain, and exclusion. The sensuality had become erotized and frightening. He frequently rushed to the toilet, where he seemed to need to evacuate his panic and hide from expected retaliation.

The self-loathing and fear escalated; Jonathan appeared to be addicted to provocation, and it was difficult not to feel drawn into being critical and feeling and sounding punitive. Then came a session that began in a state of high excitement and ended rather unexpectedly. Jonathan dislodged a piece of metal from a chair and began kicking it harder and harder, until he kicked it so hard at the window that it chipped the glass. He became simultaneously over-excited and terrified; he tried to climb up my leg like a frightened puppy, then got excited and could not stop pressing himself into me. I held him away from me and, panic-stricken, he rushed out, tried to open the doors to other rooms, and hurtled back towards me down the corridor. I said that I would I place my chair near to the door, as running out was not good for him. He collapsed in real distress, which rapidly transformed again as he began to rub himself with a hand in his trouser pocket. I finally found words to talk about the muddle when he could not distinguish between closeness and feeling sexy: not being able to stop making himself more excited made him very frightened. He became very still, went to the desk, and frantically drew a cube, and another, and another, slowing down and calming as we reached the end of the session.

The cube had appeared before. Jonathan had struggled with drawing it and had often retreated to two-dimensionality and other diversions. It was a wonderful moment when he had first succeeded, though accompanied by high anxiety. With hindsight, I think that his ability to find the third dimension, wobbly though it was, indicated a further step in the development of his imaginative capacity and a developing confidence in the existence of a space in his mind where things, people, and memories could be stored and accessed (Britton, 1989; Meltzer, 1975a). It was impressive that, after the volcanically powerful sequence of events I have described, he remembered the cube drawing and could use it to settle himself.

The turbulence of this session illustrates vividly the terrifying mental and physical upheaval of adolescence for a boy who had not really entered the latency period (Alvarez, 1992a). He had spent very little actual time in the social development that is so crucial at primary school. He was strongly attracted to "odd-balls" and disturbed children, often mimicking them and somehow conveying either that he feared being as odd as they were, or that he could use them to mock "oddness" and difference.

The transition to secondary school: opportunities for growth

Working on two issues in Jonathan's external circumstances helped him to achieve greater clarity about what he was and was not responsible for. His mother began to work part-time, so that he had to come by himself in a taxi to one of his sessions, which he managed despite recurring panic. In addition, his father sustained a leg injury and could not play football with him. Again, a real situation assisted greatly in sorting out that he was not responsible for the injury, nor would there be any punishment. He could even begin to say that he felt nervous about taking a taxi by himself—first identifying a feeling in his tummy as if he had real butterflies in there, and then linking it with feelings of fear and anxiety. He spent some time making paper butterflies: the metaphorical meaning seemed to get established alongside this physical activity, just as real external challenges helped him to be clear about the difference between reality and his imagination.

I still faced many sessions with dread. The following excerpt is from another pivotal session:

"As soon as he enters the room, he is aggressive and verbally abusive. He swears at me and tries to kick me; I feel a strong dislike of his behaviour and a sense of despair. I want to give up on him: I've just had enough. I think to myself that I will end the session if he kicks me, and I realize that I like this idea.

I sit for a moment or two contemplating the relief in ideas of escape. Then I think this is entirely the wrong thing to do. It is imperative that I do not give up. If I do, he will think that he always knew I would, and that he too need not struggle further.

I say firmly that he knows he is annoying me, he knows how to do that, but I will not let him hurt me. I add that I will not let him run out of the room, but neither will I any longer tolerate his treating me like this. He looks at me, hostile, angry, and frightened. His shirt is hanging out of his trousers, and he looks highly disturbed. I am exhausted but feel determined. We stare at each other quite hard for a time. At last he sits down. He draws a cube, slightly misshapen. He says his drawing is crap and asks me to help him. After he asks for help with his drawing, I say that he seems to feel better when he knows I want him to stay in the room with me. He then succeeds in creating an origami boat, which he has tried, and failed, to do for several weeks."

It was essential to stand up to Jonathan and to stand by him. His vulnerability and the precarious sense of confidence that he was developing are self-evident. So is the paradox that adolescence was both his terror and his salvation. The need to change schools and the fact that he was having psychotherapy linked powerfully with the catalytic effect of puberty. This meant an increase in all kinds of risk, and also a window of opportunity. Jonathan's excited reaction when things went wrong for him, together with a cynical belief in the cruelty of relationships that imply loss, separation, and reunion, made it very difficult to maintain contact with him. He had to face the real difference between himself and other children in his mainstream school (having a base in a special unit within his secondary school provided much-needed support.) Girls were sexually interesting to him before he had had any real experience of friendship with either sex. There was a dangerous period when, outside his family, I was probably his closest social contact— and it was not surprising that I was supposed to be his possession, friend, future partner, and mother figure.

At the same time, there was a more ordinary side to Jonathan's personality. He genuinely seemed relieved by calm, thoughtful responses. There were obvious developments in what he could do, and in his capacity to use his mind. The cold pleasure in human suffering that Asperger remarked on seemed to be truly modified by non-retaliatory contact. It was difficult for me to achieve the necessary non-retaliatory state of mind, because I also well understood the magnetic pull he felt towards enacting cruelty and rejection.

Towards the end of our work together I came to admire Jonathan for his courage in struggling to give up habitual coping devices that had seemed protective to his vulnerable infant self. His ego strength grew with his greater confidence in a benign figure. He regularly said that he felt comfortable in his sessions, and that we were doing teamwork. Indeed, over time he had become able to work with me in a more ordinary way.

His parents reported attending a parents' evening at which teachers praised his effort and achievements, which was a new experience for them. Jonathan repeatedly asked his mother whether she was pleased with him, which made me appreciate the genuine importance of knowing that I too shared the pleasure in his growing capacities. I came to understand how difficult it is for the parents of young people like him to feel ordinary pleasure in their children without bracing themselves for the next crisis.

Spontaneous pleasure was difficult for Jonathan as well, and was linked to normal adolescent self-consciousness. He responded well when he realized I would not collapse under his pressure. He needed slowing down, steadying, and encouraging when he withdrew in despair. Regulation was a significant factor. Anything unusual could feel as though all familiar structure had collapsed. His increasing insight into his own behaviour enabled him to stand up to real bullies at school, who took great pleasure in encouraging his misbehaviour for their own entertainment and in locating many of their own adolescent difficulties in this vulnerable boy. He became increasingly aware that holiday breaks increased the temptation to identify with a cruel, invulnerable figure that would feel no need of me. With help, he was able to battle against this internal voice and to sustain better his capacity to manage by himself.

By the end of treatment, Jonathan seemed to be both more robust and more vulnerable—in his healthy sensitivity to himself and to others. When we finished the work, he seemed not unlike a number of boys who experience some social difficulties and shyness and who tend towards the scientific and literal. They are likely to suffer episodes of self-doubt, but are recognizably part of a large group of people who have some Asperger-ish aspects without being so handicapped by more extreme states of mind.

CHAPTER THIRTEEN

On becoming of consequence

Brian Truckle

A crazy chase in circles
Ends up pursuing the pursuer.
The light at the end of the tunnel
turns out to be a tiger's eye.
A hundred disasters
mean a hundred comic somersaults
turned over a hundred abysses.

Wisława Szymborska, "Slapstick"*

T his chapter begins with a vignette about a little boy who was not diagnosed with Asperger's syndrome. However, his behaviour communicated extreme emotional experiences, including terror, which have been the subject of psychoanalytic writings on infancy and which seem relevant to the adolescent boy with Asperger's syndrome whom I go on to discuss. "Albert" had loving parents, but his behaviour impacted profoundly on their lives, and they did not know how to begin to address his worries.

---

*From W. Szymborska, "Slapstick". In: *View with a Grain of Sand* (Faber & Faber, 1996). Reprinted with the permission of the publisher.

A crazy chase in circles

A small, elfin-like face with bright, sparkling black eyes peeped round the edge of the playroom door, one foot from the ground, and startled me. A large red dummy protruded from the mouth. I had been engrossed, fully occupied by a distraught and overwhelmed mother, who was telling me of her concerns for her son of 15 months. He slept for only 20 minutes twice a day; he was hyperactive and very destructive; he refused to eat, just drank copiously from his bottle, and had a constant supply of dummies in every room—she dreaded leaving the house without at least six of them.

Albert was a problem and had been since birth. Crying non-stop as an infant; turning away from the breast; long, very slow bottle-feeds that merged into one; eye contact fleeting—a very "prickly" baby who had refused to be held.

Meanwhile a sturdy Albert had entered the room by storm. He raced around the edges of the carpet in an erratic manner. There was no response to my greeting, or to mother's pleas. She continued her tirade, holding herself in the tension of anxiety. Almost my full attention was on her, but in the periphery of my vision, Albert continued in a circle that seemed somehow to narrow a fraction as he circumnavigated the adults.

Mother continued her tale of how impossible he was. She could not take him to the supermarket because he got lost and created havoc among the shoppers. She could not take him in the car because he was terrified of the straps on the baby seat. He was constantly doing somersaults and falling over. His body was covered in scratches and bruises. It was a wonder the health visitor believed her and had not accused her of bashing the poor chap. Not that she had not considered this as an option . . . what with the sleepless nights, she was driven to distraction. I managed a word about how frightening all this was, and so exhausting.

From the corner of my eye I noticed a tiny change in Albert. He still rushed round the room, but the circle was tighter, and he seemed—or was it my imagination?—to be developing a pattern: by the radiator . . . by the door . . . by the desk . . . by the seated adults: his right hand now outstretched and fingers touching surfaces as he went. As more of my attention focused on him, the fingers touched the radiator, differentiating steel and gaps between the mesh. His route now involved stepping on and then off the doorstop, under and out of the desk, touching carpet and wooden floor.

While still talking to mother, I found myself giving a running commentary on Albert's activities: "round and round, solid and hole, in and out, on and off, soft and hard: Albert's trying to sort things out." The circle tightened; Albert was still moving fast. The tension he conveyed through his movement was tangible.

Albert circled nearer and nearer to us in his perambulations, eventually touching the wooden arm of my chair and then me, including me in his list of things to be sorted. I added "thing–person" to my own list, then "Ouch!" as he poked me on the next circuit. This prompted me to make it: "Albert wants to sort out solid/hole; in/out; on/off; soft/hard; thing/person; person–hard/person–soft and ouch!"

Part of my mind and voice was still with mother, who had not decreased the volume and volubility of her account of her difficulties. Part of my mind and voice was with Albert. This part of my mind was filled with an experience of the tightness and tension of his circling. I found myself in my imagination flattened against the spinning wall of death, held up only by the ever-tightening circle made by this little person. I began to notice the dark circles under his eyes, and although he did not look at me, I could see the tiredness in his face.

I said to mother and Albert that I saw how tired he was, and how much he wanted to rest and sleep. But he was frightened of falling if he stopped moving, and he was frightened of being crushed if he let someone hold him. The circles became smaller and were now totally centred upon the adults. He came nearer and nearer to me. I said I thought that Albert would like me to catch him and hold him but was afraid that I would crush him or let him fall. After checking with mother, I did catch him. The protest was minimal. He lay tired out in my arms, still tensing the muscles of his body. I said that I thought that Albert would like Mummy to hold him and keep him safe from falling and being crushed, until he could rest and sleep. Albert took the dummy out of his mouth, looked into my eyes, and said "yes", replacing the dummy at once. I handed him over to his mother and talked to them both about this tired, suspicious baby who got so afraid and so unsure of what or who was safe to hold him. He gently fell asleep, sucking—facing outwards on his mother's knee.

Mother whispered to me that this was the first time he had ever fallen asleep on her lap. I got her a foot-stool and a cup of tea and left the room. An hour later they were still together, resting and holding.

* * *

It can be impossible for parents, however loving and sympathetic they may be, to open themselves to their child's terrors when they are completely exhausted by his behaviour. This is the moment when someone outside the family, who is himself, unlike the parents, supported by the boundaries of his professional setting, may be able to open himself to what the child is communicating and help to make a link between parent and child. I was able to speak to Albert and his mother because my vivid fantasy that I would fall and die if Albert stopped moving—however absurd my rational mind knew this to be—helped me to imagine something of what life might be like for him, and this imaginative experience then allowed me to understand just how tired he looked and how much he must yearn to be able to rest. This is what psychoanalysts call using the countertransference—trying to make sense of the emotional experience of being with the child, but always cross-checking hypotheses against the child's observable behaviour. This kind of non-verbal communication played a major role in work with "Adam", the adolescent with Asperger's syndrome whom I discuss in this chapter.

Looking out of the window once when my train had halted, I saw a large billboard: "Experiences—great stops on life's journey". But if life's journey is to have any meaning, if we are to begin to find out who we are, we shall be involved in emotional experiences that are intimately tied to other people. If Ferenczi, Klein, or Winnicott are to believed, we can only find out who we are in relation to others by having emotional "events" or "stops". But what if the experience we have stopped at involves terror? Is there a choice? How do two people come together, and what are the costs, when even taking the first breath entails letting go of what we know and have? Bion writes about the terror involved in intimacy: "when two personalities meet, an emotional storm is created. . . . To dare to be aware of the facts of the universe in which we are existing calls for courage" (Bion, 1979, p. 322).

To take these risks when we "stop" to have an emotional experience involves needing help from our friends. Sometimes even with that first breath we need help, but certainly babies need what Hobson (2002) has called a "cradle of thought": a baby needs a primary caretaker with a mind who can help keep his body alive and his mind developing (see Introduction). Winnicott writes about facilitating environments, and later about the need for mothers to live through a stage of "maternal preoccupation" with their new baby in which they resonate intuitively with the baby's feelings. Bion talks about the mother's state of "reverie", which enables her to process the baby's experience and to provide what he calls the "containment of mental pain" and the generation of meaning. The facilitating environment that a baby requires is a mother or primary caretaker with a mind to take in who this person is becoming.

As we know, babies suck their thumbs in the womb and recognize their mother's voice. They may have what Bion called a "preconception" of something to go in their mouth, or of something that makes emotional sense. But they need help from the primary caregiver if this preconception is to be realized—if they are to find a place from which to view the world and to sort out what is "yuck" and what is "yum", instead of being overwhelmed by good and bad experiences. To be able to do this, they need the thinking function of a mother or primary caregiver who can process something for them and enable them to feel that they have been emotionally taken in.

If something goes wrong in the outside world for a particular baby (for example, if the environment is not facilitating enough, or if the caregiver cannot empathize with the experiences of a "different" child) or if something goes wrong inside the baby (such as deficits or personality problems as described by Alvarez & Reid, 1999a, or neurological impairments)—or, indeed, if both kinds of difficulty occur at once—then problems in development are likely to emerge. We know, for example, from the work of Hobson with children who are blind from birth that there can be real problems in reciprocity between mother and child (Hobson, 2002). If it is hard for the ordinary baby with a good-enough mother to take risks, how much more so for the baby where something has gone so seriously wrong. How can such a baby open his eyes, mouth, or mind to notice that "yuck" and "yum" exist and to allow enough closeness and intimacy for interchange—either at the physical level of taking the nipple in the mouth, for example, or at an intellectual or emotional level? With all babies there is a need for a filtering process—what Bion calls a mother who thinks about emotional experiences for the baby and on his behalf—so that he is not overwhelmed: not too far away and not too close, neither too hot nor too cold emotionally. This filtering, initially done by the primary caretaker, conveys the message that it is possible to develop an apparatus for thinking about emotional experiences that can give meaning to a relationship and thus lead to a feeling of personal significance. If, however, a sense of meaning cannot be achieved—if, indeed, there is no plan, no signpost, no island in a sea of confusion, no sense—then there will be no hope. All that will remain are primitive terrors of annihilation and meaninglessness.

* * *

I will now describe once-weekly work that took place over a period of some years with a young adolescent who has a diagnosis of Asperger's syndrome. I hope that this account will illustrate how this particular boy dealt with the terrors of emotional intimacy and of finding out who he was becoming. It may also illustrate a sort of "emotional dance" that has to go on between patient and clinician, with examples of some of the pitfalls and pit-stops along the way.

On becoming of consequence

A tall slim boy, just hitting puberty, stood up as I called his name, long fair hair swept back over his ears. He glanced in my direction briefly, giving an impression of dark eyes of deep slate grey. "Adam" had come because he wanted to get closer to people and found that he could not do so. His high intelligence had not helped him to know how to speak to other children in class, although he could answer questions put to him.

He sat opposite me, occasionally glancing in my direction, but he was unable to start the conversation. There was a feeling of urgency, yet he was not expressing any. My comments about this atmosphere brought a sideways smile, a gentle lifting of hands, palms outstretched facing me. The picture in my mind was one of an invisible screen between us, like a sheet of plate glass carried by two workmen in a comedy film. Was it there or not there? And on either side of it two inert forms existed. As I spoke of the difficulties in coming together as separate people and concerns of what might ensue, he sprang up to the window, looking out, suddenly alive. He said, "Now you have got me excited", in a tone that managed to convey both joy and fear.

The "force field"

Although this describes part of our first meeting, it could well be an account of many subsequent ones, with slightly differing forms and nuances. Should we begin to make an alive link between us? What would be its nature? What would be the cost? Would there be a "choice in the matter"? Would inertia or a sudden powerful force take over one or both of us? In weekly sessions we began to explore, at a very slow pace—which, incidentally, mirrored his eating disorder: very slow eating, during which he might forget that he needed to eat at all—the nature of the glass plate. Clearly there was a barrier between us. Sometimes it felt like a wide gulf that could never be crossed: sometimes, the width of a hair, when Adam would seem freer in telling me his feelings more directly. In my mind's eye I began to see this barrier as a membrane that could at times be solid and at others permeable. When I commented on this, Adam was clearly unhappy with my limited description and implied that "it" had a powerful life of its own, in a "magnetic" sort of way. Between us, we eventually agreed on "force field" as being the nearest we could get to at that moment. This force field might keep out attacks or penetrations by alien ideas and feelings, but also protect both participants, like a sort of go-between.

Adam said that he wanted to find out how to make contact with a girl in his class in whom he "had a slight interest", but she was prone to get A*s in all her tests while he could only achieve a mixture of As and A*s and would therefore be unacceptable. As with the agonizing debates between us, when we tried to ensure that we were describing and understanding enough of a shared universe, it seemed that an emotional or social mating could not be attempted unless everything matched perfectly. My comments, however nearly accurate or helpful, would be met by a nasal negative tone and a slight raising of one hand, head turned away. Inaccurate communications had to be deleted: but the notional possibility of a perfect connection seemed to be totally overwhelming also and had to be defended against by use of the force field.

Some communication did get through at a feeling level. The girl with no name had "touched" him with sensations that he could not process. The force field was "faulty": it had, Adam explained, "holes in it." These gaping tears left him extremely vulnerable to states of being very overwhelmed, and he always reacted by retreating into inertia and silence. At these times, after we had made some real emotional "breakthrough", however small, I found that I had to overcome a powerful wish just to stay silent too, drifting in and out of my own thoughts, which seemed irrelevant to the previous conversation and pointless to pursue. I would force myself to stay alert, knowing that if I did not, I might not only lose my train of thought but also the very will to retain the concept of thinking: it felt as though I might lose my mind altogether.

In the bunker

One very noticeable "failure" of our contact was my inability to marry up Adam's facial expressions with anything that he was speaking about or anything I was thinking or feeling, much as children with Asperger's syndrome are described as being unable to "read" other people's emotions (chapter 2). It was as if there were no linking between the outside and the inside of the person sitting opposite me, and no links in thinking about the communications or projections involved between us. This left me feeling puzzled, alarmed, helpless, and disabled. How could one begin to know what was to happen next? How terrifying might such an experience be to a baby looking into his mother's eyes or scanning her face. Would this baby look and be looked upon with love or with hate? Would the looking or being looked into, whether with love or with hate, feel piercing? Or might it be modulated? Eventually we came to call this state of mind "being in a bunker, but with one antenna up" (see also chapter 10). I somehow felt glad about the "one antenna", even though it implied that enemy attacks of unknown origin or content might appear over the horizon and might have to be met by an equal and opposing force.

Of no consequence

Adam would sit in his chair, eyes looking left and right as I spoke to him, trying to make contact. He might get up and pace, then settle again—but not in direct response to my words. Sometimes his eyes would dart to a corner of the room and back. I queried what was happening, but Adam would shake his head and not reply. When I persisted, he said, "It's of no consequence." The experience, however, seemed an important part of what was going on between us, or at least in the room. Pursuing this further in later sessions, he commented that his mind would follow "whatever was the stronger". I was left feeling that if I insisted on paying attention to these hallucinatory presences, it would lead to their increasing in number and therefore in power and encourage him to engage with them and not with me. On the other hand, if I did not pursue this matter at all, I might miss some vital evidence of the quality of the forces that seemed to be arrayed against the embryonic thinking part of him and myself. For most of the time, therefore, I was limited to noting the experience and wondering helplessly whether or not "it" was important. How hard for a baby to discriminate between a daydream of satisfaction and the real thing: for baby Adam, not having the unending experience of a "perfect conjunction" with a caregiver left him in the power of these "floaters". On the other hand, if such an unending conjunction had been possible, it would have carried with it its own dangers—the fear of becoming addicted to the experience, or of losing one's identity in the other person (Stockdale-Wolfe, 1993).

Entering and leaving the room often seemed abrupt. Adam arrived in a passive state and left the room as if I had pushed him "over the edge". On one occasion, when we had seemed to get nowhere in the session and there had been long, non-communicative, silences, I opened the door at the end of his time. As I did so, I felt as though the ever-widening crack around the door were becoming a void. Adam then raised his eyes and hands, smiling—grimacing a welcome to the shades and shapes that were always there waiting to receive him.

The combination of Adam's silences and my own powerful experiences of drifting into mindlessness led me to talk of Jason and the Argonauts landing on the island of the Lotus Eaters. This raised a slight smile or grimace, a turning in his chair, a leap to the window. Where had that idea come from, and how had it got through the force field? Did it feel like a defeat of his defensive system or, perhaps, an achievement? For it did enable us to consider how far he put his thinking self to sleep. How wonderful to stay on this I–land with no disturbance by thoughts or feelings to interrupt the peaceful, soft, slumbering state of being.

The coracle

These discussions led to his reporting dreams. The first dream was simply of *a bodily experience of rocking*. As Adam described it, he rocked in his chair, swaying gently from side to side. In several later sessions over a period of some months he would return to this swaying movement, reminding me of this dream. Eventually another dream emerged, very gradually over a number of sessions, with many allusive half-answers to my attempts at clarification. It was impossible to tell what had formed part of the content of the dream and what belonged to Adam's waking associations to it, as though the boundary between sleeping and waking, fantasy and reality remained blurred. However, this time there was a more elaborated thematic content: about *ancient Britons going to sea in coracles. Their original aim,* Adam said, *was to cross a river to get to the other side, as there were no bridges. Something on the other bank was "required"*. In the context, I thought that this ancient Briton was like a baby who had a notion of reaching something important—like an experience of a feeding mother. A chasm was involved, possibly implying a catastrophic separation or a fear of falling—or simply a sense that the needed person was too far away. But a means could be found of getting across and a will to attempt this movement towards something. It made me wonder if this "chasm" had been formed by the baby's attempts at avoiding a potentially overwhelming contact. But one antenna was still "up".

The coracle dreams continued, but literally "never seemed to get anywhere"; this appeared to be true of our work at this juncture as much as of the figure in the dreams. I eventually realized that this was a baby who was himself—in a coracle, *drifting*. As I spoke these words, Adam leapt up, pacing the floor, making hand and arm gestures in an alarming manner. He gradually calmed himself by idiosyncratic movements of his body, eyes, hands—incongruous smiles coming and going. My attempts to speak felt irrelevant, and eventually I just sat waiting. The baby, Adam confided at length, was in the coracle—rocking gently in the waves—but it was in the Atlantic Ocean—and he had no compass. He was lost, and could not look over the edge—because of the terror.

"Drifting" seemed to be a state where Adam attempted to have some control over the coming and going of emotional contact. It was like a sort of force-field-with-holes-in-it, a hyphenated link that enabled him to keep a protected but rigid distance. But the experience of talking about the baby-in-the-coracle's terror led directly to Adam being able to look at me eye to eye, rather than with peripheral vision, as was his wont. It was as if he had allowed us, at this moment, to come together as a powerful force for promoting growth and development of sense and meaning. The world of the shades continued to be in view, but now it was peripheral. It was as though making the choice to communicate with me, a separate person—by telling me his dreams and explaining what was happening to his baby self—instead of with hallucinated shadows had given him a sense of agency.

Fusion with the A girl*

The A* girl reappeared in the material, but the first sign was a change in the way Adam paid attention with his eyes. As we discussed his forthcoming GCSE exams, which meant that he was ageing and developing in real time (see also other children's preoccupation with development: for instance, Marco and Kane, in chapters 10 and 11, respectively) and that an actual move from school to college would soon take place, I noticed that he kept glancing upwards. He was willing to concede that there might be aspects of this that were "of consequence", but he was unable to say what. Eventually we understood it through a dream in which *a girl's face was illuminated by a dazzling light. When he looked up, he could not look away. His eyes were captured in her face and the light.*[1] What came across initially in his narrative was the beauty of what he was beholding. But this was quickly overtaken by a feeling of entrapment and addiction that spoiled the experience and robbed it of its initial meaning and significance.

Knowledge of the link to the beautiful girl, like the earlier experience of the link with the mother, came together with the insight that he did not possess her. If Adam had found this possible to tolerate, the memory of such a link could have supported his thinking self and helped him to retain a sense of balance and perspective. However, the difficulty of negotiating the right distance for emotional contact so as to avoid the dangers of unconnectedness on the one hand and engulfment on the other seemed to rob the experience of its power to sustain him. He was realizing that the beauty of intimate contact belonged to a separate person—the girl with the radiant face; and acknowledging that he must allow its warming influence to originate from outside himself. But would this realization merely rob him of any sense of power and control and leave him helpless?

The Kryptonite "factor"

Adam talked about his own conception as though it could not possibly have come about through ordinary sexual intercourse between human beings (see chapter 9). He was very aware of his cold "alien" self and fantasized about having had a father from Krypton. He was, in reality, of mixed parentage (Nordic and Celtic) and seemed to feel that his Celtic mother had in some inhuman way been impregnated by a Kryptonite "factor". His own interest in language and in punning are illustrated here, since "factor" is used as noun and verb, with different meanings. The idea of a superior, Kryptonite, alien, and powerful self-generating "factor" impregnating the host mother also led us to think about the arrogant and superior way in which Adam was looking down on ordinary, common-or-garden physical or mental intercourse, producing ordinary children or brain children (ideas): as though such a state of affairs did not at all fit with his ideas about his presumed lineage.

The knot

The idea of growth, development, separateness, and endings were summed up for Adam in the word "change". This was a word that he resisted above all others. If it were mentioned or implied, it would lead to a shaking of the head and low mutterings of "no change". Over time there were many opportunities to tease out the strands of meaning to this phrase. One such opportunity occurred before a summer break, when Adam had two dreams about *a tight-rope walker—baby who had to keep his balance on the high wire.* The baby's goal was more defined than the ancient Briton's had been in the coracle dreams: *he was supposed to reach a crow's nest at the end of the wire. Yes, the crows could all peck the baby to pieces if he got there!* (Compare Tustin, 1990, on the "nest full of sucklings"—see Introduction.) In Adam's second dream, *the baby was still on the high wire, but now in darkness. He had no balancing pole*—just as in the coracle he had no compass—*but there was at least a concept of one that was missing. The baby could not see in the darkness, but he was holding onto to a piece of string.* We thought together about a baby/Adam not seeing me in the summer break but holding onto the string-link in his mind. This second dream, however, ended with his waking up at the point at which there was a knot in the string. As Adam reported this nonchalantly, a wave of terror swept over me: I had heard the "knot" as "not"—as though the baby would *not* be able to continue holding on when faced with an important change. Any such change, including Adam's sudden transition between the states of sleeping and waking, seemed to carry within it the possibility of falling to his death in the absence of the equipment necessary to keeping his balance—the pole. Alternatively, of course, the knot could have served as something that enabled Adam to hold on to the string, and with it to his connection with ordinary human relationships and all the pain, frustration, and fulfilment that they bring with them.

The black lines

Real time did continue to impinge in the form of exams, in which Adam did well—though he did not get all A*s—and of preparations for college necessitating a change of site, people, and focus. How could he continue to look after his vulnerable infant self in a new world? How could he learn to discover and hold on to internal parental figures who could hold him up and enable him to grow into a thinking man? As we discussed this, he leapt up, pacing the room, grimacing, and wildly waving his arms. His eyes darted from one side of the room to the other in a way that very quickly alarmed me. I asked what had happened, and Adam said that black lines had appeared and moved very fast across the room. In a flat tone, he hesitantly spoke of the lines "belonging to a page". Gradually we pieced together that he had been "reading" what I said as though from a printed page, in order to gain some distance from a highly emotionally charged idea (see also chapter 5). When it became overwhelming—or, rather, just as this registered emotionally—the words became squashed and distorted: what Adam called "a sort of collapse" took place. The printed words, he said, became black lines, which seemed to be drawn out of his vision by the force field. It was as though this pull of the force field collapsed spatial structure, obliterated meaning, and so protected Adam from the notion of change with all its associated terrors—a kind of inversion of the "mighty rushing wind" in which the Holy Spirit came to the disciples of Jesus at Pentecost.

The lamp

As we continued to explore the ideas of movement, of possible change, of the need to be able to trust in the continuity of existence, Adam's material became more fragmented. There were more silences, more hallucinatory interruptions to our dialogue, and less consistent eye contact. When Adam seemed to pull away from my attention, his eye movements sometimes led to his focusing outside the window. Some months before, we had talked a great deal about the outside light on a building opposite: sometimes it was on in the daytime, sometimes it was off. There appeared to be no consistent pattern to this, and for Adam it had been a source of amazed puzzlement and alarm. One day, he gruffly commented on the absence of the light, and he went on to tell me a fragmented dream about a "lamp". His words were broken up as he related the dream, but I heard what I thought to be "fur", and "eye" or "I". In response to my questions, Adam described a diamond-shaped lantern on a T-shaped base. This seemed to be an eye/(or "I") on top of a T (for Truckle, as he said)—a representation, I thought, of an important link by means of eye contact between him and me. How-ever, this link was divested of meaning and significance, as Adam said that there was no power supply. The apparatus of relating was in place, but the significance had been dismantled. My insistence that change and loss in the external world were "real" and inevitable seemed to make Adam feel that I was about to cut off the power supply that allowed his baby self to feel alive; and the fact that the outside light on the building opposite could be switched off without any detectable reason or pattern appeared to reinforce his fears about the unreliability of anything or anyone not under his control. He seemed to take this as evidence that relationships—to a therapist or a maternal figure—ex-posed him to cruel, erratic, and unpredictable abandonment, which left him with no option but to switch off, drift, dismantle his perceptions, keep his eyes below the edge of the coracle. And yet his "one antenna that remained up" allowed him at times to perceive another world, in which a mother might understand her baby's dilemma. Such a mother would have to wait, bearing the helplessness of wanting the baby to connect with her, while she attempted to find a mode of relating that would not feel threatening to him. She would knowingly risk the anguish of possible failure while acknowledging the support of a non-Kryptonite father—and all because this particular baby was "of conse-quence". Such a world view, which implies love and some tolerance of imperfection, might make it possible to be open to experience without feeling flooded—might allow for the existence of someone who could help in bearing the terror of hope.

Adam is now preparing for life at college, where he wants to study ancient languages. There he will encounter further challenges and difficulties in his courageous attempts to make closer and potentially fulfilling emotional contact with other people. The question remains how far, in spite of the inevitable problems, he will be able to hold on to an internal life line to sustaining internal figures. Will he be able to withstand the force that has, in the past, pulled him away from internal relationships that are "of consequence" to him, and in which he, too, is "of consequence"? In studying ancient languages, which are the base of so many European and Asian languages today, will Adam be able to use his knowledge to grow in understanding and in the capacity to communicate with meaning? Or will he use it as an autistic exercise, leading to yet another I–land of illusion or delusion?

Note

1. Again, this dream, like the previous ones and those that followed, emerged very gradually, and Adam did not distinguish between the dream itself and his associations to it.

CHAPTER FOURTEEN

Psychotherapy and community care

Margaret Rustin

This chapter describes a model of ongoing support devised as a follow-up to long-term individual psychotherapy with a young woman diagnosed variously as borderline psychotic, on the autistic spectrum, severely emotionally disturbed, and learning-disabled. In many ways a diagnosis of Asperger's might have been a more helpful indication of her unusual mix of extreme oddness, hyper-sensitivity, and idiosyncratic intelligence. She was, however, given the varied diagnoses I have mentioned before Asperger's syndrome achieved its present currency, and this made her rather unusual mixture of characteristics difficult to understand.

"Holly" had been referred with a view to psychotherapy by a consultant child psychiatrist who had known her for many years. At a regular review consultation when she was 12 years old he judged that there was a window of opportunity for psychotherapeutic intervention, which should be explored. At that time Holly was in a local special school, and she lived at home with her parents and a younger sister. She was very difficult to manage both at school, where she provoked anxiety in staff and children by her very odd behaviour, and at home, where her obsessional preoccupations and frequent panics were profoundly exhausting for her parents and controlled family life to a massive degree.

She responded with relief to the regular and predictable framework of outpatient psychotherapy and was seen for many years on this basis. Her mental state improved considerably, and her capacity for relationships with other people and for an interest in the external world developed. While she remained timid and restricted in many respects, she was able to enjoy life and to feel that she had really woken up from the nightmare existence of her earlier childhood. For example, she learnt to play two musical instruments well enough to be involved in church music, and family holidays became a pleasure instead of an unbearable source of dread. At school, she particularly enjoyed creative activities, and she made some friends.

Both Holly and her parents were very attached to her psychotherapy. Holly felt that her more bizarre thoughts and feelings had been understood to some extent and that she was no longer alone in an alien world. Her large cast of imaginary characters and her idiosyncratic language had been given meaning in the course of psychotherapy, and she was fearful that on her own the more mad and contrary elements in her inner world would gain the upper hand. Her therapy was experienced very concretely as an aid to her sanity, which depended on her capacity to distinguish between internal and external reality. Her parents had come to feel trust in Holly's therapist and to recover from some earlier rather devastating encounters with a range of mental health professionals, and they greatly valued their termly meetings to talk over Holly's progress. Terminating therapy was therefore an especially difficult process. I have written elsewhere (Rustin, 1997b) about my understanding of the transference and countertransference aspects of this problem, but I now want to describe the framework for follow-up that emerged after regular sessions ended.

As background, it may be useful to give a brief picture of the main themes that had emerged by the time her therapy came to an end. Holly had lived in a fundamentally timeless inner world, and she had also had enormous difficulty in locating herself as the child of her parents, in the sense of accepting that they belonged together and that she was not part of the parental couple. She also found it very difficult to grasp gender differences and the basic fact that as a girl she could not also be a boy and have a male as well as a female body. As her therapist, I had to come to terms myself with accepting the limits within which psychotherapy could help her. Over time, I came to have a strong sense of the "hard-wire" aspect of her problems in thinking and in understanding the world, something that seemed irreducible and was not touched by the very considerable changes in her emotional life that therapy brought about. Progress could be achieved in modifying her anxieties and states of panic and confusion, and thus in enabling her to perceive the world as more friendly and more differentiated. Enjoyment of family and social relationships thus became more possible, and of course people around her could then have much more opportunity for rewarding interaction instead of feeling trapped in her nightmare versions of things or her obsessional protective manoeuvres. Life was easier for everyone, but that did not mean that Holly was free of major limitations in what she could manage. "Cure" is not a meaningful objective for these patients, and therapists have to be tough-minded with themselves in defining realistic aims for their work.

At this point Holly was living in a small community home run by a specialist agency that had been chosen with care by her social worker and parents. This placement succeeded one in a larger, more institutional, though kindly setting, which had recently been closed, and it meant that Holly was much closer to home and could spend time with her family more easily and frequently. The staff at this home have been very supportive of Holly's psychotherapy, and I had a good relationship with the head and key worker.

As Holly and I worked towards ending, I said to her that I thought it might help her to come and see me from time to time to tell me how she was getting on. This idea of an ongoing link was received with great relief, and Holly's mother was also very much relieved. I had always made it clear to the parents that I would be available for post-therapy consultation as needed, but the intensity of the worry about ending seemed only to abate when I made a definite offer of a follow-up appointment for Holly and a subsequent time for her parents. So full of material were these meetings, and so open was Holly's statement that she wanted to come and see me again in a few months, that it seemed evident that a structure for ongoing review was what was required. What emerged was a termly session for Holly and a couple of meetings a year for her parents, together with occasional telephone discussions with her social worker and the care staff. I came to see this work as my providing a range of consultation to the various people involved in Holly's life.

Before going on to try to define what kind of consultation this is, I would like to give a sense of Holly's own use of these widely spaced sessions. From the beginning, it was evident that she was fully aware that they were not like her therapy sessions. Instead of sitting on the couch, as she had previously done, she chose a chair at a considerably further distance from me and the one closest to the door of my room. If she had been brought by a care worker, she would make some reference to who it was, since I might not know that member of staff. (If she happened to be on a home visit at a holiday time, one of her parents would bring her.) She nearly always brought something with her that she wanted to refer to or to show me and quite often something she wished to give me: a drawing with some writing intended for me, and around Christmas a little present she had made for me. These objects from her ongoing outside life seemed to represent her wish to share with me her awareness of the sense of distance between us, of the passage of time and of space, and was her way of linking across several months since we last met. These events made it clear that she was able to acknowledge the difference between internal and external reality. It is striking to note that she was also demonstrating her capacity at this point to take her therapist's point of view and separate existence into account. This is interesting with respect to debates about the "theory of mind"—namely, the view that awareness of the other's point of view is what people diagnosed with Asperger's often lack. I observed that this was not the case with Holly in this later period—in fact, she quite often provided me with explicit instances of her struggles to put together different people's perspectives, and her tolerance of the effort involved fluctuated according to the balance of stress—from external and internal sources—and inner coherence she was feeling. She also showed me, at times, art work that was an extraordinary development from what I had ever seen before, including some rather lovely things. This was contrasted with other drawings that revisited her old obsessions and signalled her continuing vulnerability to being caught up in quasi-autistic and drearily meaningless rituals and thought processes, which cut her off very effectively from people and activities. For example, she would repeatedly draw the back end of a bus, next to a bus stop. We shared the understanding that this intense focus on the back of the bus (the exhaust, etc.) was in contrast to the possibility of being interested in where the bus might go (the sign at the front) or in the people on the bus. This seemed to me to represent the possibility that she might really be doing something with her life.

On one occasion, Holly leapt up as usual in the waiting-room, telling me she had brought me something that we could look at in my room. "We're going this way" she said. This was striking to me, as she would usually leave it to me to help her to wait until we reached the room rather than for her to hold forth in the corridor as if she and I were the only inhabitants of the clinic. She then explained that it was a picture of a bus that she got on when the train had broken down. She explained that they had to get on this bus, and it took them to a station where they could get on a train. I was thinking to myself that Holly, who would usually experience any breakdown as an alarming catastrophe, seemed to have been able to mobilize more ego-strength so as not to be overwhelmed. These ordinary defences, so characteristic of latency children, had been sorely lacking in her mental equipment, leaving her very vulnerable to extreme panics whenever anything unexpected happened. Holly also remarked that Mummy did not want to hear her talking about S—a fellow resident whom she does not like—all the time. At this moment, Holly is demonstrating that she can hold two perspectives—her own, which involves wanting to go on and on about S, and mother's, which is very different, "fed up to the back teeth with hearing all that old hat", as Holly would put it. This was a good example of Holly's having a well-functioning first-order "theory of mind".

I commented to her that she was bringing a lot of news about herself today, some good news and also some thoughts about how people can get fed up with her. This led to a long sequence about familiar obsessions, in which Holly recounted a dream of *getting stuck in a tunnel*—an image well known to us of the risk of her becoming immobilized in an idiosyncratic labyrinth of anxieties—and with a knowing smirk she referred to many of her private made-up words. Then, more meaningfully, she talked about a time when S had been upset and said she did not want a shower, and Holly had felt frightened. I could envisage rather well a scene of staff–resident conflict that would indeed be terrifying to Holly, who is easily distressed by raised voices or any form of overt conflict. Mixed in with this was more "old stuff" about her obsession about listening to other people using the toilet, in which she conveyed both her addiction to it, and her unease and dislike of it. She managed to pull away from this dead end and explain that "sometimes it's OK with S". She can say "Thumbs up, OK, Holly?" and Holly might reply "That's good, S. What did you do at your class today?" This exchange led to our talking about her having a new kind of friend, one she can talk to and even make friends with again after something's gone wrong. I said she was telling me that things can change, and that she and S seem to be interested in each other. "Yes!" she said. "I didn't like S, but now I'm quite friendly. But I'm glad E left. She butted me and she put her hands round my throat and pinched me. I didn't like that. She pulled my hair, and I told A about it."

These comments about her life in the home gave me a picture of Holly's growing confidence in managing the everyday ups and downs of her life, including extreme behaviour by other residents, and she went on to talk about her feelings about the approaching end of a holiday with her family. "I'm rather sad today, it's the end of my holiday at home." To my surprise, she was able to build on this to describe a visit to her grandmother, with whom she often stays for a couple of days, and how she had coped with period pains by taking some pre-menstrual tension pills. This was in contrast to many other times she had told me about visits to Granny that were dominated by her wish to exploit Granny's soft heart and make out that she was still a toddler who could not be held responsible for anything. These conversations involved a turning-away from her capacity for straight thinking that came to irritate and even madden me over time, as she was well aware. She would keep a sharp eye on me as she "wound me up". She and Granny were presented to me as inhabiting a nauseating time-warp, a particular kind of *folie à deux*, with Holly pretending to be "potty", as she would put it, and getting away with it. My role had always been to try to put her in touch with the way she was attacking her own sanity and rubbishing the relationship with Granny through this sentimentalized denigration. I found myself wondering whether the more ordinary atmosphere on this occasion might be related to the recent death of her grandfather, whom she certainly missed. Might Holly be more in touch with the reality of loss and thus more genuinely linked to the feelings of others in the family? I knew the funeral had been an important event for her. Might she be more aware of the waste involved in her horrible manipulation of Granny and more interested in something real they could share?

The idea that she was exploring doing things with people in a different way, not wholly bending them to her individual quirks—for example, choosing on an outing with mother always to go on the same bus journey and to the same shop, something that had made her mother deeply despondent in the past—was confirmed when she told me that she had been to Oxford Street shopping with her sister and her sister's boyfriend at Christmas. This boyfriend had never rated a mention before this, and indeed the notion of such an expedition seemed a very new dimension in the sisters' relationship.

Perhaps the strain of these efforts to engage with real life became a bit overwhelming, as she reverted to depressingly familiar themes in a kind of patchwork of sanity and madness. The latter would be represented by elaborate claims of how much she likes shit–faeces–urine, how "marvellous" it is, with long paragraphs of dirty talk. However, when I spoke to her about the oscillation between a thinking Holly and this mad Holly who gets stuck in a lavatory-world, she was able to tell me that shit is marvellous "because it's inside me", and to add, "I don't want to say goodbye". This insight into how anti-developmental obstinacy takes over when she is faced with the pain of separation was impressive.

One of the images Holly uses to convey her fears of being empty and disconnected is that of empty hands. Indeed, she has spent huge amounts of time in her life clutching a small object in each hand as a reassurance that she does not have empty hands, and her favourite protections are anything round and shiny. When she spoke to me about her Grandfather's death and about heaven, she explained that heaven is where you go when God calls you—this would be very much in line with the religious teaching she has received—and that in heaven she won't have empty hands. This picture of perfect safety was immediately followed by her telling me about how she had wept while she was at Granny's house because Grandpa is not there any more.

I should like to link this example of the lively, mobile quality of Holly's emotional life, so strikingly in contrast with the static repetitive dimension that remains an ongoing threat, with the question of what I hope to achieve by offering ongoing follow-up. In a highly concentrated form I think these occasional sessions provide opportunities for her both to revisit the understandings achieved during her therapy with me and to talk to me about the balance she is managing over time. She is always very straightforward about how she does not like not talking to me all the time—that is, every week—and yet the frustration and limitation of what I offer seems to be offset by the continuity. Holly always negotiates with me that she will come to see me again in a few months if she feels I have not said anything explicit enough about this, and her goodbyes when we return to the waiting-room are such as to involve whoever has brought her in the whole business. She will say something like, "I had a good talk with Mrs Rustin today, and I'm coming to see her again in the summer."

Holly's problem in holding on to her mind is not to be underestimated. The combination of unfavourable factors can be most discouraging. A good deal of the time she is not provided with helpful opportunities for work or meaningful leisure. The staffing in her home is subject to unpredictable changes and is of very variable quality. Most of the other residents are more limited than she is in terms of imagination or social potential, and some of them are aggressive or hostile. These external limitations are in addition to Holly's own serious ongoing problems in thinking and relating. She remains very vulnerable to the impact of external events, as her inner stability, though much improved, is dependent on the ongoing availability of good external figures to sustain her belief in the strength of her own inner goodness and value.

Ordinary theories about termination of psychotherapy assume that one of the aims of treatment, and thus of readiness for ending, is the development of the individual's awareness of psychic reality and the increasing strength of the capacity for containment of mental pain. I am proposing that with some patients these tasks cannot be fully taken on by the mature part of the personality in a reliable way, and some additional support is required. Most of us are, in fact, supported by a complex mixture of things when exposed to psychological stress. These include the web of relationships with other people involving family, friends, and work colleagues and the ways in which our beliefs are socially supported, which might link us to religious, political, or other community structures.

One of the deprivations of Holly's life is that she has fewer of any of these ordinary supports while in fact being in need of more. This is unavoidable, but it means that she is more at risk from the continuing fault-lines in her psychic structure. The likelihood of some regression is therefore quite significant. We are dealing with a mental state that requires ongoing monitoring, and the patient's own capacities for this task are limited. Holly's parents worry, naturally enough, about how she will cope after their deaths. This is a very common anxiety for families with a vulnerable member, and I puzzle over the degree to which my ongoing involvement may represent a collusion to do with avoiding the reality of transitions, endings, and mortality or a confusion of role, in which I take on something beyond my proper task. On balance, however, even though I cannot at this point see how this work will end, I think that a decision to withdraw would be more to relieve myself of a sense of ongoing responsibility and to feel less out-of-order in relation to usual psychotherapeutic assumptions than for any purpose designed to benefit Holly and her family. The tone of her sessions with me varies, inevitably, with some occasions or moments where there can be a real sense of her getting a grasp of something important, and plenty of patches of despair at her tendency to lose or distort the insight she has achieved. But what I am struck by repeatedly is how very hard it is to be the person that she is. My job, as she sees it, is to be alongside her and stick at it. In a recent session, after an unusually clear conversation about her desire to "cross out", "throw out of the window", "send next-door" the parts of herself that she does not like—the bully, the screamer, the lazy girl—she began to intone repeatedly "I'm so glad that Jane who used to upset me has moved next door and *that's that.*" I interrupted her to point out that she was drowning out the idea she had had earlier, when she had shown me a picture of herself dreaming, that there had to be space for the nasty Holly as well as the nice one. In the picture she had drawn a light which seemed to show how she could sometimes see all of herself, all the different bits. After another couple of droning repetitions of the statement about Jane uttered in the same sing-song tone of voice, Holly said, "I'm trying to drive you potty, Mrs Rustin. I'm trying to drive you up the wall." I could then speak to her about how dreadful it was for her to have to listen to these worn-out ideas and how the light in the picture was also showing me her wish that I would help her to keep an eye on her tricks and muddles and mad ideas. She wanted me to know that she would like to come again to tell me how she is getting on with this very difficult side of herself. "Yes", she said fervently.

Perhaps the concept that best summarizes the nature of the ongoing contact is "working through". New analytic work is not possible in such infrequent sessions, but assisting the embedding of important insights within the personality through repeated enlivening rediscovery is a valuable process.

The contact with Holly's parents, her social worker, and the care staff depends usefully on the telephone in addition to occasional meetings. I see myself as one of the team—the community mental health team, in its broadest sense—who can be consulted if appropriate. One recent example concerned difficulties arising in the home following allegations of abusive behaviour by a staff member towards some residents. These were being officially investigated, and police involvement was a possibility. The team wanted to think about ways in which Holly should or should not be involved in this process—could she give evidence to the police? What sense could one make of the contradictory things she had said? There is a shared recognition that Holly's capacity to differentiate between internal and external reality is not reliable. In particular, her terror of people who "shout" is understood to refer not necessarily to the decibels of the speaker's voice or the emotional tone of the utterance, but to the way in which she hears anything that is in opposition to her wishes or arousing a painful emotion in her. At the same time, Holly is recognized as truthful, not deceitful, and this can make deciphering her statements a complex task.

I would like to close by commenting on the pictures Holly has brought me, which are good examples of the range of psychological states she experiences. The first of them is a characteristic pageful of faces given varying shapes and expressions (see Figure 1). Anger, gloom, sadness, childlike cheerfulness, and more obviously disturbed and strange versions of the human face convey Holly's changing experience of her own state of mind and some of the ways she perceives other people. This picture also captures the way in which she sees many inanimate objects as having human characteristics—some of the shapes refer to particular things in the world by which she is very preoccupied. For example, the orange lozenge shape is like the Strepsil throat-sweet tins that she loves because they have "curved corners", and thus get rid of the sharp edges she so much fears encountering because they represent separateness and potential conflict to her. She has been drawing things like this for many years when she is in a state of mind of not being able to link things up.

Figure 1

Figure 2

The second picture (Figure 2) is an example of a much more integrated state. It is a Christmas picture of Santa Claus on his sleigh, with the reindeer drawing him along, together with some presents for people—the big box, the Teddy bear, etc. In the sky (though not visible in this reproduction) are joyous bursts of colour. What I was particularly impressed by is the way in which Santa's body lies moulded into the shape of the sleigh, providing support for his journey. We can, however, note the thin lighter layer between Santa and the sleigh which echoes the sky, and perhaps we might see this as representing Holly's slightly anxious feeling of not being able fully to trust in the solidity of whatever supports her. That little gap is the space into which her anxieties can insert themselves and dislodge her sense of safety, the safety of a belief in the solidity of her body and mind and also the safety derived from a secure relationship to the environment. This picture seems to me to give evidence of the process of "working through" to which I referred and its continued evolution, which is possible as a consequence of the vibrancy of Holly's continuing emotional and cognitive development, however patchy the outcome.

Endpiece

Maria Rhode and Trudy Klauber

At the end of this book, what do we think we have learnt? The clinical case histories and first-person accounts provide us with a detailed insight into the intimate emotional experience of children and young people with Asperger's syndrome and into their relationship with their therapists. This will be our starting-point in a final word on some of the questions that have already arisen, such as different types of Asperger's syndrome and its relation to other diagnostic entities; recurring themes across cases; the interaction between heredity, neurology and psychology; and the relevance and effect of psychotherapy.

Different types of Asperger's syndrome and their relation to other diagnostic entities

The two case histories from each age group were chosen to illustrate contrasting extremes within the diagnostic category of Asperger's syndrome. All of these children and young people recognizably fit Asperger's original description and the present-day criteria of ICD–10 and DSM–IV. They had all been given a psychiatric diagnosis. When they began treatment, Olivia, Marco, and Jonathan had major problems relating to other people—which included theory-of-mind capabilities—and in dealing with their own aggressive impulses, but they relied predominantly on controlling others by means of "bossy" behaviour and on retreating to their own obsessive "interests". Linda, Kane, and Adam—as well as Caroline Polmear's adult patients—would in all likelihood have been described as borderline before the diagnostic category of Asperger's syndrome achieved its present level of currency (see Lubbe, 2000; and also Ad-Dab'bagh & Greenfield, 2001, arguing for the category "Multiple Complex Developmental Disorder").

This second group of patients was characterized by florid, confusing, and seemingly bizarre behaviour and utterances and often by reliance on physical action. They frequently seemed to be unable to distinguish between their own fantasies and external reality, or between themselves and other people, to whom they attributed many of their own feelings. It was as though they felt violently impinged upon by their own emotions as well as by external events, and they relieved this pressure by discharging it into people around them. Contact, as Caroline Polmear has described, was felt to be immensely dangerous.

Our contrasting pairs are examples of extremes. Other case histories could have been chosen which would have illustrated a mixture of these features. In addition, as Anne Alvarez writes in this volume, some people diagnosed with Asperger's syndrome have personality characteristics that overlap with psychopathy.[1] How can this variety within the category of Asperger's syndrome be understood?

Tustin (1981b) described a group of "confusional entangled children" (as opposed to shell-type Kanner's children) who blur the difference between themselves and others by treating other people as though they represented aspects of themselves (Klein, 1946). They also blur differences by attempting to draw others into their own preoccupations and interests in a way that is largely non-communicative: communication, by definition, would mean recognition of the difference between self and other. The fear of separateness and of differentiation is not unique to this group of children. The problem is one that everyone struggles with and one that is particularly difficult for all borderline psychotic individuals who cling to the other in fantasy and whose contact with ordinary human reality is therefore variable. The drawing-in to non-communicative, repetitive activity by the "entanglers" (Tustin's term) seems to render contact safe but meaningless.

As Sally Hodges points out when she describes an Asperger boy playing with toy cars (chapter 2), the boy might desire a contact that he does not know how to establish, or how to establish safely. Such a reading is compatible with Tustin's psychoanalytically based formulation, according to which "entanglers" desire contact with another person's mental processes but cannot sustain genuine communication because difference remains overwhelmingly threatening. Tustin, as well as Meltzer (1975a), emphasized that children with Kanner's autism tend to relate to others in terms of surface mimicry, if at all—as though they had no idea of the inner, mental life of other people. During treatment, such children often realize that people—and, indeed, inanimate objects—have an inside that is not immediately visible on the surface. Doreen Weddell (1975) describes this development in a boy emerging from the autistic mode in a way that calls to mind Gunilla Gerland's momentous discovery of insides when she was 8 years old. As was suggested in chapter 4, this seems to have arisen out of feeling that one particular inside—the inside of the neighbour's garden—contained a living creature (the neighbour's cat), which responded to her. Many children with autism, in contrast, can experience everything, even toys, as though they were rivals to be controlled rather than people or things to be enjoyed (Houzel, 2001b).

Bion's theory of containment has been referred to throughout this book: adequate containment of emotional experience is vital to the growth of cognitive capacities as well as to the development of character. Containment of its nature implies the notion of a separate mind "inside" which it can take place. It also implies the possibility of bridging the gap between two people, whether by means of eye contact or by verbal or non-verbal communication. Where, for any reason, this is not possible, an ordinary gap can be experienced as a "death gap" (see chapters 5 and 12). In such situations the child may fall back on mimicry and on "sticking" to surfaces, as originally described by Esther Bick (1968, 1986): this is characteristic of children with Kanner's autism (Meltzer, 1975a, Tustin, 1994a, 1994b). Jane Cassidy's Jonathan, whose eye contact was a "sticky" way of holding on rather than one of communicating, was a good example of this: in the course of treatment, he became increasingly able to conceive of "insides", as demonstrated by his growing capacity to draw three-dimensional cubes. Olivia and Marco are perhaps the two children whose own theory-of-mind capabilities and capacity for self-reflection most obviously developed in direct response to the experience of being understood and reflected upon by the mind of another person.

This line of thought makes it understandable that children with autism should sometimes, with help from their parents (Alvarez &

Reid, 1999b) or from other sources, become children who fulfil the behavioural criteria for Asperger's syndrome—that is, they can develop a notion of "inside", so that their characteristic mode of functioning becomes three-dimensional rather than two-dimensional.

All this implies that it would be simplistic to equate the achievement of the concept of three dimensions with accessibility to treatment, though from one point of view it is certainly "progress". People in schizoid states, for example, operate three-dimensionally (Rey, 1979; Rosenfeld, 1965), but this does not automatically make them easy to help.

There are different ways of making use of another person's "inside" mental capacities: this may be an area in which personality factors (Anne Alvarez, chapter 6, this volume) have a crucial impact. Linda, Kane, and Adam conveyed their experiences in ways that left no doubt about their ability to use another person's mind and often left their therapists close to being overwhelmed. This was probably largely due to their need to communicate the degree to which they themselves felt overwhelmed (though Kane and Jonathan, for example, sometimes seemed to achieve some feeling of mastery over their own confusion by heightening it). Olivia, Marco, and Jonathan, on the other hand, were more inclined to control other people by obsessional means, which is a gentler mode. It is the mode adopted by one of the three patients emerging from autistic states who are discussed in a paper by Geneviève Haag (1997). Two other patients whom she described coped by means of more florid behaviour and fanstasies, as did Linda, Kane, and Adam and the two adult patients, Zara and Catherine.

It will be obvious to the reader that these psychoanalytically based descriptions, which are concerned with the detail of subjective experience and of self-protective devices, diverge from psychiatric behavioural categories. Indeed, child psychotherapists would speak of "autistic" or "schizoid" modes of functioning in the case of children in treatment who are neither autistic nor schizoid (see, for example, Rhode, 1997b). It may be that further research on the natural history of Asperger's syndrome makes it possible to map the psychoanalytic categories onto psychiatric, behavioural, and epidemiological ones—a step in the direction of Anne Alvarez's "periodic table". In the meantime, considerations such as these may contribute towards reconciling some of the disagreements concerning the overlap between Asperger's syndrome on the one hand, and autism and schizophrenia on the other. Similarly, children such as Karim and Jonathan make the similarities between Asperger's syndrome and ADHD understandable on the level of emotional experience. A number of the children were also dyspraxic (see Ad-Dab'bagh & Greenfield, 2001; Gillberg, 1991b), and again there might be an overlap between a neurological fragility and the emotional–physical difficulty in relaxing and creating a space between impulse and action.

Recurring themes across cases

In spite of all these differences, many similarities recur across the subgroups. An obvious one is the theme of extreme infantile helplessness (Tustin, 1981b, 1981c, 1994a, 1994b), strikingly represented in the image of a baby—or baby-like animal—with arms hanging loosely, unable to grasp and hold on.[2] A related image concerns that of a dead, brain-damaged, misshapen, or "ugly" (Meltzer, 1988)[3] baby or foetus with whom the child or young person seems to identify—and indeed many of the histories include miscarriages. This is not to say that miscarriages "cause" Asperger's syndrome any more than maternal depression does. As has been stressed in the Introduction, there are far more mothers who are physically ill or depressed, or who suffer miscarriages, than there are children with autism or Asperger's syndrome. However, these and similar factors may make it more difficult for the parents to provide the unusually high level of containment, attunement, initiative, and hope that these vulnerable or unresponsive children demand.

Bodily clumsiness is one of the characteristics mentioned by Asperger, though it is not necessary for a diagnosis. Virtually all the case histories, as well as the first-person accounts, illustrate problems in this area, and many include perceptual difficulties as well. Tustin's emphasis on physical experience in autism, as well as Haag's theories on the emotional components of bodily integration, have been summarized in the Introduction. They make it possible to subsume apparently unrelated features of autism and Asperger's syndrome under one theoretical framework. It is worth emphasizing, again, that many objections to a psychoanalytically based approach to these conditions fail to take account of developments in psychoanalytic theory over the last fifty years. Perhaps bodily terrors, in particular, provide the bridge between Asperger's syndrome, ADHD, and dyspraxia. Anxieties are often expressed physically, and the children frequently resort to physi-cal means of self-calming (see Asperger's own example cited on p. 56). It is interesting that some of the psychotherapists describe bodily expe-riences in the countertransference, which perhaps begin to provide some containment.

Other recurring images that have already been noted include that of birth—most strikingly perhaps in the case of Marco—and that of robots, sometimes with antennae. The children seem to be trying to protect themselves by physical means (such as the robot's armour—see Tustin, 1972, chap. 3) in the absence of adequate containment. In con-nection with antennae, it is worth mentioning the frequent observation that children with conditions including autism and Asperger's syn-drome can sometimes seem uncannily aware of other people's feelings. Tustin (1981b) and Meltzer (1975a) have referred to this phenomenon, and it has also been observed in some borderline or psychotic adults (e.g. Rosenfeld, 1987).

Gunilla Gerland (chapter 4, this volume) experienced other peo-ple's emotional states very vividly in terms of an idiosyncratic system of colours (compare Rey, 1994a), and Donna Williams has described what she calls the system of "sensing", as discussed in the Introduc-tion. Some children on the autistic spectrum falsely hold themselves accountable for anything wrong with others (Meltzer, 1975a) and may even attack them physically, as though trying to elicit proof of strength (H. S. Klein, 1974), when they sense vulnerability or damage (Rhode, 1999). This particular sensitivity is perhaps best seen in the case of Jonathan, who seemed to take no notice of his therapist but modified his behaviour in response to variations in her quality of attention and even unerringly attacked a hidden physical injury she had sustained.

Heredity, neurology, and psychology: the issue of "hard-wiring"

A history of severe mental illness was present on one or both sides of the family in the cases of Linda and Kane, while Jonathan—who, like Kane, was premature—suffered from epilepsy and may have sustained some perinatal neurological damage in addition to post-natal trauma. As has already been noted, Asperger's syndrome, like autism, tends to run in families (Gillberg, 1991b), and identical twin studies have led

Rutter and his colleagues to conclude that 90% of the variance may be accounted for by heredity in cases of autism (Rutter, 2000, 2001). However, he also stresses the importance of the environment in influencing the expression of hereditary factors (Rutter, 2001) and has described a minority of children, such as some Romanian orphans, who developed autistic-like responses after experiencing global deprivation (Rutter et al., 1999). At the present time, organicists and psychodynamic workers alike are increasingly subscribing to multifactorial theories of causation.

Tustin (1981b, 1994b), who thought of autism as a psychobiological reaction, never suggested that the children whom she successfully treated had not sustained any brain damage: merely that any such damage was not possible to detect by the methods that were then available. A paper by Bianca Lechevalier-Haim (2003) supports this line of argument. She describes the long treatment of a girl who received parent–infant therapy with her mother before going on to individual psychotherapy. The initial reasons for referral included serious motor difficulties as well as failure to make eye contact, and the child went on to develop many behaviours characteristic of autism. In the course of treatment she grew able to manage well at a mainstream school, both academically and socially; her motor problems were the last to improve. It was not until she had an MRI scan during adolescence, which had not previously been available, that extensive cerebellar damage was revealed—damage that has been noted in some cases of autism. As Lechevalier points out, previous awareness of this impairment would have provided a neurologically convincing explanation for the girl's motor difficulties and might have led her parents and therapist to think that psychological treatment was irrelevant, whereas in fact the motor problems did at length resolve (see Salomonsson, 2004).

Arguments put forward by Perry, Schore, and others illustrate the way in which emotional experience can facilitate the development of brain structure and function, which can, in turn, make it possible to manage even quite severe deficits. Indeed, Schore (2002) does not believe that major brain anomalies are "reversible": rather, that therapy and nurture can support the laying down of higher-order structures that make it possible to deal with the anomalies. This seems to be compatible with Bion's theory of containment and to go a long way towards resolving the traditional dichotomy between explanations on the level of psychology and of "hard-wiring".[4]

Indeed, experiences may come about for neurological or for psychological reasons, or through a combination of the two. Perhaps, in the end, the essential question does not concern the "cause" of the children's sense of terror. It may be a neurologically based experience of unintegration for which they mistakenly blame their caregiver and which was inadequately contained for them; it may be a fear of being intruded into or engulfed; it may be the terror of being dropped into the "death gap"; it may be the anxiety that their own destructive impulses are actualized in internal reality, an issue to which we return below. One of the benefits of therapy can be to tease apart some of these factors.

One characteristic of people with Asperger's syndrome on which workers with different theoretical perspectives do seem to agree is their hypersensitivity, though some emphasize the sensory aspect, others the emotional. It is tempting to think of this hypersensitivity as a neurological base (not the only one), which may then accrue emotional meaning as fantasies are mapped onto it. It might then be modified or aggravated, depending on what containment is available. Neurologically based experiences can become "personified", as in the case of the boy who covered his ears when a man came towards him and his therapist in a doorway (Rhode, 1997b). This boy was hypersensitive to light as well as sound; this was accentuated after some aggressive play with scissors, so that he shied away from the sunlight coming through a window. As Meltzer (1975a) has written, inadequate containment can leave the child at the mercy of a "bombardment of sensa".

The relevance and effects of psychotherapy: handling the issue of diagnosis

Such a line of thought goes a long way towards reconciling the seeming opposition between neurological and psychological levels of explanation. James Grotstein (1997), who is both a psychiatrist and a psychoanalyst, has proposed that Asperger's syndrome—and autism—resemble schizophrenia in being biologically based, and that the benefits of therapy may stem from helping people to manage their condition: a formulation that is very similar to that of Schore (2002) which has already been referred to. Judy Shuttleworth (1999), a child psychotherapist who has described the long-term once-weekly treatment of an adolescent with Asperger's syndrome, stresses the importance of recognizing the biological basis of the condition. Like Caroline Polmear (chapter 5), she emphasizes that the characteristics of Asperger's syndrome do not go away, but they come to be counterbalanced by the growth of other aspects of the personality that is facilitated during therapy.

Shuttleworth argues that it is unhelpful to interpret biological damage in terms of the young person's fantasies. For instance, if someone with Asperger's syndrome talks about being brain-damaged, she thinks it is important not to see this in the context of their possible fears about their personal contribution to it, which would imply responsibility where none exists. This, in our view, is a vitally important consideration, but it is also a question of therapeutic timing and tact. Young people in whom there is no question of biological damage can sometimes feel responsible for having contributed to what they feel is an impairment in their intellectual functioning (Trowell, Rhode, Miles, & Sherwood, 2003). If, as we have argued, psychological and biological levels of experience can map onto each other, then addressing fantasies of having contributed to one's own intellectual problems could help to modify any psychological component and allow one to reach whatever biologically determined ceiling might exist. Obviously, it could be profoundly harmful if this were done in such a way as to imply that the therapist actually believed the young person to be responsible, or without having first acknowledged the reality of the condition. A parallel exists with the importance of acknowledging the reality of adverse events that a child may have suffered before approaching any fantasy dimension (Rhode, 1997a).

Thus, Caroline Polmear (chapter 5) felt that her integration of Oliver Sacks's account of Asperger's syndrome with the theories she normally used marked a watershed in her work and fundamentally influenced what she interpreted. This did not mean that the development of her patients' fantasy life was inhibited. Quite the contrary: it was after this that Zara was able to experience fully, in relation to her analyst in the transference, the fear of "dead eyes" and to connect this meaningfully to the "dead budgerigar", while her previous speculations about the relationship between her mother's miscarriages and depression had appeared to be relatively sterile.

This leads on to the issue of the different emotional uses to which a diagnosis of Asperger's syndrome may be put. It can be an enormous relief to parents to realize that a name exists for the way their child behaves or fails to relate, that other people share their experience, that they are not alone with it. The young people themselves can feel the same relief—Gunilla Gerland, for example, describes movingly her previous tortured ruminations about whether perhaps she was "backward" and it was being kept from her. Even children as young as Olivia or Linda were aware of being different from their peers, though of course children can feel "different" for a wide variety of reasons. In that sense, a diagnosis is not just a means of obtaining vital extra support: it can be a validation of people's experience of themselves.

A diagnosis can also have disadvantages. Pain at the reality of impairment is one, but this may be a step towards making the most of what is possible; and, as writers from Asperger onward have noted, people with the syndrome often have outstanding capacities. It may be essential to provide ongoing consultative support, which can have impressive results (see chapter 14). What can be more problematic is the adoption of Asperger's syndrome as an alternative identity, particularly if it creates the expectation of restricted development.

Managing aggressive impulses

Children with autism and Asperger's syndrome can often experience their own aggressive impulses as being unrealistically powerful and damaging. Impaired relationships can mean that they lack the reassuring experience of having their anger accepted and helpfully dealt with by adults and other children. All the children and young people described in this volume responded well when they encountered firmness, the need for which always had to be carefully weighed against their genuine vulnerability; though they did not necessarily welcome such firmness, they began to relate much better. Caroline Polmear's adult patients were most dissociated from their own aggression, not surprisingly perhaps in view of their age and the habits of a lifetime. They were shocked by it, particularly by aggressive fantasies in relation to the analyst, and sometimes they dealt with it by what Polmear calls "cartooning"—that is, by removing any emotional significance from a cartoon-like picture. The younger patients, who were less dissociated, could be helped more quickly.

This is not to imply that Asperger children are unusually aggressive, but that they can be particularly worried about the consequences of aggression. Asperger's original statement that his children were spiteful is discussed by David Simpson and Trudy Klauber (chapters 1 and 3). As already noted, some authors (e.g. Frith, 1991a) have suggested that, when these children inflict pain on others, it is simply because they want a reaction and cannot imagine the other person's experience. (Interestingly, this is how Jonathan's parents explained his laughter when people fell down.) This explanation seems unconvincing, since there are many other ways of getting a reaction. It appears more likely that the children are seeking some degree of mastery over the pain that they have themselves experienced—what Anna Freud (1936) called "identification with the aggressor"—or that they are desperately trying to protect themselves against people by whom they feel threatened.[5] For example, Gunilla Gerland's frenzied attempt to keep supposedly hostile people out of her room by throwing lemonade at them was misinterpreted as aggression, perhaps understandably. Equally, as has already been suggested, an aggressive child may hope to elicit firm behaviour that disproves their fear that an adult may have been weakened or damaged (H. S. Klein, 1974); or they may be communicating their own fear of being attacked and hurt as a first step towards finding containment. It is when this hope of containment dwindles and external reality seems to embody the child's worst fears that children withdraw most completely. For instance, Cecchi (1990) has described a little girl who went through a total autistic-like retreat following the "disappearance" of her parents by the Argentinean secret police. Paradoxically, then, focused aggression in relation to other people can be a hopeful sign,[6] but only as long as the child is young enough to be physically manageable.

Factors affecting therapeutic outcome

Age and subgroup of Asperger's syndrome

Psychoanalytic psychotherapy certainly does not suit all young people with Asperger's syndrome, just as it does not suit all young people without it. As discussed in the Introduction to part II, a thorough assessment is necessary to see whether they respond and whether this way of working makes sense to them, to their parents, and to their teachers at school.

In general, not surprisingly, the younger the child, the better the prognosis. However, the adults treated by Caroline Polmear made dramatic gains, and both the adolescents, Jonathan and Adam, improved substantially. In both cases, the pubertal process provided a helpful developmental impetus (Howlin, 1997). However, it also makes for delicate technical problems, since ordinary adolescent sexuality, as Anne Alvarez notes in chapter 6, does not have any of the usual outlets and can easily become confused with states of mind that belong to other developmental stages. Problems in dealing tactfully with the sexual transference of an adolescent with Asperger's syndrome are cogently discussed by Hope Cooper in an unpublished paper (2003).

All the children—whichever of the two subgroups they belonged to—improved considerably. However, the results with Olivia and Marco were perhaps even more encouraging than those with Jonathan, who was older. The ultimate outcome for Kane and Adam, the two older children in the "borderline" subgroup, is more uncertain than that for the others, though Linda, the youngest in this group, achieved striking improvements. Here, again, is an illustration of the importance of early intervention, however reluctant professionals may understandably be to label a young child and however much they and the parents may hope that the child will "grow out of it" (Rustin, 1997a).

Technical issues

The importance of the therapist's countertransference has been stressed throughout the clinical histories, and is evoked particularly vividly by Brian Truckle (chapter 13). The countertransference is increasingly thought of as an indispensable therapeutic tool (Brenman-Pick, 1985; Racker, 1968), and nowhere more so than in children with Asperger's syndrome, whose emotional experience is affected at such a profound level and is so difficult to convey by means of words. The therapist can often feel despair or fear that there is no meaning in the child's behaviour. Sometimes this may be realistic, but often meaning can emerge on reflection, in supervision or through consultation with colleagues, and in these cases it is likely that the therapist's reaction was a reflection of the child's own fears. Experiences such as these make it easy to understand and sympathize with the feelings of parents when faced with their child's lack of responsiveness.

Throughout the case histories, the reader will find instances of a more active technique than would be used with non-Asperger children and adults. The need for such modifications has been discussed by writers on autism from Meltzer (1975a) and Tustin (1972, 1981b) onwards and has been extensively theorized by Alvarez (1992b, 2000) in particular. She has proposed the term "reclamation" for the therapist's role in carrying and calling into being aspects of the child that have not yet developed (Alvarez, 1980, 1992b, 1999a). Other examples of active technique include interventions to help a child who has got stuck in repetitive behaviour, the reliance on humour, and the use of means of communication, such as drawing and rhythm, which are not generally part of psychoanalytic work with adults (Caroline Polmear, chapter 5).

Most of the children and young people described in this volume were seen three times weekly. Intensive treatment seems particularly helpful in a condition like Asperger's syndrome: Olivia's treatment illustrates the benefit of increasing from once to three times a week, though after a stretch of intensive work she was able to do well on less. Adam, however, made considerable progress in once-weekly therapy, as did other children who did not exemplify the two extreme sub-types so clearly and were not included for that reason. Maria Pozzi (2003a) has described once-weekly work with a 12-year-old boy who was unresponsive and dismissive until she began to describe the minute movements of each part of his body—a technique with obvious links to the importance of bodily anxieties in Asperger's syndrome. She has also reported good results from work with a 3-year-old seen once-weekly, sometimes with his mother, sometimes with the whole family. In this case, she found it useful to combine a traditional child psychotherapy approach with more directive behavioural guidance.

* * *

Just as the contributors to this volume come from a variety of disciplines, so the outcome of each case depended on cooperation between parents, teachers, GPs, paediatricians, psychiatrists, psychotherapists, and many others. Eventually, it may be possible to develop a psychoanalytically based taxonomy of Asperger's syndrome, encompassing the coping mechanisms resorted to as well as the characteristic anxieties, which would make its own specific contribution to the continuing interdisciplinary effort that is necessary for a fuller understanding of the condition, and we hope that this book will be a step towards this endeavour. Most of all, however, we have tried to render more accessible the emotional experience of children and young people with Asperger's syndrome and to illustrate what they can achieve in the course of psychoanalytic psychotherapy.

Notes

1. It is important to distinguish psychopathy—the apparent lack of conscience in relation to other people—from the "autistic psychopathy" that is part of the title of Asperger's original paper. This is a somewhat unsatisfactory rendering of the original German, which is closer to [people with] "psychopathology". (See also Trudy Klauber's commentary on the paper in chapter 3, this volume.)

2. As already noted, this seems to be an image that appears whether or not any actual experience—such as the physical illness of Olivia's mother—has contributed to it.

3. See note 3, p. 151, for Meltzer's theorization of the "ugly" baby.

4. O'Shaughnessy (1999) has similarly discussed the growth of higher-order structures in relation to primitive aspects of the superego.

5. Identification of this kind can also be seen as counterphobic behaviour.

6. The passive type of autistic child described by Anne Alvarez (1992b) is, as Tustin (1994a) agreed, a long and daunting treatment proposition.

REFERENCES

Aarons, M., & Gittens, T. (1992). *The Handbook of Autism: A Guide for Parents and Professionals* (2nd edition). London: Routledge, 1999.

Abraham, K. (1924). A short study of the development of the libido, viewed in the light of mental disorders. In: *Selected Papers on Psycho-Analysis* (pp. 418–501). London: Hogarth Press.

Ad-Dab'bagh, Y., & Greenfield, B. (2001). Multiple complex developmental disorder: The "multiple complex evolution" of the "childhood borderline syndrome" construct. *Journal of the American Academy of Child and Adolescent Psychiatry, 40* (8): 954–964.

Alvarez, A. (1980). Two regenerative situations in autism: Reclamation and becoming vertebrate. *Journal of Child Psychotherapy, 6.*

Alvarez, A. (1990). The need to remember and the need to forget. In: *The Consequences of Child Sexual Abuse* (chap. 4). Association of Child Psychology and Psychiatry Occasional Papers, III. London: Association of Child Psychology and Psychiatry.

Alvarez, A. (1992a). A developmental view of "defence": Borderline patients. In: *Live Company.* London & New York: Tavistock/Routledge.

Alvarez, A. (1992b). *Live Company: Psychoanalytic Psychotherapy with Autistic, Borderline, Deprived, and Abused Children.* London: Routledge.

Alvarez, A. (1992c). Making the thought thinkable: Perspective on introjection and projection. In: *Live Company.* London & New York: Tavistock/Routledge.

Alvarez, A. (1993). Un approccio interazionale al trattamento dei bambini con autismo [An interactional approach to the psychotherapy of autism]. In: *Richard e Piggle* (pp. 3–17). Rome: Il Pensiero Scientifico Editore.

Alvarez, A. (1995). Motiveless malignity: Problems in the psychotherapy of psychopathic patients. *Journal of Child Psychotherapy, 21*: 167–182. [Also in: *Psychoanalytic Inquiry, 19*: 2.]

Alvarez, A. (1999a). Addressing the deficit: Developmentally informed psychotherapy with passive "undrawn" children. In: A. Alvarez & S. Reid (Eds.), *Autism and Personality.* London: Routledge

Alvarez, A. (1999b). Disorder, deviance and personality: Factors in the

275

persistence and modifiability of autism. In: A. Alvarez & S. Reid (Eds.), *Autism and Personality*. London: Routledge.

Alvarez, A. (2000). Moral imperatives in work with borderline children: The grammar of wishes and the grammar of needs. In: J. Symington (Ed.), *Imprisoned Pain and Its Transformation: A Festschrift for H. Sydney Klein*. London: Karnac.

Alvarez, A., & Reid, S. (Eds.). (1999a). *Autism and Personality: Findings from the Tavistock Autism Workshop*. London & New York: Routledge.

Alvarez, A., & Reid, S. (1999b). Introduction. In: A. Alvarez & S. Reid (Eds.), *Autism and Personality: Findings from the Tavistock Autism Workshop*. London & New York: Routledge.

APA (1994). *Diagnostic and Statistical Manual of Mental Disorders* (4th edition). Washington, DC: American Psychiatric Association.

Asperger, H. (1944). Die "Autistischen Psycopathen" im Kindersalter. *Archiv für Psychiatrie unde Nervenkrankheiten, 117*: 76–136. ["Autistic Psychopathy" in Childhood (translated by U. Frith). In: U. Frith (Ed.), *Autism and Asperger Syndrome* (pp. 37–92). Cambridge: Cambridge University Press, 1991.]

Attwood, T. (1998). *Asperger's Syndrome: A Guide for Parents and Professionals*. London: Jessica Kingley.

Bailey, A., Luthert, P., Dean, A., Harding, B., Janota, I., Montgomery, M., Rutter, M., & Lantos, P. (1998). A clinicopathological study of autism. *Brain, 121*: 889–905.

Balbernie, R. (2001). Circuits and circumstances: The neurobiologial consequences of early relationship experiences and how they shape later behaviour. *Journal of Child Psychotherapy, 27*: 237–256.

Balint, M. (1959). *Thrills and Regressions*. New York: International Universities Press.

Balint, M. (1968). *The Basic Fault: Therapeutic Aspects of Regression*. London: Tavistock Publications.

Baron-Cohen, S. (1988). Social and pragmatic deficits in autism: Cognitive or affective? *Journal of Autism and Developmental Disorder, 18*: 3.

Baron-Cohen, S. (2002). The extreme male brain theory of autism. *Trends in Cognitive Sciences, 6*: 1–7.

Baron-Cohen, S., Leslie, A., & Frith, U. (1985). Does the autistic child have a "theory of mind"? *Cognition, 21*: 37–46.

Barrows, P. (2001). The use of stories as autistic objects. *Journal of Child Psychotherapy, 27*: 69–62.

Barrows, P. (2002). Becoming verbal: Autism, trauma, and playfulness. *Journal of Child Psychotherapy, 28*: 53–72.

Bettelheim, B. (1967). *The Empty Fortress*. New York: Free Press.

Bick, E. (1964). Notes on infant observation in psycho-analytic training. *International Journal of Psycho-Analysis, 45*: 240–256. Reprinted in: A. Briggs (Ed.), *Surviving Space*. London: Karnac, 2002.

Bick, E. (1968). The experience of the skin in early object-relations. *International Journal of Psycho-Analysis, 49*: 484–486. Reprinted in: M. Harris

Williams (Ed.), *Collected Papers of Martha Harris and Esther Bick*. Strath Tay, Perthshire: Clunie Press. Also in: A. Briggs (Ed.), *Surviving Space*. London: Karnac, 2002.

Bick, E. (1986). Further considerations on the function of the skin in early object relations. *British Journal of Psychotherapy, 2*: 292–299. Reprinted in: A. Briggs (Ed.), *Surviving Space*. London: Karnac, 2002.

Bion, W. R. (1957). Differentiation of the psychotic from the non-psychotic personalities. In: *Second Thoughts*. London: Heinemann, 1967. Reprinted London: Karnac, 1984.

Bion, W. R. (1958). On hallucination. *International Journal of Psycho-Analysis, 39* (5). In: *Second Thoughts,* London: Heinemann, 1967. Reprinted London: Karnac, 1984.

Bion, W. R. (1962). *Learning from Experience*. London: Heinemann. Reprinted London: Karnac, 1984.

Bion, W. R. (1963). *Elements of Psycho-Analysis*. London: Heinemann. Reprinted London: Karnac, 1984.

Bion, W. R. (1979). Making the best of a bad job. In: *Clinical Seminars and Other Works*, ed. F. Bion. London: Karnac, 1994.

Bion, W. R. (1991). *A Memoir of the Future*. London: Karnac.

Bishop, D. V. M. (1993). Annotation: Autism, executive functions and "theory of mind": A neuropsychological perspective. *Journal of Child Psychology & Psychiatry, 34*: 279–293.

Bishop, D. V. M. (1998). Semantic-pragmatic disorders and the autistic continuum. *British Journal of Communication, 24*: 115–122.

Bleuler, E. (1911). *Dementia praecox oder Gruppe der Schizophrenien*, trans. J. Zinkin. New York: International Universities Press, 1950.

Bowler, D. M. (1992). "Theory of mind" in Asperger's Syndrome. *Journal of Child Psychology & Psychiatry, 33*: 877–893.

Bowman, E. P. (1988). Asperger's Syndrome and autism: The case for a connection. *British Journal of Psychiatry, 152*: 377–382.

Bremner, J., & Meltzer, D. (1975). Autism proper: Timmy. In: D. Meltzer, J. Bremner, S. Hoxter, D. Wedell, & I. Wittenberg (Eds.), *Explorations in Autism: A Psychoanalytical Study*. Strath Tay, Perthshire: Clunie Press.

Brenman Pick, I. (1985). Working through in the countertransference. *International Journal of Psycho-Analysis, 66*: 157–166. Revised version in: E. B. Spillius (Ed.), *Melanie Klein Today. Vol. 2: Mainly Practice*. London: Routledge, 1988.

Briggs, A. (2001). *Surviving Space*. Tavistock Clinic Series. London: Karnac.

Briggs, S. (1997). *Growth and Risk in Infancy*. London: Jessica Kingsley.

Britton, R. (1989). The missing link: Parental sexuality in the Oedipus complex. In: J. Steiner (Ed.), *The Oedipus Complex Today: Clinical Implications*. London: Karnac.

Britton, R. (1998). *Belief and Imagination*. London: Routledge.

Burgoine, E., & Wing, L. (1993). Identical triplets with Asperger's Syndrome. *British Journal of Psychiatry, 143*: 261–265.

Burhouse, A. (1999). "Me, You and It: Conversations about the Signifi-

cance of Joint Attention Skills from Cognitive Psychology, Child De-
velopment Research and Psychoanalysis." Unpublished MA thesis,
Psychoanalytic Observational Studies: Tavistock Clinic/University of
East London.

Cecchi, V. (1990). The analysis of a little girl with an autistic syndrome.
International Journal of Psycho-Analysis, 71: 403–410.

Clarke, D. J., Littlejohns, C. S., Corbett, J. A., & Joseph, S. (1989). Pervasive
developmental disorders and psychosis in adult life. *British Journal of
Psychiatry, 155*: 692–699.

Cohen, M. (2003). *Sent Before My Time: A Child Psychotherapist's View of Life
on a Neonatal Intensive Care Unit.* Tavistock Clinic Series. London:
Karnac.

Cooper, H. (2003). "Learning to Be: The Use of Psychoanalytic Psychotherapy in Treating Asperger's Syndrome in a Teenage Boy." Unpublished paper.

Cornwell, J. (1983). Crisis and survival infancy. *Journal of Child Psychotherapy, 9*: 25–33.

Damasio, A. (2000). *The Feeling of What Happens: Body, Emotion and the
Making of Consciousness.* London: William Heinemann.

Dawson, G. & Fischer, K. W. (1994). *Human Behaviour and the Developing
Brain.* New York: Guilford Press.

Dawson, G., & Lewy, A. (1989). Arousal, attention, and the socioemotional
impairments of individuals with autism. In: G. Dawson (Ed.), *Autism:
Nature, Diagnosis and Treatment.* New York: Guilford Press.

DeLong, G. R., & Dwyer, J. T. (1988). Correlation of family history with
specific autistic subgroups: Asperger's Syndrome and bipolar affective disease. *Journal of Autism and Developmental Disorders, 18*: 593–600.

Dennett, D. C. (1978). Beliefs about beliefs. *Behavioural and Brain Sciences, 4*:
568–570.

Deykin, E. Y., & MacMahon, B. (1979). The incidence of seizures among
children with autistic symptoms. *American Journal of Psychiatry, 136*:
1310–1312.

Emanuel, L. (1997). Facing the damage together: Some reflections arising
from the treatment in psychotherapy of a severely mentally handicapped child. *Journal of Child Psychotherapy, 23*: 279–302.

Everall, I. P., & Le Couteur, A. (1990). Firesetting in an adolescent boy with
Asperger's Syndrome. *British Journal of Psychiatry, 157*: 284–287.

Fonagy, P. (1999). Guest editorial: Memory and therapeutic action. *International Journal of Psycho-Analysis, 80*: 215–223.

Fonagy, P., & Target, M. (1999). Towards understanding violence: The use
of the body and the role of the father. In: R. Josef Perelberg (Ed.),
Psychoanalytic Understanding of Violence and Suicide. London & New
York: Routledge.

Freud, A. (1936). Identification with the aggressor. In: *The Ego and the
Mechanisms of Defence.* London: Hogarth, 1976.

Freud, S. (1909d). Notes upon a case of obsessional neurosis. *S.E. 10* (pp.
153–318).

Freud, S. (1923b). *The Ego and the Id. SE. 19.*

Frith, U. (1989). *Autism: Explaining the Enigma.* Oxford: Blackwell.

Frith, U. (1991a). Asperger and his syndrome. In: U. Frith (Ed.), *Autism and Asperger Syndrome* (pp. 1–36). Cambridge: Cambridge University Press.

Frith, U. (Ed.). (1991b). *Autism and Asperger Syndrome.* Cambridge: Cambridge University Press.

Frith, U. (1991c). "Autistic psychopathy" in childhood [English translation of paper by Hans Asperger]. In: U. Frith (Ed.), *Autism and Asperger Syndrome.* Cambridge: Cambridge University Press.

Frith, U. (2002). "Asperger's: Brain and Mind." Emanuel Miller Memorial Lecture, London, February.

Frith, U. (2004). Confusions and controversies about Asperger's syndrome. *Journal of Child Psychology and Psychiatry, 45*: 672–686.

Frith, U., & Hermelin, B. (1969). The role of visual and motor cues for normal, subnormal and autistic children. *Journal of Child Psychology and Psychiatry, 10*: 153–163.

Gerland, G. (1996a). *A Real Person: Life on the Outside,* trans. J. Tate. London: Souvenir Press, 1997.

Gerland, G. (1996b). Reply to *Review* [translation of an article published in the Swedish journal of psychology, *Psykolog Tidningen, 16*] <http://ashfa.cjb.net/gerland_e1.html>.

Ghaziuddin, M., Leininger, L., & Tsai, L. (1995). Brief report. Thought disorder in Asperger's Syndrome: Comparison with high-functioning autism. *Journal of Autism & Developmental Disorders, 25*: 311–317.

Ghaziuddin, M., Tsai, L.Y., & Ghaziuddin, N. (1991). Brief report. Violence in Asperger's syndrome, a critique. *Journal of Autism & Developmental Disorders, 21*: 349–354.

Gillberg, C. (1991a). Autism and autistic-like conditions: Subclassess among disorders of empathy. The Emmanuel Miller Memorial Lecture. *Journal of Child Psychology and Psychiatry, 33*: 813–842.

Gillberg, C. (1991b). Clinical and neurobiological aspects of Asperger syndrome in six family studies. In: U. Frith (Ed.), *Autism and Asperger Syndrome.* Cambridge: Cambridge University Press.

Gomberoff, M., & de Gomberoff, L. P. (2000). Autistic devices in small children in mourning. *International Journal of Psychoanalysis, 81*: 907–920.

Greenspan, S. I. (1997). *Developmentally Based Psychotherapy.* Madison, CT: International Universities Press.

Grossman, D. (1991). *See Under: Love.* London: Picador.

Grotstein, J. S. (1997). One pilgrim's progress: Notes on Frances Tustin's contributions to the psychoanalytic conception of autism. In: T. Mitrani & J. L. Mitrani (Eds.), *Encounters with Autistic States: A Memorial Tribute to Frances Tustin.* Northvale, NJ: Jason Aronson.

Grotstein, J. S. (2000). *Who Is the Dreamer Who Dreams the Dream? A Study of Psychic Presences.* Hillsdale, NJ, & London: Analytic Press.

Haag, G. (1984). Réflexions sur certains aspects du langage d'enfants autistes en cours de démutisation. *Neuropsychiatrie de l'Enfance, 32*: 539–544.

Haag, G. (1985). La mère et le bébé dans les deux moitiés du corps. *Neuropsychiatrie de l'Enfance, 33*: 107–114.

Haag, G. (1991). Nature de quelques identifications dans l'image du corps (hypothèses). *Journal de la Psychanalyse de l'Enfant, 4*: 73–92.

Haag, G. (1997). Psychosis and autism: Schizophrenic, perverse and manic-depressive states during psychotherapy. In: M. Rustin, M. Rhode, A. Dubinsky, & H. Dubinsky (Eds.), *Psychotic States in Children*. London: Duckworth.

Haag, G. (2000). In the footsteps of Frances Tustin: Further reflections on the construction of the body-ego. *International Journal of Infant Observation, 3*.

Happé, F. (1991). The autobiographical writings of three Asperger syndrome adults: Problems of interpretation and implication for theory. In: U. Frith (Ed.), *Autism and Asperger Syndrome*. Cambridge: Cambridge University Press.

Happé, F. (1994). *Autism: An Introduction to Psychological Theory*. London: UCL Press.

Happé F., & Frith, U. (1995). Debate & argument: How useful is the PDD label? *Journal of Child Psychology and Psychiatry, 32*: 1167–1168.

Heimann, P. (1950). On counter-transference. *International Journal of Psycho-Analysis, 31*: 81–84. Republished in: *About Children and Children-No-Longer* (pp. 73–79). London: Routledge, 1989.

Hobson, R. P. (1990). Concerning knowledge about mental states. *British Journal of Medical Psychology, 63*: 199–213.

Hobson, R. P. (1991). What is autism? In: M. Konstantareas & J. Beitchman (Eds.), *Psychiatric Clinics of North America, Vol. 14* (pp. 1–17). Pennsylvania, PA: Saunders.

Hobson, R. P. (1993). *Autism and the Development of Mind*. Hove: Psychology Press.

Hobson, R. P. (1994). Understanding persons: The role of affect. In: S. Baron-Cohen, H. Tager-Flusberg, & D. J. Cohen (Eds.), *Understanding Other Minds: Perspectives from Autism*. Oxford: Oxford Medical Publications.

Hobson, R. P. (2002). *The Cradle of Thought*. Basingstoke: Macmillan.

Hobson, R. P., & Lee, A. (1989). Emotion-related and abstract concepts in autistic people: Evidence from the BPVP. *Journal of Autism and Developmental Disorders 19*: 601–603.

Hobson, P., Ouston, J., & Lee, A. (1988). What's in a face? The case of autism. *British Journal of Psychology, 79*: 441–553.

Houzel, D. (1995). Precipitation anxiety. *Journal of Child Psychotherapy, 21*: 65–78.

Houzel, D. (2001a). Bisexual qualities of the psychic envelope. In: J. Edwards (Ed.), *Being Alive: Building on the Work of Anne Alvarez*. Hove: Brunner-Routledge.

Houzel, D. (2001b). The "nest of babies" phantasy. *Journal of Child Psychotherapy*, 27.

Howlin, P. (1997). *Autism: Preparing for Adulthood*. London: Routledge.

Howlin, P. (1998). *Children with Autism and Asperger Syndrome: A Guide for Practitioners and Carers*. Chichester: Wiley.

Howlin, P., & Goode, S. (1998). Outcome in adult life for people with autism and Asperger's Syndrome. In: F. R. Volkmar (Ed.), *Autism and Pervasive Development Disorders* (pp. 209–236). Cambridge: Cambridge University Press.

Jackson, L. (2002a). *Freaks, Geeks and Asperger's Syndrome*. London: Jessica Kingsley.

Jackson, L. (2002b). *A User Guide to the GF/CF Diet for Autism, Asperger Syndrome and ADHD*. London: Jessica Kingsley.

Jacobsen, P. (2003). *Asperger Syndrome and Psychotherapy*. London: Jessica Kingsley.

Johnson, D. J., & Myklebust, H. R. (1971). *Learning Disabilities*. New York: Grune & Stratton.

Joseph, B. (1982). Addiction to near-death. In: M. Feldman & E. Bott Spillius (Eds.), *Psychic Equilibrium and Psychic Change: Selected Papers of Betty Joseph*. London: Routledge, 1989.

Joseph, B. (1987). Projective identification: Some clinical aspects. In: J. Sandler (Ed.), *Projection, Identification, Projective Identification*, Madison, CT: International Universities Press. Reprinted in: E. Bott Spillius (Ed.), *Melanie Klein Today, Vol. 1: Mainly Theory*. London: Routledge, 1988. Also in: M. Feldman & E. Bott Spillius (Eds.), *Psychic Equilibrium and Psychic Change: Selected Papers of Betty Joseph*. New Library of Psychoanalysis. London & New York: Routledge, 1989.

Kanner, L. (1943). Autistic disturbance of affective contact. *Nervous Child*, 2: 217–250. Reprinted in: L. Kanner, *Childhood Psychosis: Initial Studies and New Insights*. New York: Wiley, 1973.

Kanner, L. (1944). Early infantile autism. *Journal of Paediatrics*, 25: 211–221.

Kanner, L. (1973). *Childhood Psychosis: Initial Studies and New Insights*. New York: Winston/Wiley.

Kaplan-Solms, K., & Solms, M. (2000). *Clinical Studies in Neuro-Psychoanalysis: Introduction to a Depth Neuropsychology*. London: Karnac.

Kasari, C., Sigman, M., Mundy, P., & Yirmiya, N. (1990). Affective sharing in the context of joint attention. *Journal of Autism and Developmental Disorders*, 20: 87–100.

Klauber, T. (1998). The significance of trauma in work with the parents of severely disturbed children, and its implications for work with parents in general. *Journal of Child Psychotherapy*, 24: 85–107.

Klauber, T. (1999a). The significance of trauma and other factors in work with the parents of autistic children. In: A. Alvarez & S. Reid (Eds.), *Autism and Personality: Findings from the Tavistock Autism Workshop*. London: Routledge.

Klauber, T. (1999b). Warren: From passive and sensuous compliance to a more lively independence: Limited objectives with a verbal adolescent. In: A. Alvarez & S. Reid (Eds.), *Autism and Personality: Findings from the Tavistock Autism Workshop*. London: Routledge.

Klauber, T. (2001). Glimpses of what might have been. In: J. Edwards (Ed.), *Being Alive: Building on the Work of Anne Alvarez*. London: Brunner Routledge.

Klein, H. S. (1965). Notes on a case of ulcerative colitis. *International Journal of Psycho-Analysis, 46*: 342–351.

Klein, H. S. (1974). Transference and defence in manic states. *International Journal of Psycho-Analysis, 55*: 397–404.

Klein, H. S. (1980). Autistic phenomena in neurotic patients. *International Journal of Psycho-Analysis, 61*: 395–402. Also in: J. S. Grotstein (Ed.), *Do I Dare Disturb the Universe?* Beverly Hills, CA: Caesura Press, 1981.

Klein, M. (1928). Early stages of the Oedipus complex. In: *The Writings of Melanie Klein, Vol. 1* (pp. 186–198). London: Hogarth Press, 1975.

Klein, M. (1930). The importance of symbol-formation in the development of the ego. In: *The Writings of Melanie Klein, Vol. 1* (pp. 219–232). London: Hogarth Press, 1975.

Klein, M. (1932). *The Psychoanalysis of Children. The Writings of Melanie Klein, Vol. 2*. London: Hogarth Press, 1975.

Klein, M. (1935). A contribution to the psychogenesis of manic-depressive states. In: *The Writings of Melanie Klein, Vol. 2* (pp. 262–289). London: Hogarth Press.

Klein, M. (1946). Notes on some schizoid mechanisms. In: *The Writings of Melanie Klein, Vol. 3* (pp. 1–32). London: Hogarth Press.

Klein, M. (1961). *Narrative of a Child Analysis*. In: *The Writings of Melanie Klein, Vol. 4*. London: Hogarth Press, 1975.

Klin, A., & Volkmar, F. R. (1995). Autism and the pervasive developmental disorders. *Child & Adolescent Psychiatric Clinics of North America, 4*: 617–630.

Klin, A., Volkmar, F. R., & Sparrow, S. S. (Eds.) (2000). *Asperger Syndrome*. New York & London: Guilford Press.

Kolvin, I. (1971). Studies in childhood psychosis. I. Diagnostic criteria classification. *British Journal of Psychiatry, 118*: 381–384.

Langdell, T. (1978). Recognition of faces: An approach to the study of autism. *Journal of Child Psychology and Psychiatry, 19*: 255–268.

Lechevalier-Haim, B. (2003). "Long-term Mother–Child Psychotherapy: Infantile Autism with Cerebellar Anomaly." Paper presented at the Annual Frances Tustin Memorial Prize and Lectureship. Psychoanalytic Confederation of California, Los Angeles, November.

Lincoln, A., Courchesne, E., Allen, M., Hanson, E., & Ene, M. (1998). Neurobiology of Asperger Syndrome: Seven case studies and quantitative magnetic resonance imaging findings. In: E. Schopler, G. Mesibov, & L. J. Kunce (Eds.), *Asperger Syndrome or High-Functioning Autism?* (pp. 145–166). New York: Plenum.

Lubbe, T. (Ed.). (2000). *The Borderline Psychotic Child: A Selective Integration*. London: Routledge.

Mahler, M. (1968). *On Human Symbiosis and the Vicissitudes of Individuation, Vol. 1: Infantile Psychosis*. New York: International Universities Press.

Mahler, M. S., Pine, F., & Bergman, A. (1975). *The Psychological Birth of the Human Infant: Symbiosis and Individuation*. New York: Basic Books.

Maiello, S. (2000). "Song-and-dance" and its developments: The function of rhythm in the learning process of oral and written language. In: M. Cohen & A. Hahn (Eds.), *Exploring the Work of Donald Meltzer: A Festschrift*. London: Karnac.

Mawson, D., Grounds, A., & Tantam, D. (1985). Violence and Asperger's syndrome: A case study. *British Journal of Psychiatry, 147*: 566–569.

McDougall, J. (1986). *Theatres of the Mind*. London: Free Association Books.

Meltzer, D. (1973). The origins of the fetishistic plaything of sexual perversions. In: *Sexual States of Mind*. Strath Tay, Perthshire: Clunie Press.

Meltzer, D. (1974). Adhesive identification. In: A. Hahn (Ed.), *Sincerity and Other Works: Collected Papers of Donald Meltzer*. London: Karnac.

Meltzer, D. (1975a). Dimensionality in mental functioning. In: D. Meltzer, J. Bremner, S. Hoxter, D. Wedell, & I. Wittenberg (Eds.), *Explorations in Autism: A Psychoanalytical Study*. Strath Tay, Perthshire: Clunie Press.

Meltzer, D. (1975b). Mutism in autism, schizophrenia and manic-depressive states—the correlation of clinical psycho-pathology and linguistics. In: D. Meltzer, J. Bremner, S. Hoxter, D. Wedell, & I. Wittenberg (Eds.), *Explorations in Autism: A Psychoanalytical Study*. Strath Tay, Perthshire: Clunie Press.

Meltzer, D. (1975c). The psychology of autistic states and of post-autistic mentality. In: D. Meltzer, J. Bremner, S. Hoxter, D. Wedell, & I. Wittenberg (Eds.), *Explorations in Autism: A Psychoanalytical Study*. Strath Tay, Perthshire: Clunie Press.

Meltzer, D. (1988). On aesthetic reciprocity. In: D. Meltzer & M. Harris Williams, *The Apprehension of Beauty*. Strath Tay, Perthshire: Clunie Press.

Meltzer, D., Bremner, J., Hoxter, S., Weddell, D., & Wittenberg, I. (1975). *Explorations in Autism: A Psychoanalytical Study*. Strath Tay, Perthshire: Clunie Press.

Miller, L., & Simpson, D. (2004). *Unexpected Gains: Psychotherapy with People with Learning Disabilities*. Tavistock Clinic Series. London: Karnac.

Mitchell, P., & Lacohee, H. (1991). Children's early understanding of false belief. *Cognition, 39*: 107–127.

Mitrani, J. (1993). "Unmentalized" experience in the etiology and treatment of psychosomatic asthma. *Contemporary Psychoanalysis, 29* (2): 314–342.

Mundy, P., & Sigman, M. (1989). Specifying the nature of the social impairment in autism. In: G. Dawson (Ed.), *Autism: Nature, Diagnosis and Treatment*. London: Guilford Press.

Murray, L. (1991). The impact of postnatal depression on infant development. *Journal of Child Psychology and Psychiatry, 33*: 543–561.

Nagy, J., & Szatmari, P. (1986). A chart review of schizotypal personality disorders in children. *Journal of Autism and Developmental Disorders, 16*: 351–367.

Ogden, T. (1989). On the concept of an autistic-contiguous position. *International Journal of Psycho-Analysis, 70*: 127–140.

Olsson, I., Steffenburg, S., & Gillberg, C. (1988). Epilepsy in autism and autistic-like conditions: A population-based study. *Archives of Neurology, 45*: 666–668.

O'Shaughnessy, E. (1999). Relating to the super-ego. *International Journal of Psychoanalysis, 80*: 861–870.

Ozonoff, S. (1997). Components of executive function in autism and other disorders. In: J. Russell (Ed.), *Autism as an Executive Disorder* (pp. 179–211). New York: Oxford University Press.

Ozonoff, S., Rogers, S., & Pennington, B. (1991). Asperger's Syndrome: Evidence of an empirical distinction from high-functioning autism. *Journal of Child Psychology and Psychiatry, 32*: 1107–1122.

Pennington, B. F., & Ozonoff, S. (1996). Executive functions and developmental pathologies. *Journal of Child Psychology and Psychiatry, 37*: 51–87.

Perner, J., Frith, U., Leslie, A. M., & Leekam, S. R. (1989). Exploration of the autistic child's "theory of mind": Knowledge, belief and communication. *Child Development, 60*: 689–700.

Perry, B., Pollard, R. A., Blakely, T. L., Baker, W. L., & Vigilante, D. (1995). Childhood trauma, the neurobiology of adaptation and "use-dependent" development of the brain: How states become traits. *Infant Mental Health Journal, 16*: 271–291.

Perry, R., Cohen, I., & DeCarlo, R. (1995). Case study: Deterioration, autism and recovery in two siblings. *Journal of American Child & Adolescent Psychotherapy, 2*: 232–237.

Pine, F. (1974). On the concept "borderline" in children. *Psychoanalytic Study of the Child, 29*: 341–368.

Piontelli, A. (1992). *From Foetus to Child*. London: Routledge.

Pozzi, M. E. (2003a). A three-year-old boy with ADHD and Asperger's syndrome treated with parent–child psychotherapy. *Journal of the British Association of Psychotherapists, 41*: 16–31.

Pozzi, M. E. (2003b). The use of observation in the psychoanalytic treatment of a 12-year-old boy with Asperger's syndrome. *International Journal of Psycho-Analysis, 84*: 1333–1350.

Racker, H. (1968). *Transference and Countertransference*. New York: International Universities Press.

Reid, S. (1999a). The assessment of a child with autism: A family perspective. In: A. Alvarez & S. Reid (Eds.), *Autism and Personality: Findings from the Tavistock Autism Workshop*. London & New York: Routledge.

Reid, S. (1999b). The assessment of a child with autism: A family perspective. *Clinical Child Psychology and Psychiatry, 4*: 63–78.

Reid, S. (1999c). Autism and trauma: Post-traumatic autistic developmental disorder. In: A. Alvarez & S. Reid (Eds.), *Autism and Personality*. London: Routledge.

Rey, H. (1979). Schizoid phenomena in the borderline. In: J. LeBoit & A. Capponi (Eds.), *Advances in the Psychotherapy of the Borderline Patient*. New York: Jason Aronson. Reprinted in E. B. Spillius (Ed.), *Melanie Klein Today. Vol. 1: Mainly Theory*. London: Routledge, 1988.

Rey, H. (1994a). Awake, going to sleep, asleep, dreaming, awaking, awake: Comments on W. Clifford M. Scott. In: J. Magagna (Ed.), *Universals of Psycho-Analysis in the Treatment of Psychotic and Borderline States*. London: Free Association Books.

Rey, H. (1994b). Psycholinguistics, object relations theory and the therapeutic process. In: J. Magagna (Ed.), *Universals of Psycho-Analysis in the Treatment of Psychotic and Borderline States*. London: Free Association Books.

Rey, H. (1994c). The schizoid mode of being and the space–time continuum (before metaphor). In: J. Magagna (Ed.), *Universals of Psycho-Analysis in the Treatment of Psychotic and Borderline States*. London: Free Association Books.

Rhode, M. (1997a). Discussion [of chapters on psychosis and developmental delay]. In: M. Rustin, M. Rhode, A. Dubinsky, & H. Dubinsky (Eds.), *Psychotic States in Children*. London: Duckworth.

Rhode, M. (1997b). Going to pieces: Autistic and schizoid solutions. In: M. Rustin, M. Rhode, A. Dubinsky, & H. Dubinsky (Eds.), *Psychotic States in Children*. London: Duckworth.

Rhode, M. (1997c). The voice as autistic object. In: T. Mitrani & J. L. Mitrani (Eds.), *Encounters with Autistic States: A Memorial Tribute to Frances Tustin*. Northvale, NJ: Jason Aronson.

Rhode, M. (1999). Echo or answer? The move towards ordinary speech in three children with autistic spectrum disorder. In: A. Alvarez & S. Reid (Eds.), *Autism and Personality: Findings from the Tavistock Autism Workshop*. London & New York: Routledge.

Rhode, M. (2000a). Assessing children with communication disorders. In: M. Rustin & E. Quagliata (Eds.), *Assessment in Child Psychotherapy*. London: Duckworth.

Rhode, M. (2000b). On using an alphabet: Recombining separable components. In: J. Symington (Ed.), *Imprisoned Pain and Its Transformation: A Festschrift for H. Sydney Klein*. London: Karnac.

Rhode, M. (2001). "The Use of Autistic Processes as a Protection against Schizoid States in a Boy with Asperger's Syndrome." Presentation to the Conference on Childhood Psychosis, The European Federation for Psychoanalytic Psychotherapy, Caen, Normandy, September.

Rhode, M. (2002). One life between two people: The relation of autistic anxieties to themes from the analysis of a nine-to-fifteen-year-old anorexic girl. Italian translation in: E. Quagliata (Ed.), *Un Bisogno Vitale*. Rome: Astrolabio.

Rhode, M. (2003). Aspects of the body image and sense of identity in a boy with autism: Implications for eating disorders. In: G. Williams, P. Williams, J. Desmarais, & K. Ravenscroft (Eds.), *The Generosity of Acceptance, Vol. 1: Feeding Difficulties in Childhood*. London: Karnac.

Rodrigué, E. (1955). The analysis of a three-year-old mute schizophrenic. In: M. Klein, P. Heimann, & R. E. Money-Kyrle (Eds.), *New Directions in Psycho-Analysis*. London: Tavistock Publications. Reprinted London: Karnac, 1985.

Rosenfeld, D. (1984). Hypochondrias, somatic delusion and body scheme in psychoanalytic practice. *International Journal of Psycho-Analysis, 65*: 377–388.

Rosenfeld, H. (1965). *Psychotic States*. London: Hogarth.

Rosenfeld, H. (1987). *Impasse and Interpretation*. London: Routledge.

Roth, D., & Leslie, A. M. (1991). The recognition of attitude conveyed by utterances: A study of preschool and autistic children. *British Journal of Developmental Psychology, 9*: 315–330.

Rourke, B. P. (1989). *Nonverbal Learning Disabilities: The Syndrome and the Model*. New York: Guilford Press.

Rumsey, J. M. (1985). Conceptual problem-solving in highly verbal non-retarded autistic men. *Journal of Autism and Developmental Disorders, 15*: 23–36.

Russell, J., Mauthner, N., Sharpe, S., & Tidswell, T. (1991). The "windows task" as a measure of strategic deception in preschoolers and autistic subjects. *British Journal of Developmental Psychology, 9*: 331–349.

Rustin, M. (1997a). Postscript. In: M. Rustin, M. Rhode, A. Dubinsky, & H. Dubinsky (Eds.), *Psychotic States in Children*. London: Duckworth.

Rustin, M. (1997b). Rigidity and stability in a psychotic patient: Some thoughts about obstacles to facing reality in psychotherapy. In: M. Rustin, M. Rhode, A. Dubinsky, & H. Dubinsky (Eds.), *Psychotic States in Children*. London: Duckworth.

Rutter, M. (1970). Autistic children: Infancy to adulthood. *Seminars in Psychiatry, 2*: 435–450.

Rutter, M. (1972). Childhood schizophrenia reconsidered. *Journal of Autism and Childhood Schizophrenia, 2*: 315–318.

Rutter, M. (1979). Language, cognition and autism. In: R. Katzman (Ed.), *Congenital and Acquired Cognitive Disorders* (pp. 247–264). New York: Raven Press.

Rutter, M. (2000). Genetic studies of autism: From the 1970s into the millennium. *Journal of Abnormal Child Psychology, 28*: 3–14.

Rutter, M. (2001). "As Genes Are so Important, Does It Matter How Children Are Reared?" Tavistock Centre Scientific Meeting (sound recording).

Rutter, M., Andersen-Wood., L., Beckett, C., Bredenkamp, D., Castle, J., Groothues, C., Kreppner, J., Keaveney, L., Lord, C., O'Connor, T. G., & the English and Romanian Adoptees (ERA) Study Team (1999). Quasi-autistic patterns following severe early global privation. *Journal of Child Psychology and Psychiatry, 40*: 537–549.

Rutter, M., LeCouteur, A., Lord, C., MacDonald, H., Rios, P., & Folstein, S. (1988). Diagnosis and sub-classification of autism: Concepts and instrument development. In: E. Schopler & G. B Mesibov (Eds.), *Diagnosis and Assessment in Autism* (pp. 239–259). New York: Plenum.

Sacks, O. (1995). *An Anthropologist on Mars*. London: Picador.

Salomonsson, B. (2004). Some psychoanalytic viewpoints on neuropsychiatric disorders in children. *International Journal of Psycho-Analysis, 85*: 117–136

Sandler, J. (1983). Reflections on some relations between psychoanalytic concepts and psychoanalytic practice. *International Journal of Psycho-Analysis, 64*: 35–45

Schore, A. N. (1994). *Affect Regulation and the Origin of the Self: The Neurobiology of Emotional Development*. Hillsdale, NJ: Lawrence Erlbaum.

Schore, A. N. (1996). The experience-dependent maturation of a regulatory system in the orbital prefrontal cortex and the origin of developmental psychopathology. *Development and Psychopathology, 8*: 59–87.

Schore, A. N. (2001a). The effects of early relational trauma on right brain development, affect regulation, and infant mental health. *Infant Mental Health Journal, 22*: 201–269.

Schore, A. N. (2001b). The effects of a secure attachment relationship on right brain development, affect regulation, and infant mental health. *Infant Mental Health Journal, 22*: 7–66.

Schore, A. N. (2002). (Communication during discussion.) Conference on Trauma, Dissociation and Memory, at the Clinic of Dissociative Disorders, London.

Scragg, P., & Shah, A. (1994). Prevalence of Asperger's syndrome in a secure hospital. *British Journal of Psychiatry, 165*: 679–682.

Seigal, M., & Beattie, K. (1991). Where to look first for children's knowledge of false beliefs. *Cognition, 38*: 1–12.

Shiner, R., & Caspi, A. (2003). Personality differences in childhood and adolescence: Measurement, development and consequences. *Journal of Child Psychology and Psychiatry, 44*: 2–32.

Shuttleworth, J. (1999). The suffering of Asperger children and the challenge they present to psychoanalytic thinking. *Journal of Child Psychotherapy, 25* (2): 239–265.

Sinason, V. (1986). Secondary mental handicap and its relationship to trauma. *Psychoanalytic Psychotherapy, 2*: 131–154.

Sinason, V. (1992). *Mental Handicap and the Human Condition. New Approaches from the Tavistock*. London: Free Association Books.

Sodre, I. (2002). "Certainty and Doubt: Transparency and Opacity of the Object." Conference on Uncertainty (The Melanie Klein Trust), London, 15 June.

Solms, M., & Turnbull, O. (2002). *The Brain and the Inner World*. New York: Other Press.

Steiner, J. (1993). *Psychic Retreats*. London: Routledge.

Stern, D. (1985). *The Interpersonal World of the Infant*. New York: Basic Books.

Stewart, H. (1992). *Psychic Experience and Problems of Technique*. London: Tavistock/Routledge.

Stockdale-Wolf, E. (1993). Fear of fusion: Nonverbal behavior in secondary autism. *Psychoanalytic Inquiry, 13*.

Strathern, P. (2000). *Mendeleyev's Dream: The Quest for the Elements.* London: Hamish Hamilton.

Tager-Flusberg, H. (1991). Semantic processing in the free recall of autistic children: Further evidence for a cognitive deficit. *British Journal of Developmental Psychology, 9*: 417–430.

Tager-Flusberg, H., & Sullivan, K. (1994). Predicting and explaining behaviour: A comparison of autistic, mentally retarded and normal children. *Journal of Child Psychology and Psychiatry, 35*: 1059–1075.

Taiminen, T. (1994). Asperger's syndrome or schizophrenia: Is differential diagnosis necessary for adult patients? *Nordic Journal of Psychiatry, 48*: 325–328.

Tantam, D. (1988). Annotation: Asperger's syndrome. *Journal of Child Psychology and Psychiatry, 48*: 325–328.

Tantam, D. (1991). Asperger's Syndrome in adulthood. In: U. Frith (Ed.), *Autism and Asperger's Syndrome.* Cambridge: Cambridge University Press.

Tantam, D. (2000). Adolescence and adulthood of individuals with Asperger's Syndrome. In: A. Klin, F. R. Volkmar, & S. S. Sparrow (Eds.), *Asperger Syndrome.* New York & London: Guilford Press.

Tantam, D., Monaghan, C., Nicholson, H., & Stirling, J. (1989). Autistic children's ability to interpret faces: A research note. *Journal of Child Psychology and Psychiatry, 30*: 623–630.

Testimon, P., & Rutter, S. C. (1994). A case report: Asperger's Syndrome and sexual offending. *Journal of Forensic Psychiatry, 4*: 555–562.

Tischler, S. (1979). Being with a psychotic child. A psychoanalytic approach to the problems of parents of psychotic children. *International Journal of Psycho-Analysis, 60*: 29–38.

Trevarthen, C. (1979). Communication and co-operation in early infancy: A description of primary intersubjectivity. In: M. M. Bullowa (Ed.), *Before Speech: The Beginning of Interpersonal Communication.* New York: Cambridge University Press.

Trevarthen, C. (1980). The foundations of intersubjectivity: The development of interpersonal and cooperative understanding of infants. In: D. Olson (Ed.), *The Social Foundations of Language and Thought.* New York: W. W. Norton.

Trevarthen, C. (2001). Intrinsic motives for companionship in understanding: Their origin, development, and significance for infant mental health. *Infant Mental Health Journal, 22*: 95–131.

Trevarthen, C., & Aitken, K. J. (2001). Infant intersubjectivity: Research, theory and clinical applications. *Journal of Child Psychology and Psychiatry, 42*: 3–48.

Trevarthen, C., Aitken, K., Papoudi, D., & Robarts, J. (1996). *Children with Autism* (2nd enlarged edition). London: Jessica Kingsley, 1998.

Trowell, J., Rhode, M., Miles, G., & Sherwood, I. (2003). Chilhood depression: Work in progress. Individual child therapy and parent work. *Journal of Child Psychotherapy, 29*: 147–169.

Tustin, F. (1958). Anorexia nervosa in an adolescent girl. *British Journal of Medical Psychology*, 31: 184–200.

Tustin, F. (1972). *Autism and Childhood Psychosis*. London: Hogarth Press. Reprinted London: Karnac, 1995.

Tustin, F. (1981a). Autistic objects. In: *Autistic States in Children* (2nd revised edition). London: Routledge & Kegan Paul, 1992.

Tustin, F. (1981b). *Autistic States in Children* (revised edition). London: Routledge & Kegan Paul, 1992.

Tustin, F. (1981c). Psychological birth and psychological catastrophe. In: *Autistic States in Children*. London: Routledge & Kegan Paul, 1992. Also in: J. S. Grotstein (Ed.), *Do I Dare Disturb the Universe?* Beverly Hills, CA: Caesura Press.

Tustin, F. (1986). *Autistic Barriers in Neurotic Patients* (2nd edition). London: Karnac, 1994.

Tustin, F. (1990). *The Protective Shell in Children and Adults*. London: Karnac.

Tustin, F. (1994a). Autistic children who are assessed as not brain-damaged. *Journal of Child Psychotherapy*, 20: 103–131.

Tustin, F. (1994b). The perpetuation of an error. *Journal of Child Psychotherapy*, 20: 3–23.

Urwin, C. (1987). Developmental psychology and psychoanalysis: Splitting the difference. In: M. Richards & P. Light (Eds.), *Children in Social Worlds*. Cambridge: Polity Press.

U.S. Bureau of Justice Statistics (1987). *Adolescents*. Princeton, NJ: Robert Wood Johnson Foundation (Fall, 1989).

Volkmar, F. R., & Klin, A. (2000). Diagnostic issues in Asperger's Syndrome. In: A. Klin, F. R. Volkmar, & S. S. Sparrow (Eds.), *Asperger Syndrome*. New York & London: Guilford Press.

Volkmar, F. R., Klin, A., & Cohen, D. J. (1997). Diagnosis and classification of autism and related conditions: Consensus and issues. In: D. J. Cohen & F. R. Volkmar (Eds.), *Handbook of Autism and Pervasive Developmental Disorders* (pp. 5–40). New York: Wiley.

Volkmar, F. R., Klin., Siegel, B., Szatmari, P., Lord, C., Campbell, M., Freeman, B.J., Cicchetti, D.V., Rutter, M., Kline, W., Buitelaar, J., Hattab, Y., Fombonne, E., Fuentes, J., Werry, J., Stone, W., Kerbeshian, J, Horshino, Y., Bregman, J., Loveland, K., Szymanski, L, & Towbin, K. (1994). DSM–IV autism/pervasive developmental disorder field trial. *American Journal of Psychiatry*, 151: 1361–1367.

Volkmar, F., & Nelson, I. (1990). Seizure disorders in autism. *Journal of the American Academy of Child and Adolescent Psychiatry*, 29: 127–129.

Weddell, D. (1975). Disturbed geography of the life-space in autism: Barry. In: D. Meltzer, J. Bremner, S. Hoxter, D. Wedell, & I. Wittenberg (Eds.), *Explorations in Autism: A Psychoanalytical Study*. Strath Tay, Perthshire: Clunie Press.

Weeks, S. J., & Hobson, R. P. (1987). The salience of facial expression for autistic children. *Journal of Child Psychology & Psychiatry*, 28: 137–152.

Weintraub, S., & Mesulam, M. M. (1983). Developmental learning disabilities of the right hemisphere: Emotional, interpersonal and cognitive components. *Archives of Neurology, 40*: 463–468.

Werry, J. S. (1992). Child and adolescent (early onset). Schizophrenia: A review in light of DSM–III-R. *Journal of Autism & Developmental Disorders, 22*: 601–624.

WHO (1993). *International Classification of Diseases* (10th edition). Geneva: World Health Organization.

Willey, L. H. (1999). *Pretending to be Normal: Living with Asperger's Syndrome*. London: Jessica Kingsley.

Williams, D. (1992). *Nobody Nowhere: The Remarkable Autobiography of an Autistic Girl*. London: Transworld Publishers.

Williams, D. (1998). *Autism and Sensing: The Unlost Instinct*. London: Jessica Kingsley.

Wing, L. (1980). Childhood autism and social class: A question of selection. *British Journal of Psychiatry, 137*: 410–417.

Wing, L. (1981). Asperger's Syndrome: A clinical account. *Psychological Medicine, 11*: 115–129.

Wing, L. (1988). The continuum of autistic characteristics. In: E. Schopler & G. Mesibov (Eds.), *Diagnosis and Assessment in Autism* (pp. 91–110). New York: Plenum Press.

Wing, L. (1991). The relationship between Asperger's Syndrome and Kanner's autism. In: U. Frith (Ed.), *Autism and Asperger Syndrome*. Cambridge: Cambridge University Press.

Wing, L. (1996). *The Autistic Spectrum: A Guide for Parents and Professionals*. London: Constable.

Wing, L., & Attwood, A. (1987). Syndromes of autism and atypical development. In: D. Cohen & A. Donnellan (Eds.), *Handbook of Autism and Pervasive Developmental Disorders*. New York: Wiley.

Wing, L., & Gould, J. (1979). Severe impairments of social interaction and associated abnormalities in children: Epidemiology and classification. *Journal of Autism and Developmental Disorders, 9*: 11–29.

Winnicott, D. W. (1949). Birth memories, birth trauma and anxiety. In: *Through Paediatrics to Psycho-Analysis* (pp. 174–193). London: Hogarth Press, 1958.

Winnicott, D. W. (1951). Transitional objects and transitional phenomena. In: *Through Paediatrics to Psycho-Analysis* (pp. 229–242). London: Hogarth Press, 1958.

Winnicott, D. W. (1960). Ego distortion in terms of true and false self. In: *The Maturational Process and the Facilitating Environment* (pp. 140–152). London: Hogarth Press, 1965.

Wolff, S. (1991). "Schizoid" personality in childhood and adult life. III: The childhood picture. *British Journal of Psychiatry, 159*: 629–635.

Wolff, S. (2000). Schizoid personality in childhood and Asperger syndrome. In: A. Klin, F. R. Volkmar, & S. S. Sparrow (Eds.), *Asperger Syndrome*. New York & London: Guilford Press.

Wolff, S., & Barlow, A. (1979). Schizoid personality in childhood: A comparative study of schizoid, autistic and normal children. *Journal of Child Psychology and Psychiatry, 20*: 19–46.

Yirmiya, N., Kasari, C., Sigman, M. D., & Mundy, P. (1989). Facial expressions of affect in autistic, mentally retarded and normal children. *Journal of Child Psychiatry, 30*: 725–735.

Youell, B. (1999). Matthew. From Numbers to Numeracy: From knowledge to knowing in a ten-year-old boy with Asperger's Syndrome. In: A. Alvarez & S. Reid (Eds.), *Autism and Personality: Findings from the Tavistock Autism Workshop*. London & New York: Routledge.

INDEX